W9-DGY-048

Emancipating the Professions

Also by Aubrey Wilson

The Changing Pattern of Distribution
Industrial Marketing Research-Management and Technique
The Marketing of Industrial Products
London's Industrial Heritage
The Assessment of Industrial Markets
The Art of Practice of Marketing
The Marketing of Professional Services
Marketing Audit Checklists
Practice Development for Professional Firms
New Directions in Marketing

Emancipating the Professions

Marketing Opportunities from De-regulation

AUBREY WILSON

JOHN WILEY & SONS
Chichester • New York • Brisbane • Toronto • Singapore

Copyright © 1994 by John Wiley & Sons Ltd,
Baffins Lane, Chichester,
West Sussex PO19 1UD, England

National   Chichester (0243) 779777
International +44 243 779777

Other Wiley Editorial Offices

John Wiley & Sons, Inc., 605 Third Avenue,
New York, NY 10158-0012, USA

Jacaranda Wiley Ltd, 33 Park Road, Milton,
Queensland 4064, Australia

John Wiley & Sons (Canada) Ltd, 22 Worcester Road,
Rexdale, Ontario M9W 1L1, Canada

John Wiley & Sons (SEA) Pte Ltd, 37 Jalan Pemimpin #05-04,
Block B, Union Industrial Building, Singapore 2057

Library of Congress Cataloging-in-Publication Data

Wilson, Aubrey.
    Emancipating the professions : marketing opportunities from de
  -regulation / Aubrey Wilson.
      p.   cm.
    Includes bibliographical references and indexes.
    ISBN 0-471-94437-8
    1. Professions—Marketing.   2. Service industries—Marketing.
  I. Title.
  HD8038.A1W547   1994
  658.8—dc20   93–45502
                                                           CIP

British Library Cataloguing in Publication Data

A catalogue record for this book is available from the British Library

ISBN 0-471-94437-8

Typeset in 11/13pt Palatino from author's disks by Production Technology Department,
John Wiley & Sons Ltd, Chichester
Printed and bound in Great Britain by Bookcraft (Bath) Ltd.

Just why it is customary to dedicate books I do not know. Perhaps it is a practice descended from the time of courtly love when knights wore their ladies' favour in the joust. Therefore not to break with tradition I dedicate this, like my previous ten books the last one I shall write, to my wife Gina whose contribution is to be measured in far more important things than mere words and ideas—encouragement, support, creative criticism, friendship and an unshakeable but perhaps ill-founded belief in my knowledge of the subject.

Contents

Preface

Because the professions have never regarded their practices as businesses, management was never an issue. Large firms employing thousands of people spread across the world and the smallest practices saw themselves as something apart from the rough, tough, slightly dubious world of business. As always when looking at professional practices semantics get in the way of understanding. Because a firm had clients not customers, chambers, surgeries and offices not factories and warehouses, produced an intangible service not a tangible product, usually had to react to a stream of customised requests for service often requiring a high degree of specialisation and did not for the most part engage in patterned or sequential work, methods adopted by business were seen, not just as inappropriate, but positively against the interest of the firm and their clients.

A professional was said to be characterised by the subordination of self-interest to the interests of the client (or patient). The implication is, of course, that normal commercial transactions do the opposite, yet all the evidence shows that it is where an alignment of supplier and client or customer interests occurs that the greatest benefits accrue to all parties. In business the perceived confrontational and adversarial attitudes are giving way to strategic alliances.

It has been said the company that is at the mercy of its customers deserves sympathy and nothing else, but it is equally true that customers who are at the mercy of their suppliers also deserve sympathy. And yet this has been the situation in the professional–client relationship in the past and it is only the changes forced by de-regulation which are altering the situation.

Some professions have already come to terms with the new environment and changed client ambience but the process is far from complete. Disciplines and occupations which escaped the major pressures of the last two decades, such as medicine and professions within the civil service, are now exposed to the rigours of the market place with the introduction of market testing and compulsory competitive tendering, an internal health market and fund holding.

The rules of practice for all professions started partly as a way of providing desirable protection for the public. Over time these gave way to what has been termed "blatant restrictive practices" in all aspects of professional life from entry conditions, to training, to qualification, to practice. It is only this last aspect which involves the controversial activity of marketing. For the last few years of this century and into the next one there are critical decisions for the professions to make at both collegial and individual practice level. Difficult dilemmas must be faced and resolved so that increased competition neither reduces quality nor fails to yield better services for clients.

Thus, it is the twin inexorable forces, as the book will demonstrate, of intensifying and ever more aggressive marketing and the increasing knowledge of, and questioning by, combative clients that will drive practice development forward. In a mere five years between 1985 and 1990, despite recession in the United Kingdom, the number of architectural practices increased by 59%, accountancy by 44%, management consultants by 114%, scientific and other professional services by 64% and computer services by a vast 150%. It is unlikely that the markets these professions and disciplines support increased to anything like this extent. Indeed, evidence is that the opposite occurred and in fact in many of them there was an actual decline in their size which has led to intensified competition.

The changes forced upon the professions by changes in the environments in which they operate are then the *raison d'être* for this new book which seeks to point the way in which practices can achieve satisfactory and stable levels of revenue and profit.

The overriding purpose of this book is not to advocate marketing in any form. That is for the individual practice to decide, but such a decision should be based on a knowledge of precisely what is involved in a client centred approach rather than assuming the stereotypical advertising or sales executive represents all there is to say about marketing and thus practice development. If the case is made then the book becomes a "how to" publication but "how to" set within the resources and skills which normally already exist within a professional practice.

My first book on marketing professional services stood alone in 1972 and trawled among what were patently not professions and was perhaps remarkable only for its combination of prescience and naivety and the obloquy it attracted from the traditionalist within the real professions.

The second book in 1984, published on the eve of the first major wave of de-regulation, was no longer a lone and flickering beacon so was able to concentrate on those disciplines which are generally recognised as "professions" and on what was permissible and possible given the lack of resources and skills in marketing which typified most practices at that time.

This, the third book on professional services marketing, now sits among a plethora of other texts both general and profession-specific and is addressed to a professional environment where the question of "whether" is replaced by "how". In almost all professions and in many countries regulations concerning marketing have to all intents and purposes gone or are in the process of revision and the professions, as was forecast some 20 years ago, now face two major threats—increasingly sentient clients and an intensified competition both inter- and intra-professional.

While the history, causes and implications of de-regulation are traced so that their implications can be understood and the opportunities and threats they create identified, the book concentrates very much on how practices can simultaneously improve their own performance *and* the services they render to clients and all within the skills and resources which professional practices typically possess or can acquire.

The danger which had to be avoided was turning the text into a Hollywood "son of" or *Practice Development II* way of prolonging the life cycle of an initially good idea. Apart from the fact that serial versions of excellent scripts tend to fall far short of the quality of their originals, there is no reason to invest in any tome which adds nothing to the body of knowledge which already exists. The objective, and only the reader can judge if it has been achieved, is to expand the horizons of marketing professional services using the new freedoms, to consolidate and extend those marketing methods that have been seen to work and to bury those that have, for whatever reasons, failed.

Great emphasis has been placed on best practice in different professions and could be adapted for others. Thus the research which preceded the book has involved a very wide range of disciplines indeed, with varying degrees of commitment to and success in marketing their practices. The marketing needs of in-house professional service departments are not ignored given the present trends for out-sourcing and the resultant threat to their continued existence.

There is perhaps no more fitting way to commence a book on the professions than by quoting from the seminal work of the doyen of professional services studies, Professor Carr-Saunders:

> "No man is a citizen of more than one country, and we have been mere hurried visitors to the homes of others. There is no excuse for inaccuracy in the reporting of what we have seen, but we realise that we may not have learnt the native idioms. We may call things by unfamiliar names and in a thousand ways betray our foreign origin. We would plead with those of our readers who belong to one of these worlds to be indulgent when we describe it and fail to speak as though we resided there also."

Like Professor Carr-Saunders I must ask the reader's indulgence if I have used words and language which are not applicable to their professions or adopted generics to avoid the repetition of alternative forms. Fortunately the problem of correct nomenclatures is far less than it was in 1972. After all patients are now clients, marketing can be substituted for the cosmetic "practice development" (although I use both) and the qualifying "para" in front of any professional designation—para-medics, para-legals—is accepted with only the slightest shudder.

Since the previous two books the world has become gender conscious and, while it was sufficient in the past to explain that "he" was also intended to embrace "she", this time to avoid offence the gender separation has been made, although it has been necessary at times to invoke a cowardly plural.

The two decades between this book and the previous ones has given an unrivalled opportunity to work with many professions and to observe the changes which have occurred while forecasting with some degree of confidence those that will occur. It has clearly

highlighted the need to ensure that those who never had marketing as part of their career agenda do not consider it to be an inferior
activity and beneath the dignity of their profession. Less and less
does one hear "I did not become a lawyer (an accountant, a doctor,
a civil servant) to be a bloody salesman". If the motivational
element in this book is less than that in previous books it is because
it has not become less important only less necessary.

Faced by a mountainous heap of minutiae gathered over the
years and awed by the watchful severity of colleagues, it is too
easy to take refuge in propounding interesting theories or offering
narrow specialised dissertations knowing that such small for-
tresses are easy to defend. I have attempted to avoid both havens
and have spread myself across all the professions and all the
marketing techniques, reviewed the position in a number of different countries and considered the situation for firms of different
sizes and thus with different resources available. The theoretical
has been eschewed for the practical and long-term speculation for
the problems of today and tomorrow. Only the reader can decide
if the objective has been achieved.

Their names may not be on the cover but there have been very
numerous contributors to this book which is the fruit of many
years management responsibility, consultancy and teaching in all
parts of the world. It is as much a product of learning by one's
mistakes as by the assiduous research and study in many disciplines and cultures. My gratitude to both the named and unnamed
sources is total.

It would be ungracious not to acknowledge the unfailing patience
and good humour of Dorothy Storr who had the misfortune to
receive typescripts containing an equal weight of words, staples and
adhesive tape, and drafts with corrections of Delphic imprecision.
All this she managed to turn into a near perfect and readable
manuscript. I am truly appreciative of her skills and her contribution.

There can be few more daunting tasks than that of reading an
as yet unpublished manuscript looking not just for substantive
issues but also the minutiae of typographical, spelling and other
errors. It is pushing networking and friendship to their limits to
ask that the text be reviewed while still in a state of parturition,
albeit nearly complete. Thus I must thank Ivor Hockman for
taking on the task with totally undeserved willingness and hiding
his disquiet so effectively. I am particularly grateful to Gordon

Brand who, despite being exposed to my writings for more years than either of us care to remember, expertly picked up ancient prejudices and firmly challenged new ones and made many valuable suggestions. The contributions of my reviewers are, alas, lost in the text but it has been very real and very valuable. This acknowledgement is a poor reward for their labours.

If this book is received with the same enthusiasm as its predecessors it will be a tribute to them and to the very many professional colleagues and clients in all disciplines who have made important contributions, perhaps without even knowing it. Its deficiencies are solely the result of the author's obduracy.

AW
September 1993

About the Organisation of this Book

Professionals are very busy people overburdened with too much advice and too much to read. The greatest contribution I could hope to make would be to provide highly practical guidance in its most easily assimilatable form. The work book approach has always been kept firmly in view as the objective.

While each chapter is free-standing, unlike my two previous books on this subject this time there is a considerable amount of cross-referencing to enable readers to follow through any particular issues in a logical and simple way. The cross-references can be used or ignored without affecting the completeness of the chapter in which it occurs.

Where outside sources have been used they are identified at the end of each chapter to enable readers to seek further information. This is particularly important where specialist texts have been consulted and might be needed by the reader. Just what is the best available in any particular field is very much a matter of opinion but I have attempted to be as objective as possible in assessing the sources and applying to each of them a number of key criteria: the seminal nature of the work; the authority of its authors; the applicability to the issue under consideration; its dating; its practical implications; and its readability. If it is found my selections have not always been to the reader's taste I hope they will at least be considered sufficiently valid to have justified their inclusion.

The first chapters of the book are intended to set the scene. Chapter 4 takes the health care sector on its own as being the one which has received least attention in the past and is most likely to experience the greatest change in the future. The remaining 26 chapters are entirely on marketing: concepts, activities and the enabling functions which permit marketing to be carried out cost effectively. Most chapters end with three or four bullet points to identify actions for consideration. It is to be hoped the reader will find more than those the author has selected but they are offered as a starting point.

Within the text are a great many marketing ideas which can be considered for adoption: for example, key account personnel contouring in chapter 13; the wealth seminar in chapter 25; vulnerability analysis in chapter 26.

The reader may like to use a copy of the format in Appendix 27B page 367 and write in all the ideas which it is proposed to adopt in some form or another as they are reached and complete the form so that tasks are scheduled and allocated. This is one way to be reasonably sure they will be actioned.

In order to help the reader identify what is important and to move from consideration to implementation, at the risk of mutilating the book, it is advisable to mark all points and ideas which the reader wants to action. Different coloured markings can imply different priorities or tasks for someone else in the practice. Priorities, by the way, are not necessarily just those that have a time urgency. Any ideas which can be implemented immediately at low cost or no cost and without generating any difficulties or disruption should be acted on at once.[1]

NOTE

(1) A full checklist of action points will be found in Wilson, A. *Marketing Audit Checklists*, 2nd edition, McGraw-Hill, Maidenhead (1992).

1
The Story So Far...

The professions have always held a privileged place in society; privileged in the sense of the respect and awe they commanded by virtue of their skills and in their freedom from outside interference to make their own rules and to police them. The privileges were maintained through a system of closed entry into the professions which ensured that new members would conform to the rules.

The source of professional power can be traced back to its lineal descendancy and evolution from the medieval guilds and the livery companies leading to professional associations which were formed and developed with the essential purposes of mutual aid, protecting their members from competition and the maintenance of standards. Adam Smith observed that men of the same trade seldom gather together even for feasting and merriment when it does not end in a conspiracy to raise prices against the public.

Since the professions largely evolved from trades it is not perhaps surprising that the removal of fee competition was regarded as a legitimate function of the representative organisations. This is a view which has not been extinguished with the advent of de-regulation. As late as 1992 The Institute of Chartered Accountants through their Joint Ethics Committee created new rules in an attempt to limit fee competition. They did this by placing the onus firmly on any practice to justify lower fees than competitors if a complaint was made: "Where fees were a feature [meaning a decision forming factor] in obtaining or retaining work, firms should be prepared to demonstrate to an investigating committee that the work was done fully in accordance with auditing standards".[1]

Given that one of the major objectives of the controlling bodies was the limitation of competition which might manifest itself through lower charges or fees or lower quality work, to achieve a semi-monopolistic state, a body of rules was created which prevented the professional from actively seeking business. Doing so was delineated by the pejorative "touting". There is little doubt that the majority of members of every profession would have preferred to continue the conventional approach of being a member of a gentlemen's club. That is not to say marketing was not taking place. If the professions were to have clients it had to be happening even if it was in such a low key as to be almost invisible. Perhaps the description of a prominent architect summed it up best of all: "What does a consultant architect do when he needs more work?" and, answering his own question, responded: "Traditionally he hangs around influential street corners waiting to be picked up. He must not solicit, but he can loiter with intent".[2]

But in seeking to control competition the collegial bodies and the qualifying associations actually engendered another form of competition which was to prove more destructive to their monopoly position than any activities which members might have indulged in. The new competition came from the fragmentation of the professional organisations themselves. Combinations of dissident members, those denied entry to a profession through restriction on numbers or by making the early years of practice too onerous or too unrewarding to be endured and those seeking professional recognition for similar or new disciplines and for different standards of performance were formed:

> "Observe the plethora of professional groups in medicine today. Rather an all-purpose medical craft with specialists we have a fragmented structure which, for instance, spurns physiotherapists. Observe the distinction between barristers and solicitors with all its pettifogging nonsense about representation in courts. Observe the proliferation of accounting professions where some are allowed by law to audit accounts and others are not. Observe the engineering profession which today in Britain has 15 discrete varieties whilst the French and Germans have two."[3]

As it was, the initial move towards de-regulation came not as a result of the dissatisfaction of professionals but because of both public and governmental pressure. In the USA it can be traced to a seminal Supreme Court decision in 1977 (Bates and O'Steen v. State Bar of Arizona) which removed any constraints on marketing imposed by the professional associations and which in turn opened the floodgates in all the other professions.

LIBERALISATION IN THE UNITED KINGDOM

In the United Kingdom the earliest discussions stemmed from a Monopolies Commission report in 1970 which looked into restrictive practices adopted in all professions.[4] The Commission found numerous examples which they concluded were against public interest. Among these were the constraints related to marketing which by denial of information concerning individual practitioners and practices limited consumer choice or made the optimum selection difficult or impossible. Just how tightly controlled marketing was can be judged by some of the rules of the Law Society of the time.

A solicitor shall not obtain professional business by:

- Directly or indirectly without reasonable justification inviting instructions for such business or
- Doing or permitting to be done without reasonable justification anything which by its manner, frequency or otherwise advertises his practice as a solicitor or
- Doing or permitting to be done anything which may be reasonably regarded as touting

The Bar maintained the professional rules which restricted the provision of information about the nature of services offered. The Royal Commission on Legal Services declared in 1979 "information about the services provided by individual barristers may be obtained by those who require it without resort to individual advertising". Chartered surveyors were controlled with a simple and highly unequivocal rule: "no member shall solicit instructions for work in any manner whatsoever".[5]

The medical profession was equally rigid and all embracing in their instructions to doctors. From 1902 both canvassing and advertising by doctors was classified as "infamous conduct [sic]" which could result in removal from the medical register. By 1968 the interdict had softened very slightly:

> "Any publicity by or on behalf of or condoned by a doctor which has as its object the personal advertisement of the doctor is highly undesirable, unethical and in contravention of ... the notes on professional offences issued by the General Medical Council ... A doctor shall take all possible steps to avoid or prevent publicity where it can be shown to be unnecessary or to be to his advantage as a doctor."[6]

But a decade and a half later little had changed:

> "The professional offence of advertising may arise from the publication in any form of matter commending or drawing attention to the professional attainments or services of a doctor, if that doctor has either personally arranged such publication or has instigated, sanctioned or acquiesced in its publication by others."[7]

The loss adjusters controlling association not only specifically prohibited any approach "either orally or in writing...made by a member or one of his staff with the aim of obtaining business" but also stipulated the level of hospitality which was permissible and banned the use of heavy type insertions in directories.[8]

The Monopolies Commission report engendered a wave of reaction and with a few notable exceptions, unified the members of the professions into counteracting with reasons, both valid and spurious, why unregulated marketing should not occur. High among the defence arguments were: since demand always exists there is no need to stimulate it; the public must be protected from charlatans prevailing on them to retain those who might serve them less well and disinterestedly than those who are modest about their personal attainments; unfair competition must be prevented; marketing negates impartial detachment; and, finally, the oldest defence of all, the quality of the service rendered is truly the best recommendation which can be offered without putting the public at risk.

For some 15 years the fight was joined but finally the struggle to maintain the *status quo* had to yield under the pressure of public demand, much stimulated by the media, and governmental pressure. While self-regulation was encouraged many disciplines were no longer protected by the state which, for example, in the past ensured that only solicitors may be paid for transferring interests in land and only doctors could perform some procedures.

THE BEGINNING OF THE END TO MARKETING CONSTRAINTS

The main wave of de-regulation began in 1985. It was a major *volte-face* when the British Medical Association declared that: "Patients are entitled to be given comprehensive, detailed and accurate information about medical services available to them...Doctors working within the National Health Service as opposed to private practice have particular obligations imposed on them by their terms of service by which they *must* provide both personal, professional and practice information".[9] But the advertising guidelines of the British Medical Association went well beyond just requiring advertisements to accord to the basic "truthful, decent and honest" by embargoing what might seem in the market place innocent and useful information.

The quantity surveyors who voted unanimously in 1981 not to permit advertising two years later voted unanimously to permit it. The reasons for this total reversal were given as fee competition, the desire to broaden the base of quantity surveyors' work and the Monopolies Commission pressure. (Tangentially it is interesting to note that one of the reasons advanced for this reversal of policy was fee competition, which was not supposed to be happening and which seems to have occurred despite desperate attempts to prevent it both in quantity surveying and other professions.) "Architects shall not revise a quotation to take account of a fee quotation by any other architect for the same service." Consulting Engineers "shall not knowingly compete with another member on the basis of professional charges".

Because of the domino effect, the Royal Institute of Chartered Surveyors felt they could no longer maintain their restrictions for other surveyors and their own rules were liberalised in line with the quantity surveyors. By 1988 things had gone so far as to permit advertisements to contain solicitations, as if that is not what advertising is about anyway, with words such as "contact us" or "call us".

In 1968 the Bar Council announced there was no longer any objection to practising barristers associating freely with solicitors..."who are in a position to send work to Counsel, either socially or in the course of attending professional conferences". Not exactly a giant step to de-regulation and, as late as 1989, the *Code of Conduct* purported to specify just what a barrister could put on his or her business card or compliments slips.[10]

In 1979 The Institute of Chartered Accountants of England and Wales in their *Guide to Professional Ethics* stated bluntly, "a member should not advertise his professional services or skills". By 1991 the relaxation was almost complete only requiring accountants to conform to the *British Code of Advertising Practice.* In 1992 another barrier which was concerned less with promotion than the promotional targets fell. Permission to telephone or make a personal call on a prospective client other than in relation to audit work was granted. Cold calling had arrived presumably to enable accountancy practices offering management and other consultancy services to compete with their more commercial rivals.

However a new word appeared in the regulations—harassment. "A member should under no circumstances promote or seek to promote his or her services...in such a way or to such an extent as to amount to harassment of the prospective client."[11] Perhaps fearing they had gone too far, the Institute then issued a further statement: "Harassment has not been defined", and just to pile confusion on confusion, "members should bear in mind that it is a fact that some people are more easily harassed than others".[12]

Subsequently de-regulation throughout the professions has largely followed the same course. Its history can be followed by tracing it through one discipline—dentistry. In 1982 the British Dental Association with legal sanction still maintained a whole panoply of rules to prevent any possibility that dentists would market their services: "It is strictly contrary to the Dentists Act for a dental practitioner to engage in any form of advertising".[13] By 1986 there were cracks in the total interdiction: "It [advertising] should be limited to the following items of information".[14] Two years later the only restrictions applied to advertising were those which were and are applicable to all advertising, namely that it is "truthful decent and honest".[15] The rules, interestingly enough, now stated that: "A dentist *should* not..." rather than: "A dentist *must* not..." which removed, for example, the constraint on unsolicited approaches. Whereas it was still not permissible to include the name of hygienists on professional plates, the General Council only *disapproved* of a dental practice being carried on under a name other than that of the dentists themselves. Fees *"should* not", again not *"must* not", be divided between practitioners unknown to the patient. By 1990 advertising could be combined with that of a manufacturer or providers of other products and services.[16]

In the United Kingdom a series of governmental policy documents called *Citizens Charters* have set out just what standards clients have a right to expect from their professional advisers. Among the "rights" of patients given in *The Patients Charter* is the provision of:

> "detailed information on local health services including quality standards and maximum waiting times. You will be able to get this information from your health authority GP or Community Health Council."[17]

This, it is true, is a long way from what those in the fast moving consumer goods would regard as marketing, but it is a useful start in that communication is now mandatory and goes beyond what was, in the past, regarded as the maximum necessary and the minimum which health practitioners could get away with.

Statutory legislation ensures only those professionally qualified can call themselves lawyers or doctors or architects although this aspect of the latters' privileged position is now under attack. In at least one respect this provides a considerable advantage over practitioners who are not protected by statutory legislation but who offer services which fulfil the same functions. But this advantage is being eroded in that, for example, solicitors are no longer the only discipline which legally can be paid for transferring interests in land. The construction industry is lobbying the government to end statutory registration of architects with some success and it is proposed, and will most likely be enacted, that the Architects Register be abolished. Currently the term "architect" can only be used by those who have satisfied a professional body as to their fitness to practise. If the register is abolished the title "architect" can be adopted by the humblest draughtsman. It will doubtless be argued, and not without some justification, that removing professional accreditation as an indication of competence will disadvantage the public. It is doubtful however if this pleading will prevail. Similar pressures exist or will emerge in other disciplines so that the opportunities for the supply of professional services will become more balanced and less biased in favour of those whose title is presently protected by statute.

Legal protection is not however an unmixed advantage. The extent to which, for example, architects can promote their services and demonstrate their expertise is still to some extent constrained. The construction industry is limited by nothing other than their resources to marketing their services aggressively and continuously. Members of the Chartered Institute of Building are encouraging their larger clients to adopt contractor-led design and build agreements. These give the contractor overall control, the architect either being hired as a consultant or as a member of the contractor's staff.

In looking at marketing de-regulation the tendency is to concentrate on advertising as this has always appeared to the professions to be the core of marketing. However, there were and to some extent still are other embargoes in place which were either marketing or had marketing connotations: the size and illumination of professional plates; the use of window space; the sharing of fees (this prevented representation by others or non-professionals); the revision of fee quotations to take account of a competitor's quotation; payment by results (contingency payments); naming clients to demonstrate track record; and even the claim for specialisation (this is niche marketing) are all still surrounded by restrictions as to their use.

REGULATIONS INTERNATIONALLY

The situation is further complicated by the lack of an agreed definition of a profession. In France there are nearly 100 occupations defined as professions as against perhaps 10 in other countries,[18] consequently internationally there are wide variations in restrictions and permissions, but those which control the legal professions are typical of most others. In the European Union the Right of Establishment for Lawyers, which covers conditions for Lawyers to set up practices in countries other than their own, refers specifically to the rules of conduct being "subject to the same obligations, professional rules, incapacities and incompatibilities as the lawyers practising under the relevant title in the host Member State", something the British Government in their anxiety to demonstrate the advantages of the Single Market for the professions conspicuously failed to mention.[19] Thus no matter how liberal the United Kingdom regulations may be in relation to marketing a British lawyer practising in Spain is bound by Spanish rules. These are as unequivocal and as all embracing as any which the Law Society of England and Wales imposed before de-regulation. Thus, *Estatuto General de Abogacía* (General Act for Lawyers), approved by Royal Decree as late as July 1982, states in article 31: "The advertising or dissemination of their [lawyers] services, directly or through the means of publicity ... or the issue of free legal opinions in professional magazines, newspapers or media without the authorisation of the government is prohibited".

Nevertheless in Spain, too, the pressures are manifest. In 1992 a Competition Court submitted a proposal to the Minister for Economic and Financial Affairs for reforming the regulatory framework of the professions. The idea was not to abolish all the privileges of the *Colegios* but simply those "which are used for the advantage of the professions without bringing any benefit to the consumers, such as the powers to fix a profession's fees and to prohibit or restrict advertising".[20]

In Germany current rules impose far reaching prohibitions on all forms of promotion for lawyers and most other professions. Not surprisingly however these are now being re-considered to liberalise constraints on advertising, but only insofar as it will provide factual information.

Such relaxation as has occurred in Ireland since 1988 relates only to existing clients. Most of the tools of practice development are available but, when it comes to seeking to acquire new clients, then the word "touting" appears once again (with its pejorative overtones) and almost everything is as rigidly prohibited as under the old 1955 regulations.

In Italy the rules remain rigid and unequivocal: "It is prohibited for lawyers to develop activities in order to obtain new clients through publicity or any form of communication". This prohibition also includes the use of brochures.[21]

The second principle of European competition law is that national laws or regulations do not affect the application of the Community rules. This means that even restrictive practices authorised or encouraged by national rules or regulations may be declared contrary to the rules of the EEC Treaty. Thus, step by step the controls which have regulated marketing in every profession and in most countries within and external to the European Union are under direct and immediate threat, and are being or will be modified and in many cases revoked.

In South Africa the different States can and have to some extent adopted different rulings. Natal, for example, permits members to publicise their practice or permit someone else to do so (i.e. advertising agency, public relations company) within what are normal promotional guidelines. However in the Transvaal in 1992 there was still a statement extant "Touting is not permitted", which effectively removes new potential clients as targets for the marketing effort.

In Australia, as in South Africa, there are variations in the rules applied by different States. The Queensland Law Society bans claims by lawyers for specialisation but in the Australian Capital Territories they are permitted provided the claims can be proved. In Tasmania reference by accountants to "low" or "discounted" fees is prohibited. The changes which have occurred in Australia since the 1980s are exemplified by the fact that a solicitor was then prevented from advertising on the side of a pizza box, while recently legal services advertisements have appeared on condom packets in New South Wales and milk cartons in Canberra. Barristers in South Australia are totally prohibited from any form of advertising whatsoever other than, in some States, announcements of new practices or changes of address.[22]

THE NEW ETHOS

Despite the gloomy prognostications of those who opposed the use of any form of promotion, there has not been any noticeable deterioration in service quality which can be attributed to marketing. Indeed there is ample evidence that the quality of services, in both a technical sense and in the way they are delivered, have improved while in real terms the cost to the clients have decreased. The intensified attacks and criticisms of the professions stem not from the excesses of marketing but from the greater awareness of the public both as to their rights and the way to obtain redress.

The deep seated revulsion for the market place has been replaced within sentient practices by an acceptance and indeed an enthusiasm along with understanding that there is no conflict between professionalism and all that it stands for and the development of a commercial and businesslike approach to the markets. When professional practices reach the size of medium or even large businesses then there is no alternative but to adopt the very best in management techniques. The old paternalism, nepotism and "gentlemen's club" which served the professions well enough in the past are no longer applicable. The stronger in management terms the larger practices become the greater will be the necessity for the medium size, smaller and smallest firms to emulate them. The new attitude to clients and the new approach to the market can be seen running through all disciplines and all sizes of firms from the sole practitioner to the multinational mega-organisations which are now commonplace in accountancy, and management consultancy and which are beginning to form in other disciplines such as surveying and engineering consultancy.

The General Council of the Bar had by 1990[23] accepted that both management and marketing were needed even though they saw the future of their profession as one where clients did not have direct access:

> "General direct lay access would so far undermine the whole nature of the Bar that we have assumed the continuance of the Bar as a consultancy or referral profession working almost exclusively on the instructions of other professions."[24]

This assumption is open to some doubt but there is no such reservations about marketing:

> "The policy of the Bar Council is to encourage vigorous marketing initiatives by the Circuits and Specialist Bar Associations who have a pivotal role in the development of the Bar's work, both domestically and internationally."[25]

A DE-REGULATION TOO FAR

In looking at the evolution of de-regulation there is one deeply worrying aspect. The purpose of de-regulation is possibly being sacrificed in pursuit of a situation where pure market forces can be left to regulate the market. The intention previously referred to, removing the legal protection which is afforded to the title "architect", may well presage similar moves in other disciplines. The wholesale rush to introduce the market economy into the professions and to achieve total freedom is more likely to have an adverse effect on clients than in any other commercial transaction, since the purchaser of the service in most circumstances has far less knowledge than the vendor. However, there seems little point and much danger in dismantling restrictions that genuinely protect clients.

Some barriers remain in the United Kingdom, for example the Insolvency Act 1986 disallowed remuneration to a liquidator whose appointment had been secured by "improper solicitation". There is little doubt that the relatively few constraints which remain will be dismantled within the next few years and this will almost certainly be replicated in European countries in due course. Whether to adopt marketing techniques to produce profitable and stable growth will be the decision for each practice. The techniques are there and proven; neither the cost nor the skills are beyond the reach of even the smallest practices while the yield is high in terms of both the rewards to the practitioner and the satisfactions and benefits to the clients. More importantly there is no longer a protective structure of rules and disciplinary proceedings to provide an excuse and a reason for not marketing.

NOTES

(1) *Predatory Pricing—a discussion paper*, Joint Ethics Committee, Institute of Chartered Accountants, London (1992).
(2) Eric Lyons quoted by Golzen, G. *How Architects Get Work*, p.3, Architectural and Building Practice Guides, London (1984).
(3) Wills, G. *Marketing Reality*, p.40, MCB University Press, Bradford (1991).
(4) Monopolies Commission *Professional Services: a report on the general effect on the public interest of certain restrictive practices so far as they prevail in relation to the supply of professional services*, Cmnd 4463-1/2, HMSO, London (1970).
(5) Bye-law 24(7) Royal Institution of Chartered Surveyors, London.
(6) *Report on Advertising and the Medical Profession*, approved by the representative body, London (1968).

(7) General Medical Council *Professional Conduct and Discipline: Fitness to Practice*, London (1983).

(8) The Chartered Institute of Loss Adjustors, Bye-laws Part E.

(9) British Medical Association *Guidelines to Doctors on Advertising*, London (1991).

(10) Pannick, D. *Advocates*, p.185, Oxford University Press, Oxford (1993) . This book is a seminal discussion covering many aspects of the advocates' profession and in many countries.

(11) Institute of Chartered Accountants of England and Wales, *Members Handbook 1992*, volume 2, London (1992).

(12) Institute of Chartered Accountants of England and Wales, *Help Sheet No. 12, Chartered Accountants Advisery Service on Ethics*, London (1992).

(13) British Dental Association *Regulation 8.1*, London (1982).

(14) British Dental Association *Notice for the Guidance of Dentists*, London (1986).

(15) British Dental Association *Ethical and Legal Obligations of Dental Practitioners*, London (1988).

(16) British Dental Council Amendment to *Professional Conduct and Fitness to Practise* London (1990).

(17) Department of Health *The Patients Charter*, p.10, London (1992).

(18) *Professions libérales: un nouvelle donne*, p.2, Clés pour l'Europe, Ministère des Affaires Européenne, Paris (1992).

(19) Department of Enterprise *The Single Market—Europe open for the professions*, London (1992) does not make one reference to the severe restrictions on marketing professional services which still exist in many countries within the European Community.

(20) *Competition and the Professions: Discord or Harmony?*, paper presented by C. D. Ehlermann, Director General for Competition, Commission of the European Communities, Bristol, October (1992).

(21) *Code of Conduct*, Consiglio Nazionale Forense (1993).

(22) *Advertising in the Legal Profession*, Direct Connection, Sydney (1993).

(23) *Code of Conduct of the Bar of England and Wales*, para 307.1, London (1990).

(24) General Council of the Bar *Strategies for the Future*, p.3, London (1990).

(25) General Council of the Bar *Strategies for the Future*, pp.37–39, London (1990).

2
What the New Freedoms Mean: Responsibilities and Opportunities

De-regulation has not come easily to the professions. Indeed it may well not have come at all but for strong governmental pressures in many countries because so far as the collegial bodies were concerned, there has always been a sufficient number of opposed and neutral members to ensure comfortable majorities for avoiding the legitimisation of any activities designed to obtain new clients. The widely held belief that commercialism and professionalism were incompatible was the basis for the opposition. It was stated, by way of explanation, when professional pride permitted a response at all: "A profession is a way of life, a business is a means of earning a living". The protagonists of marketing were not, it must be said, very audible in explaining that there was no dissonance between their professionalism and appropriate marketing, only between good professionalism and bad commercialism. If they had, perhaps the type of editorial to be seen as late as 1991 would not have appeared:

"General practitioners are generally dismayed at the way they have been bullied into marketing their wares. They have not quite been reduced to the level of door-to-door brush salesmen, but it is an uncomfortable experience nevertheless."[1]

Professionalism is in essence, it is claimed, a combination of disinterested dedication and learning where the motive of money making is subordinated to the interests of clients and patients. Any gap between the claims and reality can be judged by dedication and learning and by the individuals' own experiences.[2]

No one now disputes the clients' or patients' "right to know"; only their inability to choose or to assess the quality of the service received is queried. Whether this is justified or not, and it is certainly true in many cases, it does not remove the requirement for the practitioner to communicate and to at least give the opportunity of choice. The same expansion of education and communication which has diminished the sense of deference towards occupations distinguished by their higher knowledge has also enabled the users of professional services to take a critical look at these services. And if they are not prepared to ask the questions, there are plenty of well meaning (and perhaps some times not so well meaning) organisations and individuals who will ask those questions for them. What is feared by practitioners is that marketing will distort the message from factual communication to inaccurate persuasive communication in the same manner in which fast-moving consumer goods are believed to be offered to the public. That is one end of marketing but there is another polarity. Marketing can be performed with elegance and skill and does not have to be brash or obtrusive.

THE MARKETING CASE

The advocacy for marketing rests substantially on four inter-related issues which have been patchily conceded across most professions.

First, the right of the client or patient to know. Choice is destroyed by withholding reasons for choosing a particular course of action and the alternatives and the criteria by which the quality of the service can be assessed. The knowledge gap between practitioner and client which has always existed both as a source of power and a basis of privilege has been defended until de-regulation threw a shaky but usable bridge across it.

Second, the enhancement of the capability of the client to question, seek alternative and independent opinions and to obtain redress where appropriate. So much of this depends upon the ability to make comparison and therefore implies full knowledge of the total range of services available and their attributes.

Third, intra-professional competition, that is direct competition between practitioners within the same discipline, which may take the form of overt or even aggressive marketing or the development of new "products". One-day surgeries and clinics have reduced demand for longer stay hospitalisation; high specialisation such as the Shouldice hospital in Canada which only accepts patients for hernia procedures are two examples.

Fourth, interprofessional competition concerns other professions where the boundaries touch: accountants competing with investment advisers; banks with building societies, solicitors with barristers; architects with surveyors. It is, however, also necessary to take account of the growth of new occupational groups to provide cheaper and better services which were and are the core of the traditional professional service providers: legal—licensed conveyancers; accountancy—tax consultants; general medical practice—no wait diagnostic clinics. Finally there are materials, equipment and techniques to de-skill activities which were previously the sole domain of the professions—software programmes to check bank interest calculations, d.i.y. blood pressure testing, generator expert monitoring systems which compete respectively with accountants, health and consulting engineering services.

SATISFACTION ENGINEERING

In the past, when the professions served what has been described as a "privileged minority", they often possessed the means and sometimes the knowledge to choose and use professional advisers. The market for professional services today is very different. In a prescient statement nearly two decades ago and long before de-regulation was an issue, a very well-known lawyer summed up the situation which typifies conditions the professions, not just lawyers, face today:

> "Today the professions no longer serve a privileged minority. They meet the needs of, and depend upon, corporations, institutions and the public at large. Their clients are entitled to call upon them to discharge their duties, and these include assuring the client of the widest possible choice

of professional advisers and the ways in which their services are rendered. Their tasks also involve the important obligation to provide a professional service which is efficient, answerable for its activities and which charges fees closely related to the actual cost of work performed. These services must be offered in a way and upon a scale that enables them to reach the much larger corporate and individual public which are now likely to need them."[3]

These, then, are the substantive reasons why the professions must embrace marketing but if the semantics—they get worse when the word "selling" is introduced—are the unacceptable face of commercialism then perhaps the definition devised by Dr Philip Kotler would make marketing more acceptable: "satisfying human and corporate needs" or "satisfaction engineering". There ought not to be any incompatibility between professionalism and marketing. Any dissonance is caused by the way both or either are practised, not by the discipline itself. Marketing is the operation of a business (or practice) in a way that provides satisfaction, both to the clients and the practitioners, and it is difficult to argue that this should not be a *desideratum* of all professionals. There is nothing unprofessional in customer, client or patient satisfaction engineering. Organisations of every type, including non-profit organisations, depend on goodwill to survive and must learn how to sense and meet their public's or clients' needs effectively. This applies equally to all professional services because, whether it is admitted or not, professionals must (and do) sell to survive.

It is a truism that both parties in any transaction should perceive a benefit. If the wider dissemination of knowledge concerning professional practices would benefit the public, then the practitioners should themselves see an advantage in the adoption of marketing techniques to expand their practices profitably. The truth is, admitted or not, the professions must not just market they must also sell to survive. The position was stated many years ago by a clinical psychologist addressing his peers:

"Whether the word 'selling' is one that we can savour or choke upon really makes very little difference, the 'burden of proof'—that responsibility for demonstrating that our credentials really mean something and will produce genuine benefits for the clients constitutes a selling proposition that we must recognize. In short if we can't sell our credentials in the sense of demonstrating that they stand for something far more substantial than the elegant initials after our name, then we are failures not only as salesmen but as professionals as well. As professionals possessing professional skills we still have not only the requirements, but the obligation of actively and energetically selling these skills. They won't sell themselves! We have to sell them. And if we have to sell them, it is better that we do so on a conscious explicit basis rather than on an unconscious, implicit, hit or miss basis."[4]

The case for selling professional services has never been better stated. It might be assumed that the reader would not have reached this second chapter of the book if he or she had not been interested in marketing their own services and therefore the case for marketing can rest here.

THE OPPORTUNITIES

What then are the opportunities opened up by de-regulation in the professions? The values of the benefits which would accrue to professional service firms and practitioners will vary according to the organisations' or individual's needs, resources and aspirations and therefore the summary of benefits which follows is not in order of importance.

Increased Profitability

"Profit" like "selling" is a dirty word in the professions since they are, it is claimed, driven by dedication and integrity. Neither of these need be sacrificed in seeking profit and indeed, to turn to primitive economics, unless expenditure is exceeded by income the firm will cease to exist.

Improved profitability can come from a number of sources but in relation to marketing it will derive substantially from a better application of resources through the acquisition of work "mix" that uses these resources to the full. This is not just a question of the quantity of work but also the quality and regularity of engagements.

Coherent consistent marketing can yield an even flow of work to avoid the over/under demand cycle from which so many consultancy-type services suffer. "When you are doing the work you are not getting it—when you are getting it you are not doing it" encapsulates the problem for all professional service companies, even large ones where the "getting" function is separated from the "doing" function.

Other ways of increasing profits are by enriching the service "mix" with high yield services and concentrating marketing on those services: setting a minimum size of engagement or adopting a premium fee system; cross-selling services internally to substitute own internal services for bought-in ones; sub-contracting some types of work; and, needless to say, mechanisation and de-skilling tasks which might otherwise require high cost personnel inputs. (Appendix 12, page 121, gives a checklist for profitability improvement.)

Greater Work Satisfaction

Marketing can yield enhanced work satisfaction which is a factor of considerable importance to all dedicated professionals. The downside of much of the practitioner's work is the lack of opportunity to implement a planned course of action or seeing it being implemented badly or perhaps not at all which creates a high degree of frustration in those who are doers and not just advisers. By marketing those services to those clients who want partnerships with their advisers rather than a vendor–purchaser relationship it is possible to obtain a flow of the type of work that gives high job satisfaction.

An essential characteristic of professional services is the one-to-one relationship with individuals whether in their private or corporate capacities. The achievement of greater empathy between practitioner and client or patient will result in a higher degree of collaboration replacing old adversarial attitudes which, in turn, will lead to greater job satisfaction. Marketing makes a considerable contribution to identifying and obtaining clients whose work requirements and attitudes are consistent with the type of assignments from which job satisfaction is generated.

Marketing Practice and Personal Objectives

Pro-active marketing ensures the firm goes the way its owners and managers want it to go rather than being a victim of events and circumstances. Given the direction is well chosen, then a sensibly planned marketing strategy will create career opportunities which, in turn, will make the organisation more attractive both to those already working within it and in recruiting high calibre staff. It will also ensure that the ambitions and aspirations both personal and corporate of the owners will be met.

Client Satisfaction

Good marketing demands good information. If the needs and wants, verbalised and non-verbalised, of clients are known then it is possible to provide them with services that they will regard as satisfactory and cost effective. Marketing is information dependent and leads to better client service and more satisfied clients. This, in turn, has a favourable on-going impact on the efforts which are made to obtain new clients. Clients who receive value for money are always an important element in the networking system (see Chapter 20).

De-regulation means that professional firms and individuals are now free to make known their offers by the most suitable and appropriate ways and as can be seen, the rewards are considerable and sustainable. There are after all a number of dormant market sectors where assignments will only arise if there is knowledge of the service and the benefits which will accrue.

The taxonomy below provides a skeleton structure of such markets which can best be penetrated by marketing. If the actions suggested appear merely pious, the reader is assured that the encapsulation will be fully explained in later chapters.

Each market condition implies different approaches by the practice developer and, once identified, calls for positive action. Of course a firm under normal business conditions faces a combination of these situations and, while it can deal with a number of them simultaneously, in order to maximise the use of its limited resources it is necessary to place them in order of priority in terms of what the practice is seeking to achieve in the short, medium and long term.

The methods of penetrating these market groupings are dealt with throughout the book: for example, *engaged markets* in Chapter 8; Chapters 14 and 15 both deal with the choice factors in selecting a profession and a professional service firm; *lost markets* in Chapter 23;

Table 2.1 *Market dispositions*

Market type	Description	Action
Negative	Organisations or individuals who avoid using particular professional services if they can. This is particularly true of law and some branches of health care, most particularly dentistry.	Identify blockages and devise messages and methods of communication to overcome them. Emphasise benefits of use and dangers of non-use.
Unrealised	Organisations and individuals who require services which are not provided but which could be sensibly added to the existing service range.	Develop expertise in the required areas and communicate the fact it is available. Cross-sell.
Engaged	Potential clients using directly competitive services.	Identify why competitors are preferred. Add value and develop additional client benefits preferably some unique "plus".
Latent	Organisations and individuals who are unaware of the benefits a service would yield.	Promote the service concept and then the service firm.
Inert	Organisations and individuals who have professional service requirements but require stimulating into using them.	Locate potential clients and demonstrate the benefits to be obtained from using the services.
Fluctuating	Seasonal day, week, or month and time peakings.	Devise time shift incentives, market alternative engagement time or seek a counter-cyclical client demand.
Declining	Sectors of industry, organisations and individuals whose requirement for a professional service is lessening.	Establish reasons and offer services suitable to the circumstances or withdraw.
Lost	Organisations and individuals not returning to the firm.	Research reasons and if not immutable (e.g. removal, take-over, death, change of activity) correct or compensate for previous errors, restructure offer to meet requirements.
Undesired	Organisations and individuals not wanted as clients.	Re-direct any marketing activity into other potential segments.
Over demand	Client requirements exceeds capacity.	De-market less profitable services or delay demand.

Source: This table is based on the analysis provided by Kotler, P. and Bloom, P. *Marketing Professional Services*, pp. 8–9, Prentice-Hall, Englewood Cliffs (1984) and Stallard, R., Hess, K. and Scales, R. *Handbook of Dental Marketing*, pp. 52–54, PenWell Books, Tulsa (1986).

engaged markets and *latent markets* in chapter 10. These and others are all drawn together in the final chapter.

ACTION POINTS

- Are we taking full advantage of the liberalisation of practice rules?
- What activities are currently occurring which have either direct or indirect marketing implications?
- Would an intensification and re-targeting of marketing effect the results this chapter suggests are available?
- What actions should be taken to realise these benefits?

NOTES

(1) *Doctor*, 17 January, London (1991).
(2) Dingwall, R. and Lewis, P. *The Sociology of the Professions*, p.41, Macmillan, London (1983).
(3) Howe, Sir G. *Nigel Colley Memorial Lecture*, Nottingham Law Society (1975).
(4) Wittreich, W.J. "Selling—A Prerequisite to Success as a Professional", conference paper, Detroit, 8 January (1969).

3
The Professional and Ethical Framework

The foregoing, which has traced the break-up of the regulatory constraints on marketing and their implications for the professions, does not imply that the high standards of professional behaviour and ethical activities are in anyway compromised. There is no conflict between what might be perceived as commercialism and professionalism. Conflict, as has already been stated, only arises between bad commercialism and professionalism.

One if somewhat narrow view of the attributes of professionalism identified and defined many years ago still has a validity:[1]

1   *Intellectual bias.* An intellectual discipline capable of formulation on theoretical, if not academic, lines, requiring a good educational background and tested by examination.
2   *Private practice.* A foundation in private practice, so that the essential expertise and standards of the profession derive from meeting the needs of individual clients on a person to person basis, with remuneration in fees from individual clients rather than a salary or stipend from one source.
3   *Advisery function.* An advisory function, often coupled with an executive function in carrying out what has been advised, or doing ancillary work, such as supervising and negotiating, or managing; in the exercise of both functions full responsibility is taken by the person exercising them.

4 *Tradition of services.* An outlook which is essentially objective and disinterested, where the motive of making money is subordinated to serving the client in a manner not inconsistent with the public good.
5 *Representative institute.* One or more societies or institutes representing members of the profession, particularly those in private practice, and having the function of safeguarding and developing the expertise and standards of the profession.
6 *Code of conduct.* A code of professional ethics, laid down and enforced by the professional institute or institutes.

THE DEFENCE AGAINST COMMERCIALISM

It is perhaps around the fourth attribute that the discussion and division concerning the ethical marketing of professional services revolves. For a start, all professions emphasise that they place service to the individual and community above and beyond the specific situation in which they find themselves and their self interest. This, as has been observed, is good public relations and it generates respect from those who do not have the body of knowledge that has been deemed indispensable in the first place for membership of the profession. The defence against the encroachment of commercialism was that essentially the nature of the professional–client relationship was such that any question of actively seeking business would disturb the trust and confidentiality of that relationship to the detriment of both parties. The marketing of a professional service it was feared would move the emphasis from providing service to money making.

It has been said that individually and in association, the professions struck a bargain with society in which they exchanged competence and integrity against the trust of the client and community, relative freedom from lay supervision and interference, protection against unqualified competition, substantial rewards and higher social status.[2]

The essentially self protecting nature of most professional bodies has been exposed in many countries where circumstances have led to governmental or other investigations (the British Dental Association's notepaper heading states without equivocation "Working for Dentists"). This, combined

with the effect of well publicised examples of professional negligence and sometimes malfeasance in many professions, led to
the defence of the *status quo* losing much of its force.

The reluctant acceptance that practice development was relevant to all professions was achieved only after practitioners in
most disciplines were, if not actually convinced, then less cynical
that both they and their clients would benefit from good marketing communications. Except perhaps among some health care
professionals the total incompatibility of professional practice and
marketing is no longer seen as axiomatic. Why the two should
ever have been regarded as incompatible is difficult to understand
since revenue and profit are critical for the survival of the firm.
After all, without profit growth is impossible, new services can
only be added with difficulty, working conditions cannot be improved nor staff rewarded adequately, jobs cannot be made secure. It is perhaps the concept of profit overriding service rather
than the reality of profit which causes most concern.

How far this paradigm of professionalism is applicable today
with the expansion of both education and the means of communication, which together have reduced the sense of awe and respect
which was once held for the professions, is difficult to assess. As
with any other activity in which there is a supplier and vendor
and where monies are exchanged for goods and services it has
become necessary for the service provider to demonstrate that the
desired purchase is worth more than the fees for its acquisition,
while at the same time accepting that the fees paid represent a fair
return for the application of their skill and knowledge. These two
differing values are present in every transaction.

The knowledge gap between the client and professional gives the
latter considerable influence and control and the opportunity,
usually grasped, to adopt a paternalistic approach. It is the view of
one expert that "the general practitioner can only act as a necessary
mediator between layman and specialist by cultivating that trust to
a degree which makes paternalism unavoidable" and this must
apply in other professions. There is an inherent assumption that such
paternalism is justified by the overall excellence or indeed omni-
potence of the paternal figure most particularly in medicine where
the patient feels most helpless. Yet, as Proust observed of the medical
profession, ability "does not imply any superiority in other departments of the intellect, and a person of the utmost vulgarity, who

admires the worst pictures, the worst music, who is without the slightest intellectual curiosity, may perfectly well possess great expertise in his professional capacity."[3] Moreover there is no precise correlation between the excellence of advice and results. If there were, then any knowledge gap would be of little significance and paternalism would become easier to justify.

THE DEFENCE AGAINST PROFESSIONAL POWER

The Galbraithian principle that "customers' wants are created by the process by which they are satisfied" if only dubiously applicable to products certainly applies to professional services. The suppliers of such services exercised considerable power over the clients and patients and sought to control both supply and the form, if not the totality, of demand by telling them what was good for them. It cannot of course be said that such a system frustrated the real wants of the client if they themselves could not diagnose or express them. But a substantial part of the real wants, which was never acknowledged by the professions, was not simply the outcome of the service but the way the services were delivered— something clients could both comment on and assess. This was the first area where changes in attitudes emerged. In due course it will lead on to clients' ability, perhaps with independent technical support, to express their needs in terms of service content and to assess them not just for results but also to evaluate the skills and efforts of the practitioner.

There are today plenty of independent sources of advice whereby users of professional services are assisted to make judgements and to seek redress. Whether this is partly a function of the qualifying and other associations is arguable. Although the Law Society is responsible for the Solicitors Complaints Bureau nevertheless the Society is there for the benefit of its members. There is little doubt that the Bureau conducts its work impartially but there must always be concern as to whether this is the best forum for resolving disputes.

Ombudsmen, while probably being a better choice for the investigation of complaints, are not independent advisery bodies. Thus the problem of evening out the knowledge and power basis that divides the professions from their clients is still to be solved.

In a completely free competitive market for the supply of services, the natural expression of clients' choice should lead automatically to the most satisfactory organisation, and so to the commensurately lowest fee. The question is whether this model is applicable to professional services. In many respects the answer must be "hardly at all" if only because clients or patients often consult not because they want to but because they have to. Furthermore they may be referred or directed to the provider of the service instead of making a choice. Thus, unlike purchasing products and commercial services, the advantage of having a potential client pre-disposed towards the practice because they chose it is lost. While being directed or referred may represent a highly satisfactory situation for the practitioner it has a considerable downside. Clients, whether they verbalise their dissatisfaction or not, certainly resent the exercising of power in this way so that in these circumstances far from there being a pre-disposition in favour of the selected practice over another firm, the opposite may be true.

The professional's responsibility in client relationships goes beyond a duty of care. It must also include shaping expectations realistically, providing effective communication and presenting benefits (see Chapter 10) in terms of the clients' satisfaction levels not just those of the providers. These are the issues which are of major concern to clients and none of them are contrary to the norms of professionalism or in anyway are unethical. It is simply that in most professions the culture has not yet come to terms with the changed client–professional relationship.

The fears that many professionals have expressed concerning the possible deterioration in their client relationships through marketing their services have not as yet proved to have any foundation. But even if they had, the benefits to the public which would stem from better knowledge and understanding not only of the services but of the relative expertise, interests and experience of individual practitioners would more than off-set any disadvantages. Those professions that have led the way in changing their attitude to clients (and the market) have already reaped considerable rewards. While there are many concerns about bringing market forces to bear in such areas of expertise as health care, certainly one of the benefits which has accrued, as the next chapter shows, is a much more client/patient friendly attitude which itself can aid the therapeutic process.

Professional autonomy, professional charisma and professional morality are not challenged by the new ethos. They are creating a more balanced position as between the service receiver and the service provider. While it is obvious that the client benefits it does not mean the professional loses. On the contrary, the opportunities for providing better services, better relationship and greater job satisfaction now abound and should not be lost.

NOTES

(1) Bennion, F.A.R. *Professional Ethics*, p.15, Charles Knight, London (1969).

(2) Dingwall, R. and Lewis, I. (eds) *The Sociology of the Professions*, Chapter 2, Macmillan, London (1983) and Rueschemeyer, D. "Professional Autonomy and Social Control of Expertise". Macmillan, London (1983).

(3) Proust, M. *Remembrance of Things Past* (translator K. Scott Moncrieff), Vol. 1, p.536, Chatto, London (1981).

4
Health Care: a Suitable Case for Treatment

Medicine occupies a unique position among professional disciplines because nothing is more important to mankind than life itself and no other professional can lay claim to the legacy of the Hippocratic oath in the ability to heal and mastery over death. Whether or not the ability and mastery are real, at times of distress everyone perceives and invokes them. While the clients of many professions may lack knowledge of the skills involved or the ability to diagnose their own problems, none of them suffer the disadvantage of the sick or geriatric patient who may well be either incapable or at best not in the appropriate frame of mind to make clear judgements about both the service and the practitioners. For many clients of the health care professions services are paid for either by the government or by insurance; there is no financial incentive to question doctors or other professionals about the quality or complexity of investigations and treatment. Moreover, since the patient may not be paying directly for the treatment there is a distinct feeling that questioning is either inappropriate or that it would be ungracious.

Within this protective wall the medical professions might seem invulnerable to pressures generated by laymen but there is a particular reason for singling out health care and its various branches for a separate chapter. De-regulation which spread through the professions during the 1970s and 1980s, as was shown in chapter 1, did not touch the medical and associated professions.

It was only towards the end of the 1980s and gathering pace in the early 1990s that reforming the medical profession was seriously considered, forced on at a great pace in the United Kingdom by governmental determination to encourage competition, and through this competition to achieve greater efficiency in the use of resources and an improved service to patients. They did not do this by interfering directly with the governing bodies of the medical profession but forced changes by restructuring the Health Service:

> "It [the National Health Service] emphasised accountability, competition, prevention and value for money. Even those doctors who supported increased efficiency and greater cost savings greeted their new contract with wariness. They did not see how an attitude of 'bottom line' management could enhance patients treatment."[1]

One highly respected observer of the medical profession and himself a doctor, clearly identified the role of general medical practice in terms which were totally antipathetic to the profession: "General practitioners are independent contractors who run small businesses".[2]

The politics are not the concern of the author. Within the context of this book the emphasis is how practice development within the health care professions can be accomplished which will improve service to patients and provide measurable benefits to the practitioners in terms of work satisfaction, career opportunities and, last but not least, even if the words burn the lips, profitability. Implicit is the likelihood that practice development will also lead to the accountability, competition, prevention and value for money referred to above.

For those who pay for health care services, be it government, insurance companies or the individual, value for money must be a major consideration in the choice of practitioners and practices. Whether or not this will come about through competition or from other forces, there is an urgent need to organise health care activities to yield patient-satisfying services—the word satisfaction including of course the patients' perception that they have received value for money whether through taxation, premiums or direct payment.

While competition in the past was limited to varying degrees in other professions, it barely existed in health care and this was particularly true of general medical practice when, to quote one authority writing in 1989[3]:

> "Doctors are still largely paid by reference to what they do not do rather than what they do. Under any capitation scheme there was little incentive to provide a consumer responsive service as the GP's pocket was neither enriched by the provision of better service nor made poorer by its absence."

The White Paper of 1989 *Working for Patients* predicated changes in the payment basis so that financial reward would become increasingly linked to preventative medicine's assumption of entrepreneurial approaches for service development.

The General Medical Council sustained their case against any form of promotion on the grounds that the doctor who is most successful at achieving publicity may not be the most appropriate for a patient to consult. The concern for patients might have been wholly applauded were it not for the fact that the real reason for such constraints was to limit competition and reduce accountability rather than to protect patients. The game was given away in two single paragraphs in the *Code of Practice* where, paraphrased, it is stated that promotional material which was likely to attract patients to, or to promote the professional advantage or financial benefit of, a doctor would engender disciplinary action. Further, and again paraphrased, there is a clear statement that doctors through the use of promotion must not seek to gain an advantage over other doctors or to canvass their patients.[4]

As another example, ophthalmic medical practitioners are governed by the same rules as those which apply to general practitioners but specialists continue to be totally prevented from informing the general public about their services even in the same terms as are now permissible for general practitioners. This, it stated, is to "preserve the conventional referral system" although there is little to support the value of the "conventional referral system". Indeed the arguments barristers advance for being able to be retained directly by a member of the public if they have any virtue could be equally applicable to specialist medical practitioners. The system's origin can be found in the 1948 National Health Service reforms. Because of the intense resistance offered by hospital consultants they were given lucrative fellowship work; general practitioners retained their gatekeeper role. Five decades later these political settlements still apply. It has been said by one informed commentator that specialists play an almost sinister role as power brokers.

The General Medical Council's rules of professional conduct relative to advertising were challenged unsuccessfully in 1989. Even so, the judgement referred to the desirability of the President of the GMC re-considering the guidance contained in the Blue Book particularly when he had the benefit of the recommendations of the Monopolies and Mergers Commission report. The continued refusal to allow a member to place factual advertising was thus under both governmental pressure as well as pressure from groups with narrower interests.[5]

While in the United Kingdom there have been restrictions on entry to many parts of the health care professions, in the USA where some restrictions have been lifted there has been a flow of new doctors, leading to competition which may not have resulted in a reduction of fees but certainly limited the extent of their increase. If fee pressure intensifies then all health care professions will need to look at their activities and ways in which they can increase both their efficiency and profitability. One contribution to achieving this objective is marketing.

ATTITUDES TO MARKETING

But marketing is not a word much favoured by health care professionals any more than it was in other professions prior to de-regulation. The word had a censorious ring and is frequently used as an alternative to advertising or, worse, "selling" which has an even more derogatory connotation. This is clearly demonstrated by an editorial comment referred to on page 14 where comparison to brush salesmen was made and which was further inflamed with the words:

> "This [marketing] is a new style of general practice, forced on doctors, by the vulgar commercialisations of the National Health Service. It is abhorrent even to the younger generation of GPs one might have though most likely to welcome the competitive edge...It [the profession] is in no real shape to resist what many doctors see as an inexorable decline into an abysmal free for all as the battle for patients hots up."[6]

Similar reactions were commonplace in the other professions—law, architecture, accountancy, surveying, for example—but each one has in turn found to their surprise, if not actual delight, that marketing is first of all not selling and moreover is capable of simultaneously increasing profit and work satisfaction.

There may well be an intense suspicion about the market place and all it is presumed to stand for but developing a practice, medical or any other discipline, can be undertaken with grace and sophistication. Approaches need not be brash or intrusive. To repeat the words of Dr Philip Kotler quoted in Chapter 2, marketing is no more than satisfaction engineering; that is, satisfying human and corporate needs. The practice of marketing is itself a sophisticated art and discipline. Marketing is essentially concerned with delivering benefits to the patient. Obviously diagnosis, cure, alleviation, re-assurance are all part of the benefit package health care professionals can provide, but the suggestion of delivering benefits has such overtones of commercialism, the very idea is shunned and rejected as being relevant only to goods and commercial services. Yet the Hippocratic oath—which is strictly speaking not an oath but an ethical code—actually refers to "the *benefit* of my patients".

The health care profession has always believed the patient or client is not the best person to decide who is and who is not a good doctor, dentist or psychiatrist, or what is appropriate treatment and to assess its quality. The inability or reluctance of *some* patients to choose cannot be a valid basis for permitting the medical profession to restrict disclosure of information to *all* patients. It is the duty of all professions to provide their clients or patients with the information that will enable them to make informed decisions.

Perhaps patients are called patients rather than customers or clients because they have to be. Their lack of information favours and gives a power base to the doctor and as such it is only human nature to attempt to preserve it:

"This imbalance of knowledge between patient and doctor is built into the relationship. Obviously, if the patient had all the doctor's knowledge he would not need the doctor! At the same time however there is also some uncertainty on the part of the doctor: medicine is not an exact science and there are uncertainties both in diagnosis and choice of treatment. Thus the doctor also faces a high degree of uncertainty as well as the patient so why should the patient be left with a higher degree of uncertainty or ignorance than strictly necessary?* 'Ignorant patients are easier to deal with than those who are well informed and the medical machinery runs more smoothly if people do not ask questions and place themselves childlike and docile in the hands of their doctor. The power of the doctor may then be related directly to how much or how little the patient knows about what is going on'."[7]

Whether or not the client or patient has the ability to choose wisely does not remove the requirement for the practitioner to communicate and to at least give the opportunity of choice. The danger perceived by doctors is that the persuasive element in marketing will submerge the factual aspects of communication. Any argument that bad or unscrupulous health practitioners will exploit advertising is a tacit admission that bad or unscrupulous health practitioners already exist. Clearly if this is true then the public is already at risk and David Green asserts[8] the dangers which flow from a lack of knowledge must be set against the risks that flow from misleading advertising, an equation that has not been solved. The methods, the message and media which are used for many types of consumer goods are one end of marketing, but it is the other polarity which health care practitioners should be considering.

Now that medicine has lost much of its mystique the defence of a fortress that no longer protects is without much purpose. Television, health journalism, manuals and publicity for alternative remedies are leading to a minor rebellion among patients. Complaints to family health service authorities have doubled in the past decade. Perhaps more significantly, many people have lost faith in conventional medicine's ability to cure all their ills; even the sceptical are turning to osteopathy or homeopathy or acupuncture. Perhaps most significant has been the development of powerful patient lobbies united by the AIDS/HIV epidemic.[9] Many AIDS patients, it is claimed, know more about therapies than the doctors who treat them and are demanding a say in what type of care they receive. These empowered patients are part of well educated and usually militant activist groups who regularly demand or refuse treatments thus challenging the hegemony of the medical profession. Faced with a life or death issue, sufferers

---

* The problems and opportunities engendered by client uncertainty are included in Chapter 5 and Chapter 15.

want access to new and often unproven therapies and demand to be involved in how and where new drugs are tested. Other groups suffering life-threatening illnesses are learning rapidly to emulate the tactics of the militant organisations.

In an attempt to provide both the individual and the community with better value for money, a series of reforms have been forced on to the British medical profession which involve new systems and constraints among which is that of fund holder. This gives general practitioners control of their budget allocations and the right to retain for their surgeries any savings they achieve. This has generated a change of attitude among fund holders. They now have an incentive to control their costs. The additional funds they generate by remaining within their budgets is leading to an improvement in patient care through the provision of better surgeries and equipment. A potential spin-off is that others in the health care system such as hospitals, consultants and alternative medicine practitioners must now vie for a share of the doctors' disposable funds, and are faced with the need to market to doctors irrespective of whether the latter choose to market their own practices to patients. The effect can already be seen. Hospitals under the new arrangements are required to cost their surgical procedures and the more enterprising are now marketing them to fund-holding general practitioners.

It is also necessary to take into account the growth of new occupational groups to provide cheaper and better services which were and are the core of orthodox general practice as well as the current emphasis on primary healthcare terms. In America it is possible to see the emergence of "nurse practitioners" acting independently of physicians (which is also occurring in the United Kingdom), podiatrists and pharmaceutical-care, described as an umbrella definition of patient care, including drug prescribing, sourcing, monitoring patient compliance, detecting adverse reactions and checking the therapeutic outcome.[10]

Finally, there are products, equipment and techniques which are changing the locus of medical specialists or de-skilling activities. Examples are the development of electronic equipment which substitutes surgical procedures for haemorrhoid treatment by a single out-patient visit and the now ubiquitous d.i.y. blood and pregnancy testing equipment. On the horizon are sensors for diabetic blood glucose monitoring which will replace invasive techniques. There is also the erosion of the monopoly which general practitioners hold over the issue of prescriptions. More and more drugs are being switched from "prescription only" to "over the counter" (OTC) availability and with this change will come greater consultation with the pharmacist on health requirements.

SKILLS AND RESOURCES

Another new element is entering the health care scene—the appointment of practice managers, not themselves qualified professionals but experienced managers able to systematise the administrative and financial aspects of a practice or an institution. Among the skills many of them bring to these new appointments is some knowledge of marketing. Just like the non-qualified senior managers within other disciplines, they have an immense task in overcoming the barriers of not being professionally qualified and the grave suspicion of attempting to turn the organisation into a purely commercial activity with the bottom line the only criteria for success. It would be absurd to dismiss such fears totally, but substantially the practice manager strata within health care organisations of all types will add significantly to the push for sensible promotional strategies that neither compromise the integrity or culture of the profession nor turns doctors, nurses, dentists, hygienists, paramedicals and others into "brush salesmen".

These then are the forces of change, some providing threats to be avoided and others opportunities to be grasped. Both these can be achieved by developing and implementing a cohesive, consistent and concentrated programme of practice development. This does not call for skills beyond the capability of doctors and others to develop nor for resources that they do not possess or could not acquire. Doctors must accept that patients will now begin to shop around. In the United Kingdom they will take the National Health Service principle of a second opinion to its logical conclusion. They will want the best doctor, the best hospital, the best medicine. Some will seek private services, and others may be sent to private hospitals, their treatment paid for by their health authority. Consultants, who have seen their income from the private sector increase enormously in the past few years, will become richer still—as long as they win popularity with increasingly assertive patients. "Winning" in this context means ensuring both referrers and patients have knowledge of the skills and believe results can be delivered irrespective of the way information has been obtained. The nomenclature the professionals choose to adopt to describe the communication method is irrelevant. (Chapters 6, 20 and 24 are just three of the later chapters which deal with this issue.)

Whether it is desirable or possible to hold back the tide of reform in the health care professions is doubtful to an extreme. It is no longer a question of whether doctors, hospitals and other organisations should acquire the skills (which must include marketing) to manage their activities with the same level of efficiency they expect from other organisations. To do so is now a necessity. There is nothing in this book that is not appropriate and indeed possible to accomplish for all health care organisations and practitioners and much of it needs to be adopted now in order to meet the rapid changes which are occurring.

RESIDUAL CONSTRAINTS

While some branches of health care have gone a little way to de-restrict promotional activities, as was shown in Chapter 1, there still remain important prohibitions. Innocuous in itself the rule which states, "doctors must not compare or contrast the quality of services with those provided by other doctors" has significant implications. Those who offer services not usually available, for example screening or counselling for cancer sufferers, cannot bring this information to the attention of potential patients without the risk of disciplinary action. Extend the rule to hospitals and it will be found that it is not possible for those treating particular diseases or providing specific surgical procedures to make a comparison of success or safety records or for them to suggest that some forms of treatment are superior to others, for example the use of non-invasive techniques or where radical mastectomy is avoided in favour of less disfiguring approaches.

It is however worthy of note that nursing agencies, not bound by the strict rules of health care professions, have neither been slow nor ineffective in marketing their services, some even reaching the holy grail of marketing—unaided instant recall.

Those who deliver health care services on behalf of an employing organisation—nurses and other paramedicals, hygienists, radiographers, midwives, pharmacists, for example—are not directly involved in marketing efforts although their role has a pervasive effect on the acceptability of the service as Chapter 19 clearly shows. Marketing is essentially a task for the employing organisation or equity partners or their managers.

Three *desiderata* so far as the promoting of health services are concerned have been offered:

- Factual or comparative information should be available and should not mislead by omission
- The deliberate building of "brand" loyalties should be permissible. This enhances loyalties that already exist for local and often old established clinics, hospitals and surgeries
- Promotional regulations should not be controlled by the well-being of the professionals which cannot be said to act as disinterestedly as they would claim[11]

In the United Kingdom the so-called *Patients Charter*[12] has pushed open the door a little further by endowing them with the right to be given detailed information on local health services including quality standards and waiting times. It would now take a judgement of Solomon to decide whether a hospital stating that its admission time for the replacement of hip joints was half of that of other institutions was not breaking the rule on contrasting or comparing quality of services. For health care there is still much to be clarified, but at least the professions are at last facing the right way.

This chapter has considered practice development as being directed at the main players—patients, potential patients, general practitioners, specialists, hospitals, primary health care teams and others. There is, however, one more target which has to be considered; that is, the providers of funds be they government or private health insurance:

"General practitioners will need to develop the skills to enter into…discussions, and they will lose out if they fail to learn the new language of managers of family health services authorities...The views of the profession will be simply sidestepped if general practitioners do not contribute constructively to these debates."[13]

These same skills will have to be acquired by all in the health care sector in relation to other funders who set scales and whose power is sufficiently great as to be able to determine the success or otherwise of practitioners. And since the discussion referred to will of necessity be of a persuasive nature, what is it but marketing?

ACTION POINTS

- Undertake an overall appraisal to establish if the practice would benefit from professional management to release practitioners to concentrate on patients
- Develop a client database (see Chapter 7)
- Set up a programme to keep patients informed on all aspects of the service
- Develop "patient friendly" physical and personnel ambience
- Offer an augmented service range

NOTES

(1) O'Connor, C. "Changes in the NHS", *Professional Practice Management*, London, May (1992).
(2) Marinker, M. *Greening the White Paper*, The Social Market Foundation, London (1989).
(3) Charles, C. "Advertising by Medical Professionals—a health outlook", *International Journal of Advertising*, Vol. 8, London (1989).
(4) General Medical Council *Professional Conduct and Discipline: Fitness to Practice*, paras 62 and 94, London (1987).
(5) An excellent review up to 1989 of advertising in the medical and other professions will be found in Bosanquet, N. "Advertising and the Medical Profession in Britain", *International Journal of Advertising*, No. 8, Bradford (1989).
(6) *Doctor*, 17, London, January (1992).

(7)   Charles, C. "Advertising by Medical Professionals—a health outlook", *International Journal of Advertising*, Vol. 8, p.61, London (1989).

(8)   Green, D. *Should Doctors Advertise*, p.26, Institute of Economic Affairs, London (1989).

(9)   The HIV/AIDS situation has had a pervasive effect on all marketing as is shown in a detailed study, see Wilson, A. and West, C. "Permissive Marketing: the effects of the AIDS crisis on marketing practices and messages", *Business Strategy Review,* Summer, London (1992).

(10) Curston, G.L. *An Assessment of Future Educational Need for Community Pharmacists*, SRI International, Menlo Park, CA (1991).

(11) Green, D. *Should Doctors Advertise*, pp.29–30, Institute of Economic Affairs, London (1989).

(12) Department of Health *The Patients Charter*, London (1992).

(13) Roland, M. "Fundholding and Cash Limits in Primary Care: blight or blessing!", *British Medical Journal*, London, 20 July (1991).

5
On Being Client Centred: Attitudes, Activities and Benefits

No amount of exhortation will change a firm's attitudes to its clients and its markets unless there is a substantial reason for doing so. After all, it can be argued, the professions have always prospered without the need for the cosseting of clients. This is perfectly true but the tense is important. "*Have* always prospered" implies that the past is a reliable guide to the future. This it is not, given the reasons advanced in previous chapters. But being client centred does not simply provide benefits to clients. Far from it. Benefits are divided perhaps equally between clients, the equity partners in the practice or firm and other stakeholders, and all staff. Moreover many of the benefits are measurable. What then does a practice have to be or not to be, to do or not to do, to win the rewards which are on offer? Being client centred implies meeting client *needs* but there is also the question of client *wants* and that of client *expectations*. These are not the same and often overlap. An important part of the professionalism of a practice is its ability to make all three coincide. This should be the objective of client care.

SENSING NEEDS

First, the entire organisation from the most senior to the most junior has to be able to sense client needs, even those they cannot or will not verbalise. Technical needs which call upon the skills of the discipline are not too difficult to identify although not infre-quently the client may have made a wrong identification. In fact, problems which can arise from the technical aspect of an inquiry can be easily shown in a schematic form, as is illustrated in Table 9.1, page 80.

Some of the needs whether expressed or not will be obvious: efficiency needs—that is, the requirement to conserve resources, the saving of time and money; safety needs—that is safety in a physical and resource sense; management needs—the desire to be involved in the process and not to lose control over their own affairs; experience needs—the emotional impact of the use of a professional service.

It is unexpressed needs which require the greatest sensitivity. These fall into three categories and their validity is easily tested if each practitioner were to consider him or herself as another pro-fessional's client or patient. The three categories[1] are:

1 *Minimising uncertainty.* A professional service must make a direct contribution to the reduction of personal or business uncertainty. The proper assessment of a service, unlike that of tangible good, must take into account the impact of its perfor-mance on the client.
2 *Understanding problems.* Practitioners must come directly to grips with the fundamental needs and problems of the client, associated with the purchase of the service. Successful perfor-mance depends on understanding the client's needs and busi-ness.
3 *Being totally professional.* A professional service can only be purchased meaningfully from someone who is capable of ren-dering the service. Selling ability and personality by them-selves are meaningless.

There are many sources of uncertainty and the client-centred professional and all the support staff will seek to understand these and to mitigate them. This and the importance of accurate and agreed problem definition and the need for total and unremitting professionalism are considered in more detail in Chapter 15.

One other client need which falls between that which is ex-pressed or implicit and that which is not verbalised is the desire for activity. While it is true clients want a favourable result they also want activity. The majority of complaints made against professional service firms can be traced to a real or apparent lack of activity which in turn may derive from poor communication. An insurance company providing private pension schemes admitted it could take up to six months to respond to letters from customers. Clients like to feel their situation, problem or requirement will not result in a mechanistic approach but will receive a quick and creative pro-active response and that the activities necessary to accomplish a result will move forward at a reasonable and appropriate pace.

There are many ways of creating activity all of which, will add to client satisfaction and build towards client loyalty to and enthusiasm for the practice and the practitioner. Some examples are:

Projecting Activity

- Copy to the client all documents received (if necessary, edited).
- Return clients' calls immediately.
- If working on private cases outside office hours, call them at home with questions so they know you are devoting "personal" time to them.
- Bill at regular intervals.
- Make client visits.
- Visit commercial clients at their premises to gain an understanding of their business. Do not charge them for "learning" but charge for conferences or consultations at place of business.
- Go with clients to the scene of an accident in personal injury or compensation cases.
- Ask for annual reports and comment on them.
- Keep clients informed of any changes in law or technology which may affect them.

It is not of course sufficient to sense needs. It is necessary to demonstrate to clients that their needs have been perceived and that the service both in content and the manner of its delivery will match the needs. (These issues are dealt with in more detail in Chapter 15, page 148.)

RESPONDING TO ENQUIRIES

Second in the hierarchy of client-centred activities is responding effectively to clients. That does not just mean promptly but of course it includes that too. It implies communicating with clients in terms which have a meaning to them. That is, the knowledge gap between the practitioners, which traditionally was kept as wide as possible, has to be narrowed and closed. *It is not the client's job to understand—it is the professional's job to be more understandable.* In following this dictum it is important not to appear patronising or to be treating the client as a lower form of intelligence who must be humoured. A skill those involved in professional services must develop is the ability to achieve the correct balance between the information to be conveyed and the listener's ability to understand it.

The less familiar clients are with the subject matter the greater the uncertainty they will experience although not necessarily exhibit. Thus, the practice representative needs to develop a mental scale of the "state of knowledge" or knowledge gap between themselves and the client:

- Ignorant (of the subject matter)
- Below average
- Average
- Above average
- Expert

A discussion which has misjudged the knowledge gap by more than one category has every likelihood of failing in its objectives to achieve some pre-determined action. Thus, if it is pitched at average level to an expert, it will be largely wasted and will result in impatience, aggression, and even ridicule. An above average level of presentation of the firm's approach to a below average knowledgeable potential client will not achieve an understanding, and without understanding a client would be foolish to take any action. Moreover to expose, however unwittingly, their lack of knowledge is hardly likely to produce a favourable atmosphere.

SEEKING OPPORTUNITIES

The third element of a client-centred programme is the seeking out of opportunities to provide additional or improved services. The greatest possibilities for enhanced profitability for all practices is increasing the volume of work undertaken for existing clients. It is claimed that it costs between five and seven times as much to obtain a client as to retain one. Even if the arithmetic is suspect the relativities cannot be too far out. Thus, there is every incentive to seek additional work. Asking the question "what services do our clients purchase which we do not supply but could do so profitably?" is likely to open up more possibilities than the most sophisticated marketing.

Marketing, as its practitioners well know but rarely admit, has a *penchant* for giving new titles to old concepts. While the now much quoted "relationship marketing" appears to do no more than re-express what marketing is about anyway, it does have a refining quality. Its application is based on developing a continuous relationship with clients by supplying a range of related services. Its purpose, like marketing in its totality, is to create loyalties for mutual benefit. Relationship marketing requires a very detailed database (see Chapter 7) and continuously tracks and monitors the practice's relationship with each client using lifetime value to the organisation calculations to set the extent of client nurturing.

A checklist[2] for obtaining additional business from existing clients has been devised and can usefully be adopted but will obviously need adjusting to the circumstance of the individual firm. Chapter 21 deals with this subject in depth.

VALUE FOR MONEY

The fourth aspect of being client centred is that of satisfying needs through the delivery of high quality services at commensurate fees. "Commensurate" is, of course, the substantive issue in that what may well be commensurate to the service firm is perceived as anything but commensurate by the client. It should be quite clear, sentient clients do not seek cut prices; they know that with services by and large you get what you pay for. What they are looking for is value for money and the onus is on the practice to provide this.

There is a general perception throughout business and society generally that professional service bills are far too high, which is a view reinforced by the very high rewards some professions generate for many of their members and by the sumptuous premises they occupy and life style they adopt. The fact that professional service fees are considered not to be value for money stems from two reasons, both of which can easily be counteracted. The first is that the client only sees a small part of the operation. The infrastructure of many professions can be as large or larger than that which the client is exposed to. Thus the cost of the service appears disproportionately high compared to that part of the organisation which is visible and the amount of time the professional spends with the client. The second reason is an apparent lack of activity. The client is all too frequently unaware of the activities taking place on his or her behalf.

The antidote to these two client perceptions is for those who present the practice to be sure the client does know of the existence and contribution of the infrastructure, for example researchers, quality control systems, information technologists, equipment, continuing professional development and their respective roles in adding value to the service delivered. Apparent lack of activity can be corrected by the use of the techniques previously referred to.

SATISFACTION AUDIT

The trap of assuming client preference equals client satisfaction and client satisfaction guarantees client retention is a very real and dangerous one. When clients appoint a practice the only statement which has been made is that they prefer that firm at the moment of time to any other of which they know. But such a preference may be based on a compromise between what is offered and what is really wanted. If that gap can be filled by another organisation the client is lost. The second half of the equation is just as toxic. Clients may well express satisfaction but nevertheless change advisers. American studies have shown satisfaction rates of up to 85% existed among client defections. The message is clear. No practice can afford to relax its efforts to ensure satisfaction *and* loyalty.

Being client centred implies that the level of client satisfaction is monitored constantly. Service quality auditing requires the setting of practical standards, rating the importance of these issues to clients and measuring or evaluating performance against the quality objectives and in conjunction with the importance of that issue to the clients. (Because this aspect of professional services is so critical, the subject is covered in depth in Chapters 17 and 18.)

There is no point in pouring in time, money, skills and strategic thinking unless there is some measure, however crude, of performance standards as perceived by clients. It is, after all and in the final analysis, only their views that matter. Checking service quality standards can be done by interrogating clients on their experience as measured against their expectations and by observation. The techniques vary from a simple questionnaire given to clients at the end of a matter or project to sophisticated independent marketing research on one-to-one or focus group basis. This last technique can of course also produce comparative performance with competitors which will reveal strengths and weaknesses. An example of this can be found in Figure 16.2, page 170.

Every practice can adopt the first method at virtually next to no cost, and from it rapidly build up an accurate picture of how they are performing and how clients react to their services. A model questionnaire is included as Appendix 5 and can be adjusted for the needs of the individual practice by, for example, substituting "professional" and "people" in questions 4 and 8 by the discipline "solicitor", "surveyor" or whatever is applicable, and "client" for "patient" or "owner". It will be found that clients, far from minding being questioned on their view of the firm's performance, welcome the interest which is shown.

Many professionals would be reluctant to ask question 12 either because it would seem to invite a negative reply or because it is far too commercial. A tangential comment is appropriate here and links with Chapter 22. If the firm is reluctant to ask the question the overriding reason is that they themselves are unsure about whether the client will consider the fees as fair for the work undertaken. Such uncertainty will almost invariably communicate itself to the client. If clients are unhappy about their bills, the practice should be the first to know if only because research has shown that a satisfied client tells three to four people and an unhappy client tells eleven to twelve. The research figures may not be wholly accurate but they are certainly indicative.

BENEFITS

The benefits to clients of their professional advisers being client centred are easily deducible from the foregoing and are dealt with in detail in Chapter 10. But to return to the issue raised at the beginning of the chapter, the practice developer must then ask whether the efforts to deliver benefits have a pay-off for the practice, its partners and staff. Indeed it does.

First and foremost it leads to more regular and better quality business and thus greater profitability. Repeat engagements, engagements taking up other services and new clients obtained through the referral network are all generated by a genuinely client-orientated approach. Even the more traditional practices and professions, who regard their calling more as a way of life than as a means of earning a living, are not averse to increased profitability.

There are, however, well defined beyond-profit gains. Being client orientated can also yield a "mix" of work which has greater compatibility with the skills within the firm, its resources, any specialisations and with the interests of all its members. Such a mix generates greater work satisfaction, which is a benefit not to be understated, and improved career opportunities for staff at all levels. Everyone wants to belong to a successful organisation—an organisation which is held in high regard by its clients, its peers and by other professionals. Success engenders success.

ACTION POINTS

- Identify the major uncertainties of clients utilising different services and develop a scenario for dealing with them.
- Set a standard for speed and comprehensibility of response to inquiries.
- Research what other services clients purchase, or could be shown to need but do not purchase, that could be profitably supplied.
- Ensure clients understand what fees purchase besides consultation and reports.
- Generate activity programmes for each assignment.

NOTES

(1) All three issues are considered in depth in Wilson, A. *Practice Development for Professional Firms*, Chapter 7, McGraw-Hill, Maidenhead (1984). This contains a comprehensive list of uncertainty factors.

(2) Wilson, A. *Marketing Audit Checklists*, 2nd edition, list 11, McGraw-Hill, Maidenhead (1992).

APPENDIX 5

CLIENT QUESTIONNAIRE MODEL

Thank you for consulting us. We very much appreciate your trust and confidence. We always want to improve our services. It would assist us if you could complete this questionnaire and return it in the stamped addressed envelope enclosed. Your response will be kept confidential.

YES/NO

......1   Were our office personnel friendly and were you treated courteously?

......2   Were you seen punctually?

......3   Why did you select our firm originally?

....

....

......4   Did the professional dealing with your business set out the situation, options and consequences to your satisfaction?

......5   Did the professional express a view and give a recommendation on the optimal course of actions?

......6   If "no" would you have liked him/her to have done so?

......7   Did you consider the professional spent sufficient time with you on your business?

......8   Do you feel the people handling your matters understood your business and/or personal situation?

......9   Are you satisfied that enough attention and care was devoted to your requirements?

......10   If you made telephone enquires were they answered to your satisfaction?

......11   Were you kept adequately informed of progress?

......12   Do you regard our fee for the services performed as value for money?

......13   We would appreciate any comments that will help us improve our service to our clients. Please use the reverse side of this sheet if necessary.

Thank you very much for your time and courtesy in filling out this questionnaire.

6
Understanding the Marketing Process

"Marketing", it was said by one cynic, "begins with a concept and ends with a catastrophe". While it cannot be denied that not all professional firms who embraced marketing in the early days of de-regulation did so with consummate success, it was not because marketing for the professions lacked relevance. Rather it was that practitioners lacked understanding of what marketing is, can do and how it is used.

Rather than definitions it is far more useful to disaggregate the marketing process from what is termed the "marketing concept" to see precisely what is involved in adopting what for many professionals would be a somewhat revolutionary approach to their actual or potential clients or patients. Some seven stages are involved.

1 *Mission (or vision) statement.* This is a somewhat pretentious title for what is a basic and important step in practice development—namely, producing an enduring statement of purpose that distinguishes one practice from similar practices and is a declaration of the partnership's "reason for being". The statement is a formal document of the vision of what the owners or stakeholding partners want the organisation to be and what it should be.

The process of developing a written mission statement forces everyone to consciously contemplate, debate and articulate the nature of the activity, the clients who are being served and who should be served, and services that are being and that should be offered, the rewards and quality of life for employees. This process has an inherent risk. It can lead to disagreement and dissent among participants. But the benefits of formulating a written mission statement generally outweigh this danger. A mission statement can serve as a tool to guide strategy formulation and implementation and it unifies expectations, plans, performance evaluation criteria, and objectives.

The statement, once agreed, ensures that everyone within the firm adopts the same approach, the same standards, the same "messages" and the same means of disseminating them. Without it the practice development activities are likely to disintegrate on the rocks of differing criteria and aspirations. The components and benefits which will be derived from taking time to consider the purpose and aspirations of the owners are summarised below and the relationship of the statement with all else that is involved in marketing will be obvious.[1]

Components of mission statements include reference to:

- Clients served
- Services performed and where
- Technology involved
- Survival and growth of practice
- Philosophy
- Self-concept
- Image sensitivity
- Concern for employees

Benefits of mission statements:

- Creates unanimity of purpose
- Gives basis for a standard for allocating resources
- Helps develop a culture
- Provides a focal point with which individuals can identify
- Translates organisational purpose into objectives
- Translates objectives into a work action plan

However, if a mission statement contained all these issues it would lack conciseness. Only those which are most relevant to the organisation should be used. Examples show how the appropriate issues can be incorporated.

Gerald Eve

To establish and maintain mutually successful relationships with clients that endure through the provision of professional surveying services which are flexible, efficient and cost effective and to provide a high quality challenging and rewarding working environment where teamwork is encouraged.

Blake Dawson Waldron

Blake Dawson Waldron aims to be Australia's pre-eminent corporate law firm, providing quality, effective, timely legal services. Our services are distinguished by a high degree of partner involvement and delivered in a manner which reflects our genuine respect for our clients.

Allied Irish Banks

Our Mission is to be the premier Irish financial services organization capable of competing world-wide by consistently delivering high quality service on a competitive basis to our customers in Ireland and throughout the world.

Unfortunately a concomitant of concentrating on the reason for a firm's existence is to give the statement something of an aura of piety. Thus to give it greater precision firms have tended to add what are termed "guiding principles".

Bank of California (Legal Department)

1. To provide comprehensive, pro-active legal services through early and active involvement with our clients.
2. To be creative problem solvers, mindful of our responsibility for identifying legal risks and formulating

alternatives to achieve our clients' business objectives,
advising against business actions only where acceptable
solutions cannot be found.
3. To communicate effectively with our clients.
4. To foster a climate of mutual respect and a team approach
to meeting our clients' business objectives.
5. To collaborate with other members of the Division to
utilize our collective expertise and skills.
6. To provide Senior Management with a second set of eyes
by surfacing risks or potential problems which we believe
have not been adequately addressed.
7. To engage, manage and monitor outside counsel to provide defined, cost-effective, high quality legal services.
8. To promote efficiency and productivity within the Division to achieve timely and cost-effective services.

2 Market target identification. "Lord Ronald flung himself upon
his horse and rode off madly in all directions", wrote Stephen
Leacock. This sums up the technique of many professional organisations in approaching their markets. The waste of limited resources is on a truly grand scale if a total market is regarded as a
suitable target. Breaking it down into more homogenous sub-sections permits the practice to focus on those sectors which are most
likely to yield the result which is desired. A very simple division
of the veterinary market can be made between large and small
animals or pet and working animals, but an equally valid but
complex division can be made by relating the veterinary services
to the emotional needs and attitudes of pet owners.[2] In financial
services there is a world of difference between messages and
media used to attract "blue collar" customers and high net worth
individuals.

The purpose of targeting, or to give it its marketing title,
segmentation, is to be able to approach groups with similar characteristics using the same messages, media and methods thus
exploiting to the full the whole marketing activity. However segmentation variables are numerous, and if too many are applied it
will be found that the market has been reduced to such a small
number of prospective clients it cannot yield the results wanted.
Moreover it is possible so narrowly to define a market that it
becomes difficult or impossible to locate companies or individuals

within it who meet the segmentation criteria. A target comprising commercial concerns employing sales agents on a commission basis only to sell semi-manufactures for retrofit in heavy engineering in the USA would be difficult to locate and would be unlikely to comprise many establishments.

In practical terms, and in the majority of instances, some three to four segmentation criteria will be sufficient to narrow down a market to practical proportions. Deciding what the criteria will be is of course the essential step and this can best be done by relating what the practice has to offer and the attractiveness of the offer to different groups. It is thus possible to identify where the marketing can be applied with maximum effect.

Segmentation implies that some groups of potential clients exist which are less attractive to the practice than others. Few major architectural practices would be interested in a commission to undertake a loft conversion in a suburban house. But to suggest that there could be potential clients who are more desirable than others is an anathema in some professions, most particularly health care and the Bar. This is because "more desirable" implies that different types of patients or clients may be undesirable. Such a distinction offends the culture of these professions. This is one view, but the other, which does not offend any of the ethics of the medical and other professions, is that the skills and interest of the practice, if directed towards the most appropriate patients or clients, would yield very considerable benefits to them and to the practice such as those set out in Chapter 2. It cannot be said that it is unethical to seek out and serve patients who would most benefit from the skills, experience and resources of a practice. As already pointed out the Hippocratic oath itself uses the phrase *"for the benefit of my patients"*. The Shouldice Hospital in Canada, referred to in Chapter 4, which treats only hernia cases could hardly be called unethical because they have deliberately sought out one group of patients:

> "By segmenting the market of sick people according to their complaints, the concentrating on one segment that is inexpensive to serve, Shouldice has optimised its operations *fulfilled its mission* [author's italics] and enjoyed a handsome return."[3]

An idea of some of the segmentation variables can be deduced from Table 6.1.

Table 6.1 Segmentation variables

	Business clients	Private clients
Geographical	x	x
Demographic	x	x
Operational methods of clients	x	
Form of organisation of clients	x	
Specialisation of the practice	x	x
Size of client company	x	
Extent of use of services	x	x
Client activity/occupation/market	x	x
Psychographic factors (life style)	x	x
Benefit sought	x	x
Seasonal utilization of service	x	x
Size/value of matter or project	x	x
Reasons for purchasing the service	x	x
Client's occupation or function of decision maker	x	x
Referral source	x	x
Need for full range of services	x	x
Frequency/regularity of use	x	x
Type of client problem	x	x
New/old clients	x	x
Age/sex/ethnic/religious/		x
Socio-economic group		x
Family size and life cycle		x
Education		x
Degree of security required	x	x
Emotional needs		x
Fee sensitivity	x	x

The weight of a segmentation criterion will obviously vary from discipline to discipline with, of course, some being common to all, such as geography and size of engagements. While for veterinary surgeons segmenting clients by their emotional needs and reactions could be of dominant importance, this is unlikely to be of such significance as to form a target for pharmacists.

As with many aspects of marketing, most particularly when they attract academic disputation, definitions and boundaries become difficult to agree. Thus new concepts, although some might argue they are just new words, such as "relationship marketing" (defined in Chapter 5, page 45) and "niche marketing" have to be accommodated.

There are difficulties in deciding just how "niche marketing" and "segmentation" differ. If they do, and this is arguable, it is only that it might be said that niche markets would tend to be smaller than a market segment and that the organisation supplying the needs of the niche market would have to adopt a greater degree of specialisation. It is also suggested that niche marketing is developed bottom-up as opposed to segmentation which is top-down. That is a niche market begins with a few customers and then built by identifying other customers with the same specialised or limited needs. Segmentation starts from the non-homogenous whole and seeks to identify smaller groups within it. Few professional service firms need to make such sophisticated distinctions and should not be confused by the esoterics of marketing academics.

3 *Client attitudes, behaviour and need analysis.*   In creating and meeting the demand for professional services, knowledge of clients' needs and attitudes may be formed on impressionistic evidence. Folklore rather than fact can hinder the development of the services offered, prevent identification of accurate segmentation criteria and differentiated appeals being devised. Increasingly, practices recognise that knowledge of a client's perception, activities, policies and requirements are not yielded without some form of enquiry. National and individual stereotypes are a poor guide for developing elegant approaches. Accurate and up-to-date information is a prior condition for the successful practice development and is perhaps the one aspect of marketing which is rarely disputed. The need for data on clients, on the competition

and on the environment, whether its collection is formal or informal, dominates and influences every aspect of the practice development plan and the application of every tool available.

While it is commonplace in the USA for professional service firms to seek client opinions on how well their service and personnel performed, it is unusual in most other countries. Yet this is a quick, low-cost method for obtaining reliable actionable data. An example of a client questionnaire in Appendix 5 can easily be adjusted for any discipline.

Apart from formal inquiries, a great deal can be learned, which may not be directly related to the subject of any consultation, in normal discussions and for corporate clients, by perusal of trade or professional press and through business networks. Client dossiers can be easily and cheaply developed by the simple process of filing all relevant information whatever its source and then creating composite statements so that it is only a matter of a few minutes to update all practitioners or members of the support staff on the client before a client contact occurs. Chapter 7 refers specifically to the use of information on clients to enhance relationships and marketing opportunities.

4 *Differentiated advantages.* There are few absolutes or incontrovertible statements which can be applied to marketing. One such "absolute" is that every practice and every practitioner who is actively engaged in the provision of professional services has some unique competence resource or facility which distinguishes the individual, firm or partnership from all others. Only relatively rarely and usually in an emergency is a professional service chosen in a totally random manner. The basis for choice may be trivial or may be fundamental, real or perceptual, but a distinction between those who offer what are perceived as similar services is almost invariably made because of some preference or an aspect or a combination of aspects of the offer. Every practice must consider what elements in its resources, capabilities, experience or reputation will create special and unique values in the minds of its clients. There is no suggestion of searching for a pot of gold at the end of the rainbow. A differential advantge always exists except under the most rare and unusual circumstances.

Because services cannot be patented, there is little opportunity to achieve a lasting differentiation by some technical innovative aspect, although short-term and valuable advantages can be developed. Differentiation is likely to occur through personnel, "packages" of services, the way which information on the practice is presented, benefits offered, types of clients which retain the practice, referral sources, location, availability and perhaps the creation of an attractive ambience. The development of unique selling propositions or packages is explained in Chapter 8.

5 *Selecting appropriate, permissible and acceptable methods for contacting clients.* Communication channels are diverse as are the methods of reaching, explaining to, and convincing potential users of the services. Personal contact and public relations are just two methods, press and direct response two media, from perhaps a range of 20 obvious possibilities and 30 less obvious ones. Marketing financial services, for example, can be effectively carried out through the use of intermediates of various sorts. It is still mandatory for barristers to obtain their clients through the intermediary of the solicitor. In general, medical, dental and veterinary practice intermediaries between the patient and the professional have no role. Banks and opticians have been able to develop unique merchandising techniques for their services, but these are inappropriate for architectural services. The presentation of the service, the frequency of approaches to prospective clients and/or exposure, the time and place of practice development activities, all require careful aligning to the target segments and their needs. Many methods and media are rejected by professional service organisations as too brash, too costly or too ineffectual, without any real consideration of their relationship to the services and markets. This unnecessary reduction of alternatives reflects a distaste for marketing rather than a considered view of what is appropriate and permissible. Extreme examples drawn from the most strident parts of the consumer goods industry's communications methods are used to confirm the opinions of the inappropriateness of many techniques. The various tools of marketing should not be judged by either their title or their association with consumer goods marketing.

Table 6.2 lists some of the tools which have been used by professional practices with success, most of which are not beyond the resources and skills of even the smallest practices.

Table 6.2 Practice Development Tools

Personal contact	Financial aids and incentives
Telephone contact	Direct mail
Public relations	Lead time
Merchandising techniques	Fee strategies
Newsletters	Range strategies
Brochures	Sponsorship (events, books, academic)
Audio/visual	Marketing research
Secondments	Education campaigns
Presentations	Inward visits
Directories	Selected media advertising
Outdoor (posters)	Conferences and meetings
Interpersonal network	Signage
Distribution and branch offices	Packaging
Backing services	Speculative consultancy
Demonstrations and reference plant	Entertainment
Lotteries	Off-premises displays
Posters	Loyalty schemes
Couponing	Client training

While it is conceded that some of these tools will be considered totally antipathetic to professionals developing their practices and possibly to the users of their services, others will be found, if examined objectively and free from their image connotations, to have a direct applicability so long as they are used with skill and sensitivity and do not offend the culture of the profession or its clients. More detailed considerations of methods and media will be found in Chapter 25.

6 Integrating the practice development activities. Despite its small scale, in comparison to business generally, practice development activities by professionals can nevertheless have a cancelling-out effect unless the various techniques adopted are integrated both with each other and over time. The role of the co-ordinator has been compared to that of a conductor of an orchestra. The analogy is not a good one since most usually the conductor, while integrating and co-ordinating the musicians, is interpreting someone else's composition. The practice development task should include that of devising strategy and tactics as well as ensuring their efficient implementation. In the context of the marketing concept, "efficiency" must embrace timing and integration of the various elements that comprise practice development and also with the other activities and policies of the practice.

The simplest and most effective way to ensure that there is neither duplication nor omission is to list all the tasks to be undertaken, indicating the lead person and the date for full and successful completion and ensure that everyone involved is privy to this information. Appendix 6 is a format for ensuring that co-ordination and processing occurs. It should be used in conjunction with Appendix 27B, page 367.

7 Continuous information feedback. The information-gathering process, formal or informal, is continuous in all business activities. Most product manufacturers or distributors use their salesmen, research departments, outside research organisations, advertising agencies and informal contacts to monitor changes in their environment and their own performance. Professional service practices tend to be more casual about collecting these vital data.

This is particularly true relative to developing a client or patient database. While in health care, for example, medical records will always be available, it is also important, and far from difficult, to collect other information which can be particularly valuable in building and holding loyalties since it demonstrates an interest in the patient that goes beyond their medical requirements. For all professions the client database should include their interests, family, business activity and any other relevant facts that help to establish a rapport (see Chapter 7). Information must be collected, integrated and stored in a databank and collected from externally and internally originated sources which is required for the effective operation of the practice. However, it is vitally important that the collection, integration and storage should be purposeful, and that the information should be easily retrievable when needed and, as appropriate, available to all levels of management. The rule must be that it does not have to be interesting, it has to be useful. Appendix 27A contains a checklist for possible inclusion for control purposes.

This schematic of the marketing process obviously requires considerable expansion to be wholly practical and this will be found in the chapters which follow. It is hoped, however, it has now been demonstrated how practice development for professionals, some operating under conditions of mandatory and self-imposed restraints, can be accomplished without demanding skills or resources which cannot be found in or acquired by most firms, or in anyway circumventing the rules or breaching the dignity and integrity of professionals or the culture of the profession. Marketing is not, as is often incorrectly presumed, only to acquire more clients. It is to obtain the "right" types of clients whose needs and wants are compatible with what the practice offers and with the aspirations of the firm and its members.

ACTION POINTS

- Decide who in the firm will develop the mission statement (individuals or committee) the issues to be included and circulate to the whole practice
- Incorporate a client version in brochure or other appropriate publications and display it on the premises
- Identify market targets in order of priority
- Identify the unique advantage the firm enjoys and exploit with those types of client who would benefit most

---

Other action points which emerge from this chapter are included on the appropriate sections later in the book.

NOTES

(1) David, F.R. "How companies define their mission", *The Journal of Long Range Planning,* Vol. 22, No.1 (1989).
(2) Van Tilborgh, C.A.H. "Marketing for Veterinarians—Success by Customer-orientated Management", *Proceedings of the XVI World Congress of the World Small Veterinary Association,* Vienna, October (1991).
(3) Davidow, W.H. and Uttal, B. "Service Companies: Focus or Falter", *Harvard Business Review,* Cambridge, Mass., July–August (1989).

APPENDIX 6

PERSONAL ACTION PLAN

Action to be taken	Why?	Who is to do it?	How is it to be done?	Must be completed by?	Results and comments

7
Client Databases: the Key to Cost Effective Marketing

"Know your client" is one of the oldest maxims in marketing and most professional practices do. However, critical information is all too frequently not gathered and recorded in a formal manner and thus is often lost through memory lapse or because the holder of the information leaves the practice or moves into another department where client contacts change. Depending on the profession, typically there is only a recording of the basic information required to conduct a client's business or personal matters. As a result, information which has considerable marketing value is not used.

If relationship marketing which centres round developing *continuous* relationships with clients across the whole offering of a practice is to succeed, then databases have to be detailed, accurate and constantly updated as new information is received or obtained. Bonding clients is infinitely more effective if the firm holds and uses creatively intelligence on individuals and on corporate clients.

The contents of client databases will obviously vary between that which is gathered for private clients and that for commercial clients. However there is an important cross-over which is frequently overlooked and which, if properly used, can yield a considerable competitive advantage. This is the gathering of background information on the individuals within the corporate client organisations who are involved in decision making as well as intelligence on the organisation itself.

A detailed knowledge of the corporate client's policies, activities and aspirations can lead to increased use of the practice by the client and opens opportunities for cross selling (see Chapter 21). These bonuses are in addition to the values gained by being able to impress the client by the knowledge the practitioners have of their business, its problems, its markets and its opportunities and of the personal circumstances and interests of corporate decision makers.

Needless to say the type and extent of information gathered will vary for each discipline and each type of client. There is little point in offering a comprehensive checklist of information to be gathered because the differences between the professions will be considerable, for example: a lawyer might want information on the adverse party; an accountant, details of any trusts; a doctor, previous medical history. However there are some general issues worth recording which can be incorporated into most client data sheets irrespective of the profession. The listing contained in Appendix 7 covers many factors which should be included and which have implications for practice development. These, apart from such obvious requirements for information needed for administration and consultancy purposes can form the basis of a client data sheet specific to the practice needs (see also the "Preparation Checklist for Client Briefing" Chapter 24, pp. 282–4, for other issues that could be considered for the client data sheet).

The cross-over referred to above occurs when it comes to gathering personal information on decision makers and influencers in corporate clients. The decision maker within a corporate client organisation is an actual client but also a potential private client for those firms that serve both business and individuals. Small animal vets tend to have very few corporate clients while the largest accountancy and legal practices either avoid or discourage private clients. In both instances, however, information on the individual will measurably improve marketing responses.

THE IMPORTANCE OF PERSONAL INFORMATION

In many professions, while initial information gathering can be personal as in the case of doctors, accountants, solicitors and executive search, it is not likely to be formally recorded where the professional has no requirement for it, for example architects or computer consultants need little or no personal information. Nevertheless much personal, indeed intimate, information is obtained in the social conversation that often precedes a consultation as well as that which is revealed during other personal contacts. But what is the point of recording yet more information into systems often already choked with data in one form or another?

Most people respond positively to any form of recognition, that is turning them from file numbers into people. The demonstration of an appropriate level of interest in people as individuals and beyond the requirements for the engagement makes a positive contribution to building client relationships. Moreover this wider knowledge often assists the practitioner in protecting clients' concerns by being able to react on clients' behalf to changes which might affect them in a positive or negative manner. In a sense it is no more than creating the good feeling individuals experience when being addressed by name in a hotel or by airline staff: the recognition of the individual not just as a revenue producing client but as a person.

All this is as true for companies as it is for private clients. After all, managers are still a group of individuals making decisions alone or together on which practice they will use, what they use them for, and even whom within the practice they wish to be assigned to their business. Being able to talk with a client about personal interests or activities gives the client a message—the professional is interested in him or her as an individual. This takes on an even greater significance if the interest is time related, that is, remembering some issue which was mentioned in a previous discussion. Asking after the family is nothing like as powerful as asking how a child performed in what was a forthcoming examination or how successful what was an imminent journey turned out to be. Relationship marketing, which is referred to and explained in Chapter 5, page 45, depends on detailed information on clients.

But a sound client database has more than an interpersonal value. If the interests of individuals are known, newsletters can be personalised by simply drawing attention to relevant sections, articles or other published information which the client might not have seen and which can be sent to them; direct mail can be more focused and, therefore, the lists become more efficient, and attendance at seminars or conferences can be attracted. In fact there are few marketing tools where their yield would not be considerably enhanced if fuller information were available on the target's interests and activities. If the firm decides to adopt database marketing, which is explained in Chapter 25, page 313, the inputs to be derived from the client database will have an enhanced value.

It is not difficult to create a low-cost client database. It requires discipline rather than skill. Moreover, even the smallest practices now have access to technology that makes data storage and retrieval highly efficient and cheap. The advantages of having a detailed information base on individuals are real. With many clients and a range of services to deal with, unless a practice has a systematic method for collection and retrieval, important details may never be remembered or found in files and even less likely in the recollection of the practitioners.

MONITORING AND UPDATING

Databases are not, however, self generating. It should be mandatory that every practitioner should set out what is known about each client and then monitor and update it. While it is not usual for professionals to prepare interview and meeting reports except perhaps on the subject of the discussion, it is valuable to be able to refer to a report to see whether any change is required in the records. Chapter 24 explains the value and utilisation of contact reports from face-to-face and telephone contact. It is totally counter-productive to use out-of-date information. To take the example already given, asking a client about a child's examination performance five years after they have left full-time education is not likely to create an impression of either interest in or knowledge of the client's circumstances.

Unless those who contribute to the client database have evidence that the information is being used, their enthusiasm for collecting and updating it will soon be dissipated. Therefore any system should ensure that feedback occurs in order to keep everyone inputting data fully motivated.

The rule with information has to be "need to know", not "want to know" and in deciding what to seek and what to include or to exclude, the following "test" questions might be usefully applied:

1   What information do we already hold in a formal system?
2   How is the information gathered—can it be systematised?
3   Who uses it?—if no one uses it, it is not worth the effort of gathering.
4   Who ought to use it—can the exploitation of client data be "sold" internally?
5   How often is it used—is it sufficiently frequently to justify its collection monitoring and updating?
6   How is updating carried out and with what frequency?

Apart from a formal data sheet, information which is of only limited or time sensitive nature can be used by a simple expedient of noting it on a "post-it" slip which can then be removed without cluttering up the file. One dentist does exactly this, marking the patient's dental chart and even when a year has elapsed, is able to say to the patient, "How did the visit to Australia go?" which, without knowing how it is accomplished, appears to be both a feat of memory and a demonstration of interest.

The type of personal information to record should be confined to that which might be normally used in social intercourse. For example, occupation, commercial family composition and life cycle, occupation of client, spouse, children, commercial interests, personal interests, e.g. sports, music, collecting, home owner/tenant, other property. While all these are obvious enough there is an additional series which can guide the practice by giving an advanced insight into the personality of the contact, something which may not be known to others in the practice who may deal with the client. Is the client contact conservative, cautious, progressive, adventurous, abrasive? If a compatibility with the firm's personnel is to be ensured, what are the language requirements, social background, educational level and experience which will best fit the client profile?

INFORMATION SOURCES

Obviously most important information sources on clients comes from the clients themselves. However, careful monitoring of trade and professional press either internally or through an abstracting agency will also yield a great deal of usable information on individuals, companies and markets. A request to be put on clients' circulation lists for their newsletters can provide a positive goldmine of usable facts.

Company reports are another valuable source of inputs for the database for corporate clients as well as information emanating from their trade or professional associations. Although the likelihood of collecting information on private clients, other than those who are in the public eye, is not particularly high, national, regional, local and enthusiast press could yield items of interest.

SECURITY

It is obvious that client databases are valuable documents and must therefore be given the same type of security and protection as other sensitive material. However, in some countries legislation requires that clients have access to their own records. This, then, calls for care in the way information is recorded—a thought that should be kept in mind but not allowed to inhibit the development of detailed, accurate and timely client information.

However, none of this effort is justified unless the client or prospective client's situation holds out the opportunity of sufficient business to recoup the cost of the surveillance. The extent and complexity of a client database must be related to its cost-effective use. Under no circumstances, however, should their development and maintenance be allowed to become an in-house industry.

ACTION POINTS

- Decide information inputs that would contribute to the marketing effort
- Decide how the information is to be used
- Develop system for inputting new and updating existing information and give named person responsibility for implementation and monitoring compliance
- Check at frequent intervals who uses what information and with what frequency intervals
- Feed back to contributors how the information is being used

---

APPENDIX 7

CLIENT DATABASE

The client database is the most important marketing tool and should be developed and maintained to a high level of effectiveness. Apart from the obvious information required for administrative and professional purposes (e.g. name and address, matters dealt with, etc) the following should be considered for inclusion, although it is emphasised just what is collected and incorporated depends upon whether the client is a business or an individual and upon the discipline involved. Information must be constantly updated and its use checked. The guiding principle is that it has to be practical.

Include	Commercial	Private	Both
Name of client's secretary			
Name of any referrer involved			
Whether and when the referrer was acknowledged and by what means			
Credit control status: excellent/good/fair/caution/do not act			
Inclusion on mailing list			
Names and addresses of other professional advisers			
Form of address: formal/informal			
Billing basis and rates: hourly, fixed fee, retainer, *ad valorem*, contingency			
Client's own services/products			
Market position and profitability			
Size of operation			
Opportunities for other service engagements			
Inquirers: position in company and job title			
Professional qualifications			
Use of client name/engagement for publicity			
Marital status			
Children (names, sex and ages)			
Occupation			
Name of employer			
Where self-employed type of business/size/location			
Home owner/tenant			
Other property			
Investments			
Date last seen and outcome			
Banker's address			
Critical dates for auto reminders			
Personal interests (e.g. sailing, chess, gardening)			
Commercial interests (Lloyds member, non-executive directorships, Member, Chartered Institute of Marketing)			

8
Developing Unique Competences and Resources: the Capability Gap

In Chapter 6 reference is made to the fact that there are few things even the most enthusiastic marketing experts can be dogmatic about, but one which arouses no controversy is the statement that there must be a reason why anyone buys anything from anybody. It would be an extraordinary and rare circumstance for two professional firms to be exactly similar. The fact that a client chooses one adviser rather than another is indicative that there is a strength or attraction (which may be hidden) which the chosen firm commands. As was pointed out in Chapter 6, searching for that resource is not akin to looking for a pot of gold at the end of the rainbow. It is very real. The reasons for the choice may be trivial or substantive.

In product terms, this could not be better illustrated than by the Polaroid instant camera. If a customer wants instant still photography there is no alternative but to purchase a Polaroid. This is its unique selling proposition—a concept which has been known for 50 years, and it is just as applicable to professional services as it is to products. However, for professional service firms, it is not usually the possession of one particular feature, competence or resource which represents the distinction in the sense that a patented, innovative product is unique to its manufacturer. Much more typically it will be a mixture of a number of components of the firm's activities which will provide that unique difference and which will be of significance.

The purpose of developing a unique "package" of *features* is to deliver a unique package of *benefits*. Unless the client wants the benefits which will be made available neither the services nor the fact of uniqueness will have any marketing value. Experience shows that combining a knowledge of clients with a certain amount of introspection can, for most firms, identify a capability or resource gap between themselves and their competitors. The advantages of so doing are very real. It provides a differentiation where otherwise the market might see identical services, it increases the impact of the practice message and, as a consequence, there is an improvement in the productivity of the practice development effort.

In essence what is being done is combining and promoting existing resources and skills and relating them to client needs while emphasising the benefits which will accrue to the client by taking advantage of the unique package. If a practice has something the client wants and believes it can only get from that firm or practitioner, its possession will give a huge competitive advantage and will certainly bring the client to the practice. The strongest emphasis must be given here to the fact that the package does not have to be unique—it only has to be perceived as unique. The fact that competitive firms *could* offer the same "package" is of no consequence. How, then, is this highly desirable situation of having something unique which clients want to be achieved?

The initial task is to identify all the resources the practice possesses—skills, experience, services, qualifications, language capability, facilities, track record, network, special software packages, geographical coverage. These are just a few aspects which could be considered.

There are however important, less-tangible areas of differentiation that may not be so easily identified but which can give the crucial advantage over competitors.

Capability gaps include:

• *Business systems gap:* the ability to perform individual functions more effectively than competitors and their inability to follow
• *Position gap:* reputation, image, awareness, track record, reference clients

- *Regulatory/legal gap:* service marks, operating licence, quotas, governmental factors, accreditation
- *Organisational/managerial gaps:* ability to innovate, adapt and re-position quickly

CREATING THE PACKAGE

The guidelines to identifying and bolting advantages together into a unique beneficial package are:

- The combination of skills and resources should be *seen* to be unique
- They are applicable to clients' needs or problems under consideration
- They will be a quantifiable benefit from the applications of a unique "package"

The advantages and the dangers of the approach are obvious. Any system of opportunity identification by the relation of skills or resources to the market must be modular, that is, the skills and resources should be capable of being rearranged to open up a number of sectors not just lead to a single market or client. A strength audit will reveal components which, when related to the targeted makers, can be bolted together to form a unique proposition.

An extreme situation may be one in which a firm has no particular skills or resources other than capacity to meet a demand at a particular moment. An accountant able to handle immediately an urgent back duty investigation offers a unique advantage over any other accountant who cannot undertake the work at once. In fact, capacity or "lead time" is a common advantage firms can provide in a given situation when all else seems to be equal. However, it is not a "plus" which can be built on since its very existence tends to destroy it.

A unique selling package for an accountancy practice might look like the following:

- Familiarity with and experience retail businesses operations
- Knowledge of logistics*

- Extensive knowledge of capital allowances
- Inter-disciplinary skills*
- Excellent relations with other professionals*
- Contacts with sources of finance
- Availability*
- Offices in main commercial centres
- Partner involvement in all matters*

It is obvious that each "plus" increases the degree of specialisation but the concomitant aspect is that it also appears to reduce the market potential. This is by no means the case, since the various modules which are involved can be re-arranged, and with additions and deletions repackaged for different types of targets. Thus, while the example above might be particularly attractive to a national retailer, some of the elements can also be used for an international freight company:

- Partner involvement in all matters*
- Availability*
- Excellent relations with other professionals*
- Language capability
- Associated offices overseas
- Commercial knowledge and experience
- Inter-disciplinary skills*
- Knowledge of logistics*

The asterisked items are common to both packages.

Another example, this time taken from surveying might be as follows, but is now related to the benefit the clients receive:

Segment: Educational Establishment

Package content	*What the client receives*
• Special experience in needs of educational establishments	• No "learning curve" costs
• Close links with other professional advisers	• Cost-effective co-ordination without overlaps or omissions
• Detailed knowledge of local conditions	• Insightful problem-solving approaches

- Partner involvement in all matters
- Special software specifically developed for automatic measurement, risk analysis and project forecasting
- Total acceptance of responsibility
- Speed, punctuality

It can easily be seen that many components of the package can be re-used for other business sectors.

The firm must be capable not only of assessing its own strengths and weaknesses objectively, but also of appreciating how they compare to the client's needs. Thus the move from the generic to the specific is now required. The identification of the individual prospect will be a key requirement for the practice developer. The method of achieving this is a combination of two related approaches. The first step is to structure the particular advantages or, as they would be described in marketing terminology, "pluses" of the firm and to relate them to the market segments most likely to respond to them and to be able to use them. This is the area of unique competence or resource every firm possesses and which distinguishes an individual or practice from others.

UNIQUE SELLING PACKAGES AS SEGMENTATION CRITERIA

As is suggested in Chapter 11, a profile should be drawn of prospective clients to assist in identifying them and their location in the geographical or activity area selected for the segment. This is to isolate those features of a service provided by a firm or individual—but most particularly the appropriate combination of them—which apply to a given situation and then to communicate and promote these to the prospective clients.

The whole purpose of identifying unique aspects of an offer is to provide a criterion for segmentation for any professional service with claims to an area of specialisation. The human resource consultancy with a known reputation for outplacement counselling has segmented a total market for human resource services to a narrow sector perhaps offering a unique competence by virtue of extensive experience in this activity exceeding that of other practices. The surveyor with special knowledge, experience in and staff familiar with expenditure programming and resource allocation has segmented the market by a particular type of client and benefit needs. These segmentations may be obvious and they may be intentional yet still not spring from a deliberate attempt to isolate the sector of the market most likely to respond to the firm's unique offering. As was explained in Chapter 6, page 58, every firm without exception has some aspect of uniqueness which differentiates it from competitors.

It has already been emphasised that for most professional services, it is necessary to divide a market positively in order to concentrate resources on the segment offering the best potential opportunities compatible with the service company's corporate objectives and aspirations. If an offering is unique it must bring the client to the firm if the skill, resource or facility need or benefits sought outweighs other factors which might make an alternative profession or professional preferable.

None of the foregoing implies that creating a unique competence for a service guarantees it will remain so. Having found or devised a unique aspect to the service it can be copied by others, but with varying degrees of difficulty. Services cannot be protected by patent. Expertise might be matched by acquiring personnel with similar skills or experience, by opening offices near competitors or increasing the range of services available. These "pluses" are relatively easy, if not always cheap, to replicate. More difficult to follow and surpass are any image advantages that exist or can be created. For example, the introduction of new "lead" services—and many such services appear every year—projects an attractive image for the firm of being innovative, creative, professional, authoritative, as well as unique.

Thus, having achieved a differential advantage, the practice development personnel must remain aware of competitive matchings, and must constantly review their offering to develop new inputs and new combinations. Like most marketing activities it is a dynamic, on-going activity.

It has already been stated that a unique selling package does not in reality have to be unique. It has only to be seen to be. Thus if real differential advantages do not exist—invent them.

ACTION POINTS

- List out our salient strengths
- Match strengths with client and potential client needs
- Segment total potential market using the USP as a criterion
- Devise promotional platform to emphasise the combination and benefits it will yield to the client

9
The Decision-making Process

Before there is an exchange of goods or services for money, the prospective purchaser has to take five positive decisions. These may occur in a single moment of truth, often without the buyer even being aware that the continuum has been spanned and sometimes they will form a series of incremental steps, each one being subject to the most careful scrutiny and negotiation. A simplified practical summarisation of the whole task of marketing a professional or indeed any other service or product cause can be summarised under these headings:

- A need (or want) must exist
- The service (or product) must meet that need
- The supplier must be capable of delivering the purchase
- The timing must be right
- The fee (price) must be acceptable

In an impulse purchase the buyer instantly makes these five assessments without consideration. Standing at the supermarket check-out queue and picking up a bar of chocolate or a magazine the buyer has said, "I have a requirement for something sweet or something informative, this chocolate or magazine will meet the need; the supermarket can provide it since I have it in my hands now I can get it when I want it which is at this moment; and I'm prepared to meet the cost". This decision making is neither formal nor even sequential but it has nevertheless happened in a brief moment of time.

If, however, the ramifications of the decision are of importance or concern in terms of commitment, risk, personal or business security, then each stage will be subject to the most detailed examination and criteria will be established to enable the decision to be reached.

The continued viability of an internal architect's department is under consideration. "Do we have a need for such an internal facility?" Many aspects of corporate activity immediately become involved in this first and basic choice. Next, "can an external practice meet our needs?" It is a frequent comment of internal clients of internal services that outside suppliers cannot understand the business and are therefore less cost effective. "Given our needs can be met by a private practice do we know of any which would be suitable in every respect?" Each external firm will need to be assessed as to their skills, resources, experience, facilities and track record. "Can they provide the service when we need equal to or better than our internal facility? How will their fees compare to the costs of the internal department?" A subsidiary point is how will these costs be absorbed—central overhead, departmental/divisional charge based on use or some other financial arrangement?

The very considerable difference in terms of consideration of the factors involved between the purchase of the chocolate or magazine and a decision to purchase architectural services are obvious. The information needed, the implications and the reasoning are far greater but the process is unchanged. Each step has to be accomplished to reach the final decision.

STAGE 1: A NEED (OR WANT) MUST EXIST

In Chapter 5 the importance of being able to sense client needs was emphasised as well as the complex overlap between needs, wants and expectations. For the decision process to commence, there has to be an awareness of a perceived "want" if the initiative is to come from the client, but in fact it may well be a need. A need or a want may be obvious but on other occasions and in other circumstances clients may not even know they have a problem. The situation is summed up in Table 9.1:

Table 9.1 Problem matrix

Client	Professional
Believes there is a problem when it does not exist.	In these circumstances the professionalism of the practitioner will prevent an offer of service being made. However, the client has to be convinced that there is no problem or else they may seek help elsewhere.
Only parts of the problem are observable or understood by the client.	The task is to integrate the various parts of the problem into its substantive whole.
The client has made an incorrect assessment of the problem.	A transfer must be achieved between the given and the real problem and client must agree the problem as re-stated is correct. Without this agreement any solution is unlikely to be considered satisfactory.

One of the essential skills of a professional adviser is to help identify that a problem does indeed exist and to understand the fundamental situation. The symptoms of a situation may well disguise the cause; an apparent cash flow problem could stem from failure to make up bills which, in turn, could be the outcome of bad time management or poor prioritisation by revenue-earning professionals. Each of these situations require different problem-solving approaches.

Need (or want) identification comes in various forms. The client may well be able to identify a need with accuracy or the stimulus may come from external sources. Many purchases both in business and by individuals are made as the result of advertising or some other form of promotion identifying and making overt an unappreciated or unverbalised need. The legal audit or preventative law is an excellent example of this. It is not on record that any client ever approached a legal practice and asked that an audit be made of all their documentation and activities to ensure compliance and protection for the company. Once the idea was announced, preventative law became part of many solicitors' service "mix".

Thus, to return to the first level of decision "a need must exist". This may not be a stated need but it must exist in some form or another before the next steps in the continuum can be accomplished. The role of the professional at this stage is to ensure the need (or want) is understood, formulated and expressed.

There is a fourth situation. The client is not aware they have a problem. This cannot be grouped with the other three and must be treated separately because in these circumstances there is not likely to be any approach to the practice. However, this situation is a considerable marketing opportunity since it provides the ambience for the professional to demonstrate both knowledge and concern. Moreover, it may well signal its existence among other clients. This is considered in Chapter 14 .

STAGE 2: THE SERVICE WILL MEET THE NEED

However unambiguous or complex, obvious or latent a need may be, the ways of meeting it or the types of practice to use are anything but obvious. Different disciplines will offer different approaches to problem solving; different types of organisations will offer similar services. A problem of declining market share could attract offers to help retrieve the situation from accountants, management consultants, marketing experts, information technologists, R&D and designers. Financial planning services are available from banks, accountants, consultants, insurance and pension companies; healing or therapy is offered both by general practitioners and a bewildering array of alternative medicine and methods—acupuncture, aromatherapy, homeopathy, herbalists. The choice for some needs can be bewilderingly wide.

By way of a more specific example, a company or an individual subject to a back duty investigation has a very well defined problem—to defend themselves against a suspicion or claim that their full income position has not been declared or has been evaded. Are the services of an accountant, a lawyer, a tax consultant appropriate or could the client resolve the matter him or herself with perhaps some product support, e.g. software, law books?

The decision as to which service would provide the most cost-effective results then requires the most careful consideration and indeed consultation. Is the problem wholly technical or interpretative, is there any likelihood of criminal charges ensuing, can the law be challenged as an alternative to defending a position, how important is precedent?

These and other issues will very much influence the view taken by the client as to which service will meet the need. This of course begs the question: how is the lay client to know which of these and other approaches is likely to be the most effective? Expertise is needed to choose expertise when the client does not have the necessary knowledge to arrive at an unequivocal conclusion. The difficulty is frequently aggravated by conflicting claims of different services which honestly believe they have the solution since they have interpreted the original problem in terms of how their discipline would solve it.

This is one dimension of the problem, the other being the polar opposite—the traditional reticence of some professions, notably medicine and its associated disciplines, to either explain themselves or their services. This professional arrogance is still manifest among some practices and in some professions despite the strength of the consumer movement and the decline in the deference traditionally accorded to the professions.

In either circumstance the client is left in the hands of the "experts" to decide which "expert" will best suit their needs. Information on different types of services and disciplines will therefore often come from intermediaries, the solicitor will recommend the barrister, the dental practitioner the endodontist and, of course, and importantly, from other people's past experience.

STAGE 3: THE SUPPLIER MUST BE CAPABLE OF DELIVERING THE PURCHASED SERVICE

Once a decision is taken as to which particular skill would be most appropriate for the problem resolution, there will then begin the search to achieve the next affirmative.

"Who can deliver the service needed?" This may be formal or informal, beginning always with professionals who have previously delivered services regarded as satisfactory. To continue the example above, if the decision is taken to use the services of a taxation specialist then information will be sought to locate where such practices or practitioners exist. A number of them will be approached to obtain information on some key issues:

- Are they willing and interested in undertaking this particular case?
- What is their depth of experience or expertise in cases of this type?
- What are their links with other professionals whose services may be required?
- What is their track record of successes?
- Is there an empathy between the professional(s) and the client?

The information and perceptions may come from face-to-face meetings, ranging from informal chats to full scale presentations and "beauty parades", from brochures, articles and any other communication methods. The method or the media can itself often have a significant influence on the choice. An advertisement in the professional press may carry the authority and influence of the journal in which it appears but, in contradistinction, advertising in the trade journal of a client implying special knowledge of that trade can be equally influential under other circumstances. An understanding of the catering business might appear just as, or more, important than a membership of the Institute of Taxation to the restaurant owner suspected of making an under declaration of income.

Given the seriousness of the situation, the choice of adviser will not be made without the most careful consideration of all the facts. For those firms which, as a result of their communications and contact, fail to convince the potential client they can deliver the service the continuum ends here.

STAGE 4: THE TIMING MUST BE RIGHT

The selected practice or practitioner has to be available to meet the time requirements set by the circumstances. "Right timing" in this context is that which the client and circumstances demand, not that which is convenient to the practitioner. It is possible to go from the extreme of "now"—a solicitor required to advise and represent an arrested person—to perhaps months or years where a problem can be anticipated ahead of its emergence, or the natural course of its resolution will take a period of time. In either circumstance before a commitment is made the client will need assurance that time requirements can be met and the practice has the appropriate capacity and, if needs be, back-up. Not all events will necessarily await the availability of a single professional.

In the example which is being used, no matter how many postponements the tax consultant can obtain for a hearing before the Commissioners of Inland Revenue, in the end the demands of the investigators will have to be met. The last thing a client wants is to find on the actual day that a substitute has replaced the original practitioner. Many a client has bitterly considered W.S. Gilbert's Lord Chancellor's words:

"My learned profession I'll never disgrace
By taking a fee with a grin on my face
When I haven't been there to attend to the case"

The prospective client will always make a mental trade-off between the advantages and disadvantages of a one-man practice with no professional back-up and a large firm. In the first case the client will be serviced by the practitioner retained but that person is vulnerable to *force majeure* and lack of capacity to meet demands. The latter possesses a wide mix of skills and resources and alternative practitioners but cases can and are "passed around" for the convenience of the firm or undertaken by professionals less able than those who "sold" the services to the client.

One of the most common criticisms made of many professional services is that "you see the top man when they are trying to get the engagement and after that you get anyone available". Unfortunately this is all too true for many professional and semi-professional services. The almost criminal irresponsibility of some firms in accepting assignments on the basis that "God will provide" the capacity makes the more experienced client probe capacity and skills in some depth. "What happens when the professional assigned to my project is away or unavailable?" It is increasingly difficult to fob clients off with vague promises on timing or completion or excuses for failure to meet deadlines.

The problem of substitution for the larger firm is not too difficult if the original contact takes the appropriate steps to assure and reassure the client that, while another member of the firm may take over part or all responsibility perhaps because of greater specialisation, they will nevertheless remain as the client's adviser and main contact and will monitor and progress the course of the assignment or matter. In many circumstances a total hand-over becomes possible with no client loss of confidence. Chapter 21 contains a number of suggestions which are relevant to this particular problem.

For small practices it is important to promote the fact that all professional staff are of equal competence and that knowledge is shared if, of course, this is the reality. If it is not then there is no alternative, if the client is uncertain, than to set out the risks against the benefits of the small practice such as those explained above which can off-set the down-side. This applies with particular force to the one-man firm.

STAGE 5: THE FEE (QUOTED, ESTIMATED OR PERCEIVED) IS ACCEPTABLE

In circumstances where it is possible to quote a fixed fee or to undertake the assignment on a contingency basis (fee contingent on obtaining a given result, for example estate agents selling on commission) the client makes a decision if the charges are both affordable and regarded as value for money. In some circumstances there may be a comparison with competitive charges. Of course a great deal will depend on the urgency of the decision. A patient undergoing a heart attack is not likely to want to negotiate medical or hospital fees. A developer seeking an architect can make fee comparisons.

In many professional services, however, it is quite impossible to quote a fixed fee or indeed offer much more than wide estimates. There are few if any purchases where the vendor metaphorically asks the purchaser for a signed open cheque, but where fees cannot be stated this is virtually the situation. Whether the fee is based on an hourly/daily billing rate with the number of days open, *ad valorem*, or any other method, the client will have to make a judgement as to whether they are justified by the situation, the skill level of the professional or the work to be done. Such judgement in many instances is more likely to be subjective than objective. It should never be forgotten that what the client is seeking is not cut prices, low fees, long credit or any other financial arrangement. Their needs in terms of service fees are easily summed up—value for money. This is the only assessment the client will make at the end of the continuum.

OBTAINING A FAVOURABLE DECISION

To return to the original examples, it can be seen that, between the purchase of the chocolate or magazine and the choice of a professional service by a client with a back duty problem, there is no difference at all between the various stages which will lead to the selection. What is different is the consideration and time which the client gives at each level.

Complex as this is there are still further factors which can influence the choice pattern. In the tax example it is assumed that it is a new (to the client) service required but in reality the client faced with the alarming possibility of having to appear before the tax commissioners would probably go straight to his or her appointed accountant rather than seek a new firm. The problem and thus the need is obvious, the choice of a service (accountancy) is pre-empted as indeed is the choice of practice since the client is returning to his or her existing practice; timing might require further consideration as would fees. Given a past history of business between vendor and purchaser the level or method of fee setting will be known to some extent. Thus, the various decision-making stages have been merged or truncated but never to the extent as that which occurs in an impulse purchase. The decision-making continuum can vary all the way from instant to prolonged. Perhaps the best visual analogy is that of an accordion which can be compressed totally, extended fully or different parts of the instrument can be compressed while other parts are extended. Thus, for the marketer of professional services as for his peers involved with other services and products, the task can be encapsulated as directed to obtaining those five critical affirmatives. However, corporate decision making, while following this process is complicated by other decision points explained in Chapter 14.

ACTION POINTS

- List likely needs (problems) of existing and prospective clients, most particularly any which they themselves have not identified
- Check and/or adjust service to meet identified needs
- Decide techniques to demonstrate your ability to solve client problems—prove that the features of your service will deliver benefits sought
- Ensure all information provided to clients and prospective clients addresses all the decision factors

10
Communicating the Practice Message

"The greatest problem of communication is the illusion that it has been accomplished."

George Bernard Shaw

Shaw's truism is as applicable for practice development as it is for other aspects of commercial and social contacts. A practice cannot be wholly successful unless it is capable of communicating convincing messages to its public and it can deliver the precise services clients need.

In the past, messages were communicated through referrals and by face-to-face meetings since all the professions were debarred from promoting, or to use the preferred description, "touting" their services. Under the conditions of de-regulation the only embargo on methods and messages is they do not bring the profession into disrepute. Best practice can be summed up in the words of the *Advertising Code of Practice* which states that advertising must be "truthful, decent and honest", a phrase which has already been used in a previous chapter. These must be the mandatory rules for all forms of promotion—not just advertising.

In looking at the communication process for professional services, three aspects must be considered: *methods; message* and *media*.

METHODS

Any consideration of methods of communication has to be preceded by an understanding of just how the communication system works. Communication, whatever its form or purpose, consists basically of taking the target audience through a series of stages leading towards the ultimate purpose of the communication—that is, some knowledge is conveyed or the action desired is taken. Commencing with a situation where the recipient of the message has no knowledge at all of the sender or the subject, the first stage is to move them from a state of unawareness (of the sender or subject) to one of awareness. There are few, very few, absolutes in marketing, but it can be said for certainty that, unless people are aware of a service and a service provider, no transaction can occur. The first critical point which must be passed is for the communication system to advance the sender from a condition of invisibility to visibility.

However being visible does not produce clients. The audience has to understand the message. The contents of far too many professional service communications are incomprehensible or only partly comprehensible to the would-be user of the service. The importance of the issue is such as to justify repeating the statements made in Chapter 5 that it is not the task of the client to understand, it is the task of the professional to be understandable. Many target audiences, particularly private clients, are diverse in their interests and knowledge of the professions so that the only messages which can be addressed to them must necessarily be basic and simplistic. Conversely, a quantity surveyor's practice promoting its services to architects can with little risk be highly technical. An audience consisting of property developers for the same service may require something more commercial than technical. Practice developers must know their audiences and adjust their messages to be comprehensible to each one. (See also the comments on page 272.)

Having gained visibility and comprehension the result is not an engagement. There are still more blockages to be overcome. The information being conveyed must be relevant to the client's perceived needs. Visibility and understanding may be absolute for an industrial psychologist with highly developed skills in psychometric testing. This would be seen to be of little relevance to firms not using testing techniques or using different methods in their recruitment procedures. Professionals have to demonstrate the relevance of their service to the potential clients for that service.

The last hurdle is that of "conviction". When the whole process has been successfully achieved, the only way to obtain a decision to commission the service is for the client to be convinced that the service will meet their needs and that it represents value for money. It is claimed that, in most developed societies, each person on average received more than 500 sales messages each day—radio, television, newspapers, posters, direct mail, telesales—and rejects the vast bulk of them. Unfortunately, valid messages become immersed in the clutter and are also rejected. In what now seems like the pre-history of marketing, Theodore Levitt identified one of the verities of marketing:

"We sell eagerly, but we buy suspiciously. Our first reaction to a sales situation is fear…In a nation where buying is so popular, why is selling so unpopular? You can't have buying without selling yet people who enjoy buying don't enjoy sellers. Certainly the distaste and distrust of selling and salesmen are not things that were bred in primeval man on the original day of creation. He has learned them somewhere. Chances are his opinion is based on costly experience."[1]

Again the onus falls upon the professional to convince the potential client that the service will be rendered as specified and that the benefits offered will be delivered. Only when the prospective purchaser of a professional service has been drawn through the various stages—from invisibility to visibility to understanding to applicability to belief—will action follow. This of course suggests that there may well be a sort of gravitational effect which draws the prospective client down through these stages. Nothing could be further from the truth. In fact there has to be a driving force if favourable decisions are to take place and the driving force, of course, is the tools of communication.

But if there is no gravitational effect leading prospective clients towards a decision, there are very real countervailing forces pressing against such a decision. Professional service firms are neither uppermost nor constantly in the minds of clients, most particularly when services are used at infrequent intervals; clients forget about firms, their very existence, their services and their personnel. Because practices do not operate in a vacuum, the communication activities of many firms become confused with those of competitors. Indeed, communication can as easily market a competitor's services because of clients' confusion. Markets are in a constant state of attrition; firms lose clients all the time, not because they have failed in anyway but because clients move away from districts, die, decision-making units in commercial concerns change with promotions, retirements and recruitment and the company's themselves merge, cease to trade or relocate.

Thus, the communication process can be seen as a series of forces bringing the client to the decision stage and countervailing forces propelling them back towards the invisibility level. To be successful a professional practice has to ensure that their communications cancel out and overcome the negative countervailing forces.

All marketing is a communication process and the success of the marketing effort is totally geared to the success of the method, form and content of the communications which occur between seller and buyer. There are three types of communication however: factual; persuasive; and dissuasive.

The marketing effort is concerned with communicating factual and persuasive information and avoiding dissuasive communication. The purpose of communication is to convey ideas; ideas that seek to persuade, coax, cajole, arouse, stimulate, motivate or that simply inform. The situation can be best illustrated by a flow diagram (Figure 10.1), but it is emphasised that the suggested tools of communication in the bottom line are just that—suggestions. They must be chosen on the basis of their appropriateness and cost.

BEST PRACTICE

Many, indeed most, marketing campaigns developed by professional service firms fail because the ground rules, long since learned in consumer goods marketing, have not been followed. Irrespective of the methods and media adopted and the message itself, there has to be an accord with the basic precepts of good practice whether the service is a highly technical one operating in niche markets or a simple one in a mass market.

1 Promotional objectives must be clearly defined and agreed. Unless everyone agrees just what the promotional activity and

92

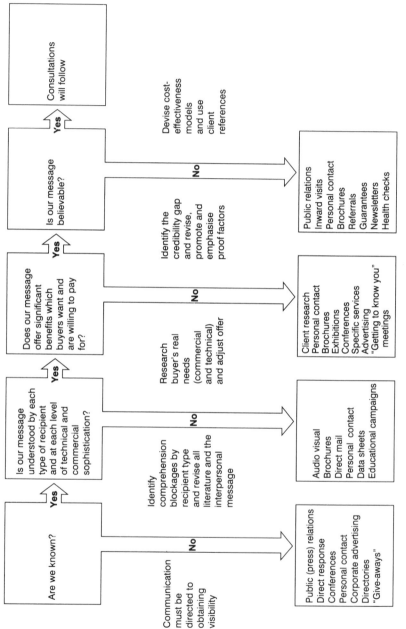

Figure 10.1 *Communication process and communication tools*

message is supposed to achieve then assessments of success will vary. It may be obvious to the practice development manager that the purpose is to obtain new clients, while the personnel partner believes it is to attract the best graduates. Others in the firm may see it as an opportunity to improve the quality rather than the quantity of engagements and yet others an enhancement of cross-selling opportunities. If the communication succeeds in any one of these, the others would nevertheless regard it as a failure. The success or otherwise of any form and content of communication must and can only be judged fairly against the objectives which were set.

2   Targets must be identified and are practical. Here again the same conditions apply. Everyone must be aware of the communication targets which, of course, must be compatible with the communication objective. A target of older people in the "C" and "D" socio-economic groups for a dentist seeking to provide private cosmetic dentistry is unlikely to yield worthwhile results no matter how well the message fits the parameters set out above. This is equally true for a legal practice offering Privy Council expertise to any but the few remaining dependent territories or personal injury expertise to clients concerned with intellectual property. Moreover, and as with segmentation (see Chapters 6 and 27) the target group has to be attractive to the firm and they must be accessible.

3   The message must be effective in the sense that it is easily understandable, relevant and convincing. This, then, raises the timing dimension. For some types of professional services there will be a seasonality factor—auditing, loss assessing and adjusting, a range of medical services and educational consultancy—while others may also be sensitive to timing but on a more unpredictable basis. This itself is one reason why those involved in practice development must scan both the immediate and outer environments within which the firm operates, as illustrated in Figure 26.1, page 335.

4   There has to be total co-ordination in all the communication activities. The larger the organisation the greater risk that this will not occur. Co-ordination implies the linking of communications between different departments of the practice and with external conditions and events. The annual budget analyses published or distributed by many accountancy practices could

easily draw attention away from perhaps the quarterly news-
letter or a departmental promotional effort.

5 Unless there is feedback to indicate if the communications are
both being received and are each achieving objectives, the
chances are that there will be more wastage than benefit. There
is no virtue in pouring in limited resources in pursuit either of
unattainable objectives or to inappropriate targets. In due
course the questions must be asked. How has the firm's position changed as a result of the communications? Are we more
or less visible? Do our communication targets have a better
grasp of the subject we are contacting them about? Is it appropriate to their needs? How do we demonstrate such a relevance? Have we achieved a level of belief in the message which
will lead to a favourable decision to appoint the practice? These
are the basic questions which feedback must answer but, needless to say, there are many more, as the checklists in other parts
of this book indicate.

This then is the communication process and although it has
been focused on external targets, there are also important internal
targets. Good communication is critical both horizontally between
peers and departments and vertically between different hierarchal
levels; these issues are covered in Chapters 17, 18, 19 and 21. What
has as yet not been designated is the marketing message.

THE MESSAGES

So far as these are concerned they can be summarised into a single
category. The client, the patient, the customer, whether individuals or corporations asks only one question to which few professional firms provide a direct answer: "What is the benefit to me?".
No one exchanges money for goods or services without perceiving
a benefit in so doing. Even giving money away provides benefits;
the feeling of generosity, commitment, magnanimity or just the
reduction of guilt generated by a high standard of living. There
has to be a reason why anyone should purchase a professional
service from anyone else. Thus the message which must be conveyed is that of the benefits which will ensue from the application
of the service to each client's situation.

There is an understandable but incorrect and almost universal approach to the messages which are sent by practices to their different publics. Indeed the same approach which was for many years used in industry and, until destroyed by the acceptance of the marketing concept, was known as *product orientation*; that is, extolling the technical, aesthetic performance or other aspects of the product, not what the product would do for the purchaser.

In the professions and stemming back to the attitude "the only advertising we need is the quality of our services" (a view which has been considered and rejected in Chapter 1), service providers tended to emphasise the skills, the resources, the experience and the qualifications of their partners and professional staff. This is the service equivalent of product orientation, or in the arts, "artistic integrity". Both phrases do no more than camouflage the real purpose of the features of a product or service. This is to provide direct or indirect proof that the service will deliver benefits. What the firm offers and sells and what the client's buy can be two very different things. Five examples given in Table 10.1 for accountancy, surveying, financial, computer services and law demonstrate the differences.

An insurance company's centralised database, which is a feature, can yield very real benefits to some users of its "products". Military personnel, for example, who are constantly redeployed do not have to find new agents in each area they are assigned to and the company does not have to transfer records or create new ones. There are mutual benefits.

The message must convert the features which the practice possesses into benefits which the client buys. In a sense the client does not care how a result is achieved so long as it is favourable. The fact that the firm has skills and contacts to acquire finance is of little consequence. If a favourable outcome could also be obtained through a casual social conversation the client would be just as satisfied. Their only interests are the end result, not how they are obtained.

A simple test most professional firms can try is to take any of their communications—brochures, direct mail, newsletters or formal presentation material—and mark in one colour every feature mentioned and in another every benefit identified. Most firms would find that the features, of which they are rightly proud, exceed the benefits by a factor of seven or eight to one. If this

Table 10.1   *Examples of features and benefits*

What the practice offers	What the client buys
Accountancy (segment: corporate finance)	
Tax mitigation	Higher retained profit
Knowledge of tax law	Problem solution
Availability	Peace of mind
Commercial knowledge and experience	More efficient business operations
Excellent relations with other professionals	Quick results
Surveying (segment: developers)	
Project cost advice	Value for money
Knowledge of tendering procedure	Increased certainty of price
Project control	Time saving; cost saving
Advice on documentation	Security
Valuation of work in progress	Risk reduction
Financial Services (segment: retailing)	
Offices throughout the region	Availability
Skills and experience in working with other professional advisers	Integrated response
Understanding of retail business needs	Insightful problem solutions
Assistance in acquiring finance	Profitable expansion
Partner involvement in all matters	Assumption of responsibility
Computer Services (segment: local government)	
Fast repair and regular maintenance	Improved operational efficiency
One-stop supply	Easier administration
Knowledge of local government	Better problem definition
Skilled technical staff	Effective problem solutions
Computer integration skills	Waste elimination
State-of-the-Art knowledge	More accurate planning
Law (segment: marine)	
Ability to provide maritime lawyers to any part of the world at short notice	Speed and continuity
Network offices throughout the main trading nations	Accessibility
Skill and experience of working with other professional advisors	Integrated response
Partner involvement in all matters	Assumption of responsibility
Experience in Charter Party and other disputes	Insightful problem solutions
Knowledge of the commodity market	Reliable advice

should be the case then the whole message needs re-sequencing. "Sequencing" is important because the features too have their purpose. Because the service cannot be assessed until it has been completed, clients will use features as surrogates for the proof they cannot obtain as would be the case with a product. The client is unlikely to believe that a career guidance counsellor can provide reliable advice without a knowledge of psychological testing techniques or a quantity surveyor can deliver increased certainty of price without a full understanding of tendering procedures. Features indicate, but no more than indicate, that the firm can deliver the benefits.

The task of converting features into benefits is not an easy one unless it is known precisely what benefits clients desire. These will vary widely between different types of clients and over time. Promoting a benefit that is not wanted is not only ineffective but can be counter productive. Not all clients who utilise the same service necessarily seek or desire the same benefits. A feature can translate into a number of different benefits and, in communicating with clients, it is obviously important to know which are the benefits the client would regard as a suitable trade-off for the fees charged.

There is, however, one group of professionals who have a special problem and dichotomy in meeting client needs. These are veterinary surgeons. "Animals have the most to endure from so-called animal lovers. There are, of course, exceptions but most people love animals because they love themselves and the animals are victims of their pleasure."[2] While veterinarians want to meet client needs and solve client problems they also have a duty towards the animals they treat. This is perhaps best and most easily demonstrated where a vet feels that euthanasia is the best course but the client wants to keep the animal alive. A vet must always give the client's expectations and needs priority but only against the background of their best judgement as to the animal's welfare.

Although not usually considered a marketing message or a medium, there is an important element in the operations of many firms which is usually overlooked. This is the *Terms of Business* which can say a great deal to a client about the practice. These are mostly drawn up by lawyers to protect their clients against claims and themselves against charges of professional negligence. Unfortunately, the language of the legal professions and the language of marketing and the art of persuasion have about as much in common as Swahili and Swedish.

A typical anti-marketing clause drawn from an actual *Condition of Business* document reads as follows: "Services provided by us and which are shown to *our* [author's italics] reasonable satisfaction to be defective...". Anyone with market sensitivity would know that, to meet client needs, the definition of "reasonable satisfaction" has to be mutually agreed so that there is at least a semblance of equity.

Marketing personnel are often accused of using jargon. As a condition of business the following would take a great deal of matching: "It is hereby declared that if any part or parts of condition 5 shall be found to be void or unenforceable such part or parts therefore shall not affect the validity of the remainder of the provision of this condition". In other words, if the lawyers have made an error in drafting the clause, the rest is still valid. Who is protecting whom now?

A typical condition is that the contract shall be interpreted under the law of the jurisdiction the firm is located in. This might be critical for some firms and in some markets, but there are few professional service suppliers that would turn down a profitable on-going assignment because the client insisted that the contract was read under the law of other stable and fair jurisdictions such as Scotland, Holland or Sweden. If the client sees it as preferable or beneficial for the contract to be read under the law of the client's own jurisdiction, then under most circumstances it should be offered.

Contracts for services, as opposed to products, often state that in the event of premature termination the whole fee is chargeable. It is easy to understand a firm seeking to recoup lost profits, but would they seek to do so at the expense of losing a good client when they can, with apparent fairness, recover the cost of work done and disturbance caused by aborting the service? A simple statement that premature termination will only invoke the cost of work completed or in hand at the time of cancellation, contains no element of penalty which can be bitterly resented. On the contrary it can offer an unusual or even unique benefit.

There is a very easy test any firm can apply to their contract conditions. Would they litigate with a good client on the clause concerned? If the answer is "no" then the clause can be struck out without losing anything and, at the same time, perhaps making an image gain. Indeed, one organisation, as part of its unique selling package emphasised "no restrictive contract clauses" thereby breaking away from the profession norm where the usual conditions of business look more like military Queen's Regulations.

Of course, there are also the not-so-good clients and some circumstances when a supplier might justifiably litigate over a substantive issue. All that this implies in marketing terms is that there ought never to be inflexible standard terms of business, but terms tailored for key groups of clients and key clients which yield benefits to them.

MEDIA

The third "M" in the components of communication process is media. This however is dealt with in some detail in Chapter 25. Suffice to say at this juncture that the choices are extremely wide as the list in Table 6.2, page 60, will have already indicated. However the practice developer's choices, not commanding the huge appropriations to be found in industry, particularly the fast moving consumer goods sector, are somewhat limited. Nevertheless even those that might on the surface appear to be culturally inappropriate or financially impractical may well be found on consideration can be used. An example of the first constraint, culture, is the use of outdoor posters. This has been adopted very successfully by some legal practices on appropriate sites such as station platforms. The second group, media advertising, tends to be considered as very expensive. Nevertheless, there are some media where cost is low and readership intensive. These vary from classified sections of the press to limited but dedicated readership associated with special interests. Examples of these media will be found in Table 25.2, page 302. This is not to suggest that advertising can be taken to the extremes adopted by some Australian legal practices referred to in Chapter 1 which have used the sides of pizza boxes, milk cartons and even condom packets to promote themselves. While the technique is appropriate the media are most certainly not.

This chapter began with a quotation from Bernard Shaw warning of the dangers of assuming the message sent is the same as the one received. The decisive element in any marketing communication is not what is said or written but what is heard, read and understood. Thus, all messages using whatever communication channels and methods are appropriate should be tested to ensure that the meaning to each type of recipient is that which was intended.

ACTION POINTS

- Check the level of visibility of the firm, services and personnel along with the extent to which messages are understandable and relevant to the target group
- Decide the objective of type of communication (see Table 25.2)
- Establish a system to monitor results against objectives
- Tightly define the targets for each type of communication
- Regularly review all communication to ensure that benefits are emphasised and features only used as evidence that the benefits will be delivered

---

NOTES

(1) Levitt, T. *Innovation in Marketing*, McGraw-Hill, New York (1962).
(2) van Tilbergh, C.A.H., van Meer, R.A. and Smets, M.R. *Van Dierenarts Practicus naar Praktisch Dierenarts*, Brocacef BV, Maarssen, The Netherlands (1987).

11
Identifying High Prospect Clients

An inordinate amount of time and money is spent in marketing professional services to inappropriate target groups. They may be unsuitable for a number of reasons: the volume and quality of business given does not meet the practice's needs: timing or the speed for completion does not fit their work loads and schedules; the type and level of service is inappropriate; the target group is more demanding than their engagements justify; creditworthiness is suspect; pressure on fee levels is too high; lack of personal chemistry; these are all typical examples. It is obvious that if unsuitable targets can be identified and removed from the "trawling" then there are benefits to be gained.

This, however, is a somewhat negative approach. A positive one is to identify those types of organisations or individuals who are most likely to retain the practice to apply their professional skills to client problems. Market segmentation has been defined in Chapter 6. It is the activity which divides disparate markets into more homogeneous sub-sections to allow a concentration of marketing resources. This chapter (based on material in the author's previous titles *Practice Development for Professional Firms* and *New Directions in Marketing*, which have been updated) concentrates on locating *within* the segments individual *potential* clients where there is a high possibility of obtaining business. Chapter 13, where segmentation is again relevant, deals with the nurturing of what substantially are *existing* important clients.

Marketing resources are too few to be spread evenly across the whole of the client and potential client target base and, therefore, there has to be a stratification in importance terms. Potential clients can be targeted in terms of the likelihood of them actually retaining the practice. This is best achieved by a process whose relative simplicity disguises its effectiveness. It is called *profiling*.

The service firm can start the individual prospect identification process either from its own history of successes and failures or, if it is a new activity or practice, from an examination of the characteristics of clients in the market segment.

THE PROCESS

First a list of potential clients, must be compiled which can be coarse-screened quickly to remove misfits and low possibilities of business. Small companies are unlikely to require very large span buildings; speculative developers tend to concentrate on one type of use structures, e.g. housing, commercial buildings, or service industries that do not usually require cranage; pet owners will not seek the services of large animal or farm veterinary services; and the number of occasions a private individual is likely to require the skills of a town planning consultant will be very few. A sensible consideration of the values to potential clients of different elements in the offer will enable the list to be narrowed down quickly.

From here on, the firm can fine screen by using its own experiences or by examining the characteristics of the companies in the segment concerned. Based on its own experiences, the practice can identify those salient groupings which appear again when image research is undertaken as Chapter 16 explains:

- Regular clients
- Transactional clients—sporadic or inactive
- One-off clients
- Lost clients
- Discontinued clients

- Non-clients (failed offers)
- Non-clients (no invitation to submit offers)

Further self-questioning is required:

1 What reasons underlie our being invited to present our service for any particular enquiry?
2 What reasons underlie our successes?
3 What reasons do we, and does the potential client, ascribe to our failure to obtain their business? How far do the reasons accord?
4 What are the reasons for sporadic rather than regular business or periods of inactivity?
5 What is the history of each discontinued or lost client in the category under consideration?
6 What inquiries do we know have been made by actual and potential clients for our type of services and where we have not been considered?
7 What reasons do we and the prospective client attribute to explain this situation?
8 How many individuals or organizations exist which use a similar service to that which we offer, but with which we have no contact?

An examination of the characteristics of clients for engagements successfully obtained and fulfilled will provide an identification profile. But even without previous experience it is still possible to devise indicators of the existence of potential clients. Precisely which indicators are relevant is, of course, impossible to suggest without knowledge of the profession and the specific segments, but they will certainly be widespread and perhaps as many as 50 variables will be needed.

Appendix 11A at the end of this chapter lists a number of profiling factors for consideration which have been found to have a significant effect, alone or in combination, on the susceptibility of a firm or an individual to the offer of services by an organisation. Obviously others must be added as appropriate. The relevant issues should be selected but it is not suggested that anything like this number will be needed or would be necessarily obtainable.

MATCHING

If the characteristics of known, satisfied, regular clients can be identified and then a match sought with non-clients with similar profiles, the high possibility potential will be revealed.

The original experiment with this technique conducted by SRI (Stanford Research Institute) in the USA is worthy of explanation. Like most organisations marketing professional services, SRI quickly realised that client interests tend to be very diverse and numerous, and that categorisation is extremely difficult. However, it proved possible to reduce the categorisation problem to manageable proportions. Seventy-eight companies, whose membership status (client or non-client) was known, were used for "training" a pattern recognition system by in-putting information on a number of key profiling factors such as size, location, activity, form of organisation, degree of specialisation and so on. After 30 iterations through the data, the system became stable, forming two large groups of "likely" and two smaller groups of "unlikely" client companies. Then, an additional 59 companies were classified through the system. Of these, the client/non-client status of 30 was known. The system correctly classified 23 of these companies. Two of the companies selected by the system as being unlikely but which were actually clients when the data were collected several months earlier, had subsequently ceased to be clients. In addition, four unknown companies were selected as being likely prospects.

The situation can be illustrated as follows. Without placing any values on the axis, it has been found that the extent of marketing activity in many organisations tends to produce a preponderance of effort at the lower end of the scale of business possibilities. Above average performers with perhaps a higher empathy, motivation, knowledge, entrepreneurial flair and a more knowledgeable approach to the task show a greater contact rate in the middle reaches of the possibilities of success. The profile method would seem to move both the average and above average into the sectors where their concentration through better targeting is heavily on high prospects for business.

Even if firms do not have the resources to indulge in long computer-based exercises, the fundamental ideas underlying the prospect identification have clear implications for all professional

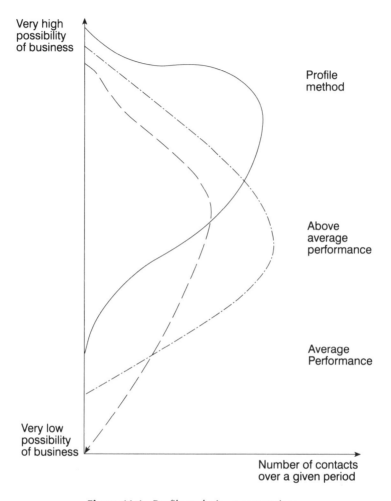

Figure 11.1 *Profile technique comparison*

service firms. The difficulties of correctly selecting the key criteria are not under-estimated and are no less than obtaining the information both on client and non-client companies but, even with inadequate data, much can be done on these lines.

The task can be summarised as identifying the characteristics which good (using whatever criteria are appropriate to define "good") clients have in common because there is then a high probability that non-clients sharing these same characteristics will be converted to clients since there is a match between their characteristics and what the practice offers.

Experience shows that if there is a match between as few as six to nine characteristics, not all the 100+ listed in Appendix 11A, then the opportunity for business is extremely high.

By way of example, a profiling exercise revealed the characteristics of the "best" clients for an engineering consultancy to be: medium sized company (2,000 employees); semi-specialised in one area of activity; international but with high local autonomy; products with a very short life cycle; policy of approved supplier lists but multiple sourcing. These five factors were sufficient to help them identify similar organisations in a number of countries. That is not to say they were necessarily converted to clients but the possibility of this happening was infinitely greater than among the generality of potential clients.

OTHER USES

The value of the profiling technique does not end with the identification of high potential clients. It can also reveal a patterning which can provide very valuable intelligence on the other categories. For example, a sporadic client may use the service irregularly because of periodic shortages of capacity of their regular supplier of that particular professional service and thus the firm is considered on an "emergency reserve" basis only. If a practice is sufficiently well regarded to be used in such circumstances, then there is a strong possibility of moving the sporadic client into a regular client category. Similarly, questions can be asked to see if there is a pattern of discontinuances which can be eliminated by some change in activity or indeed personnel. Does one particular service, one particular professional, create lost client situations? Perhaps a record of unpunctuality or poor communication may be the cause. These and other factors if identified are capable of correction and thus of improving client retentions. Chapter 23 deals with this particular problem in some depth.

The next category is that of non-clients but with whom contact has been maintained. They too may well yield to similar questioning. What were the reasons for rejections of offers made—cost, perceived lack of expertise or experience, over-specialisation, no empathy between professionals and clients? Again a patterning might emerge which will give guidelines to corrective action.

Finally, the non-clients who have never considered the professional firm. Is it lack of visibility? Was there a failure to understand the message? Was the message irrelevant or unconvincing? Information of this type, if it can be obtained (and it can be, given the resources are made available), gives an invaluable guide to practise development techniques and activities.

In addition to these benefits which derive from a profiling exercise, the information obtained can make a considerable contribution if the firm adopts database marketing, which is explained in Chapter 25, pages 313 to 314.

Following early experiments, SRI's use of the system by other types of services, professional and non-professional, as well as for products, produced an improving level of accuracy and more than justified the earlier optimism for this type of market analysis. Prediction scores are constantly improving. It must be said, however, that the system will not work for all firms and in all circumstances, but even at a lower success level there will be an improvement in the concentration of practice development resources which must result in both lower costs and a higher rate of success. Profiling used in a fairly simple form will involve very little in the way of time and money investment even if it fails to produce spectacular results. Thus, it is well worthy of examination and possible use by all professional service firms.

In identifying the prospective private client the professional firm has, then, in the majority of cases, also identified the decision maker. The position is different with the commercial client. Identification of a company does not, of course, lead to the important decision makers in the company. The decision-making unit (DMU), as Chapter 14 describes, can vary from purchase to purchase, from time to time and, most importantly, as a result of the situation which occasioned the purchase. Thus, it is quite impossible to designate in specific terms how a DMU may be composed at any particular moment. However, it is possible to build up a dossier over a period on DMU compositions, by job title or definition under varying circumstances, so that a pattern emerges.

The information is extremely useful as a guide to the profile of the correct people to contact in a would-be purchasing company and it is always relatively easy to identify the individual by name once the job title or function is known.

EASE OF ENTRY

There is, however, a difference between targeting likely clients and the ease or difficulty of penetrating a particular business or market. While a potential client may fully align to the "best" client profile, there can be many reasons—objective and subjective—why they will not purchase from a particular professional practice. Perhaps it is seen to be too close to their competitors, to have an insufficient asset base to handle a project of a particular magnitude, or a funding authority may insist upon the appointment of a firm of that authority's nationality or locality. It is, therefore, again necessary to do a coarse screening to eliminate all targets which, for whatever reason and despite the match, are unlikely to provide business.

After this there will be other issues to be considered: availability of budgets to finance an assignment; climate of competition; requirements for customised service; visibility and credibility of the supplying practice. The screening process, since not all factors identified will be of equal importance, has to be undertaken on a weighting and rating basis to enable the comparative scores for different target clients to be compared. An example of a weighting rating and score sheet will be found in Appendix 11B.

It is necessary to keep prospect identification, once obtained, in perspective because it is unreal to examine it outside the context of the total and continuing practice development. It is part and parcel of a two-way communication process since informative and persuasive communications can materially assist in locating individuals and organisations which offer opportunities for business to the professional service firm. Thus, identifying applications for a service and the individuals both private and within a company with whom the decision-making authority lies is one part, albeit an early one, of the practice development activity, but it is one which will govern the strength, direction and content of the whole effort.

ACTION POINTS

- List good existing clients
- Identify any characteristics they have in common
- Compile a list of potential clients for profiling, removing any obvious misfits
- Seek information on key issues identified for good clients
- Screen for matching

APPENDIX 11A

PROFILING

Possible Factors for Inclusion in a Profiling Exercise to Identify Non-clients with Similar Characteristics to those of Regular Clients[1]

These are just some suggestions and many will not apply or cannot be ascertained in a particular instance. Each firm should develop its own factors using this as an *aide-mémoire*. The list focuses on business-to-business organisations but a number of the questions will also apply to private clients. It is suggested the exercise begins with the "best customer" profile and can then be extended to all categories listed on pages 102 and 103 and at the end of this Appendix.

1 Size of organisation by any or all of the following:
   - Turnover
   - Profit
   - Assets employed
   - Numbers employed
   - Number of establishments
   - Size of establishments
   - ROI
   - Other

2   Form of organisation:
  - Government—local, central agency
  - Owner-managed
  - Limited company
  - International/multinational/national/regional/local
  - Extent of verticalisation
  - Co-operative
  - Other

3   Extent of specialisation:
  - Full line
  - Associated products/services
  - Complementary products/services
  - General suppliers

4   Types of distributor:
  - Retailer
  - Wholesaler
  - Cash and carry
  - Merchants
  - Factor
  - Dealer
  - Importers
  - Exporters
  - Stock holder
  - Rack jobber
  - Voluntary group
  - Mail order
  - Fulfilment house

5   Buying organisation:
  - Central purchasing
  - Central selection—local commissioning
  - Local autonomy
  - Committee purchasing
  - Approval body
  - Susceptibility to inducements (above and below the line)

6   Activity:
  - Construction
  - Manufacture (including energy) (by SIC)
  - Consultants
  - Commercial service company
  - Educational

- Defence
- Research
- Other institutional
- Transport
- Utility
- Extraction
- Importers
- Exporters
- Professional services
- Industrial/commercial services
- Commission packing

7 Psychographic factors:
   - Ultra-modern
   - Modern
   - Old-fashioned
   - Receptivity to new service
   - Sensitivity to aesthetic factors
   - Changing requirements
   - Static requirements
   - Transitional

8 Source of information:
   - Referral
   - Advertisements
   - Exhibition
   - Editorial
   - Direct mail
   - Telesales
   - Other

9 Seasonality of demand:
   - Nil
   - Moderate
   - Intense

10 Types of usage:
   - Heavy
   - Medium
   - Light
   - Regular
   - Sporadic
   - Emergency

11 Service purchasing reasons:
   - Financial difficulties

Service purchasing reasons (*cont.*)
- R&D assistance
- Managerial problems
- Market position
- Storage problems
- New product requirements
- Competition
- Recruitment/downsizing assistance
- Litigation
- Adaptation advice
- Testing
- Legal requirement
- New material appraisal
- Safety
- Improved performance
- Insurance/security
- Compatibility with existing operations, facilities, staff systems
- Skill updating or training
- Others

12 Buy class:
- First purchase
- Modified re-buy
- Straight re-buy

13 Demographic (private clients)
- Socio-economic
- Marital status
- Age
- Sex
- Occupation
- Education
- Ethnic/religion/nationality
- Life style
- Family composition
- Family life-cycle state
- Home ownership

14 Other:
- Geographical location
- Seasonality of demand
- Frequency/regularity of purchasing
- Benefit received
- Size of contract

It is suggested that the exercise begins with the "best customer" only profile: that is those in the first group below. It can then be extended to the other categorisations given:

- Regular clients
- Sporadic clients
- One-off
- Discontinued
- Failed quotation
- Non-invitation to quote

NOTE

(1) Wilson, A. *Marketing Audit Checklists*, 2nd edition, pp. 26–28, McGraw-Hill, Maidenhead (1992).

APPENDIX 11B

SCREENING FOR EASE OF ENTRY INTO A MARKET

Industry/application	Weighting	OEMs rating	OEMs score	Chemicals rating	Chemicals score	Medical Equipment rating	Medical Equipment score	R&D rating	R&D score	Aerospace rating	Aerospace score	Pharmaceutical rating	Pharmaceutical score	Environmental rating	Environmental score	Educational rating	Educational score
Factor																	
Product compatibility with existing or proposed production methods	2	+2	+4	+2	+4	+2	+4	+2	+4	+2	+4	+2	+4	+2	+4	+2	+4
Availablity of funds to purchase	3	-1	-3	+2	+6	+2	+6	+1	+1	+2	+6	+2	+6	+1	+3	-2	-6
Climate of competition	3	+1	+3	-1	-3	-2	-6	0	0	+1	+3	-2	-6	-2	-6	0	0
"Visibility" and "credibility" of company	1	-2	-2	-1	-1	-1	-1	0	0	+1	+1	-2	-2	-2	-2	0	0
Availablity of operating skills	1	-2	-2	-2	-2	-2	-2	-2	-2	-1	-1	+2	+2	+2	+2	+1	+1
Attitude to new technologies/ products	2	-2	-4	+1	+2	+2	+4	+2	+4	+1	+2	+1	+2	-1	-2	-2	-4
Requirement for customised products	1	+2	+2	+2	+2	+2	+2	+2	+2	+2	+2	+2	+2	+2	+2	+1	+1
Benefit received from the product	3	+2	+6	+1	+3	+2	+6	0	0	+2	+6	0	0	+1	+3	0	0
Economic climate within prospect industry	3	+1	+3	-1	-3	0	0	-2	-6	+1	+3	+2	+6	+1	+3	-2	-6
Service backing and/or suitable distributors in area/region	1	-2	-2	-1	-1	-1	-1	-2	-2	-2	-2	0	0	-1	-1	+2	+2
Cost of sales	2	+2	+4	+2	+4	+1	+2	-1	-2	+1	+2	-1	-2	+2	+4	-2	-4
Add others																	
Total rating/score		+1	+9	+5	+6	+5	+14	0	0	+1	+26	+6	+12	+5	+10	+1	-7

Source: For a full description and examples of this screening technique, see Wilson, A. *New Directions in Marketing*, Kogan Page, London (1991).

12
Client Value Analysis

The previous chapter showed that to regard marketing potential as a single monolithic whole is both unwise and can be expensive. But, equally, believing every client producing the same volume of revenue is worthy of similar treatment and concern is less than cost effective. What must be assessed are quality, frequency and timing of engagements.

It must be said, in parenthesis, that not all comments in this chapter can necessarily be applied to all professions, most particularly branches of law and medicine. It was pointed out in Chapter 6, page 55, that strong objections and constraints can and do exist in the selection and targeting of potential clients by marketing and management criteria. Doctors would not like it to be thought that they would not accept geriatric patients because they make heavy demands on time and are unprofitable. Barristers must comply with the "cab rank" rule whereby they cannot select clients in terms of personal preference and must accept them to appear before any court in which they practise. These exceptions aside, what follows on client selectivity will be found to be applicable in almost all professions.

It is not difficult to appreciate that professional services clients have different values and in this respect the reader is referred to Chapter 13 which sets out criteria for key client classification. One of these factors is profitability. Two clients producing identical volumes of work can yield very different profit. One client absorbs a great deal of non-billable time in obtaining the engagement, uncharged meetings or telephone calls, changed specifications and adjustments, unrealistic time requirements and is extremely slow in settlement of its account while another states its needs, accepts the work without unjustified quibbling and pays promptly. The effect on the bottom line can be considerable. "Loss leaders"—accidental or intended—in professional services are almost as common as in fast-moving consumer goods, only they are dignified by less disparaging titles such as "offset pricing". It is, however, one thing to set out deliberately to encourage business by sub-profitable fee strategies on the basis that this will be compensated for by additional profit generated by other services to the same client or in a later assignment, and quite another to be unknowingly devoting resources to clients who provide little or no profit. Only by client value analysis is it possible to identify this position and to take steps to rectify it.

Most organisations are familiar with and have experienced the Pareto effect where a small proportion has a disproportionate effect on the whole. It is frequently referred to as the "80–20 rule", 80% of volume from 20% of clients, 80% of service uptake over 20% of the range. Moreover, for most firms there will be a Pareto curve where it will be found that perhaps 20% of the client base provides 80% of the profit.

An interesting study[1] revealed that a major unit trust company found that 80% of the 250 professional intermediates through whom the "products" had been sold for many years were providing less than 10% of the business. Since the intermediaries required considerable sales support effort, they were unprofitable in both actual and comparative terms. The dead wood was cut out, and a relatively small number of new key accounts acquired. Turnover rose by an amazing 50%. Yet the increase in business could still be handled satisfactorily, and without deterioration in the service to other key accounts because of the resources released by ceasing to service unprofitable intermediaries. Had there been no such restriction of the distribution channels it would not have been possible to recruit sufficient new staff in time to cope with the extra growth. In the volatile environment of the financial services sector, this would have meant that the new business transferred to competitors as quickly as it had been acquired.

Such analyses, which can easily be conducted, may well be the starting point for a client value analysis. Are the same 20% of clients who take up 80% of demand the same corporations and individuals which yield 80% of the profits? If not then the case is made for conducting the analyses suggested.

The value analysis technique developed by engineers, which has saved industry huge sums every year can be adapted with considerable effect to clients which, in turn, will ensure that the practice development effort is correctly aligned to client potential and profitability. Too few professional practices take advantage of the richness of information available on clients, such information being frequently embedded and hidden in the firm's own records and some of which is frequently available from public sources.

PROFIT PROFILE

The first stage is to create a client profit profile; that is, what, in precise terms, does it cost to service a client? Every factor which has a cost implication needs to be taken into account and evaluated. While it is recognised that these cost factors are variables depending upon the assignment, the client personnel involved and their predilections and efficiency, it will nevertheless be found that a profile emerges. This pattern will almost invariably reflect the culture and the psychographics of the client. While the marketer should not look for absolutes, they should certainly look for, and will find, patterns.

By no means will all important cost inputs be available since few practices analyse the cost of client servicing, but a start should be made to develop the data so that in due course (and this can be relatively short term) clients can be classified by their profitability, actual and potential.

Among the issues which should be considered are:

- Frequency and length of meetings and telephone calls that are not billable
- Extent, frequency and seriousness of complaints and settlement and/or rectification costs
- Level of personnel deputed to deal with client
- Changes between quoted fee, fee agreed and fee paid
- Credit required and credit taken
- Entertainment and travel cost
- Emergency (disturbance costs) requirements—extent and frequency
- Administration
- Disbursements
- Fixed expenses

While the summation of these costs as applied to individual clients will give the first guidelines as to their value, it is also necessary to examine the sources of profitability. In some respects these will be the mirror opposites of the cost centres:

- Extent to which the full service range of the firm is utilised
- Volume of business let
- Frequency regularity and type of demand
- Timing of demand (cyclical or anti-cyclical or seasonal)
- Share of client's available business
- Size of individual engagements
- Quality of assignments

There will be a correlation between some of these elements of profit and level of profitability. It has been pointed out[2] that identifying the sources of profit requires a high degree of skill, innovation and insight. It is necessary to develop a familiarity with the situation and the supply position of each client must be subject to the analysis. In most cases, a client interview programme as well as in-depth internal analyses are required to develop profitability patterns. The internal analysis will also direct external research towards uncovering the reasons for differing profit levels among similar clients generating the same type and volume of assignment.

BEYOND PROFIT

However, a mechanistic approach cannot be adopted because every firm has to consider the "beyond profit element". Again the reader is referred to Chapter 13 where it is emphasised that profitability is not the only criteria for designating key clients. There must always be an allowance for the beyond-profit element which could justify special treatment. When a profit and beyond-profit analysis has been conducted it will then be possible to rank each client, though such a ranking will not necessarily parallel the monetary value ranking. For further comments on beyond profit analysis see Chapter 22, pages 248 to 249.

The next task, once the rankings have been developed, is to probe any reasons which account for any difference between the profit yield of clients generating the same turnover value and between different market sectors and different services. If the source of differences can be isolated, then it is possible to consider and apply methods which will improve the situation so that costs are reduced to leave a bigger surplus. Thus if clients are taking a considerable time to settle accounts, most particularly disbursements, it is always possible, firmly but tactfully, to achieve an improved settlement period which will impact on the bottom line. There is also the possibility of charging a disturbance or premium fee for emergency or urgent work.

Along with client value analysis it is also advisable to conduct a similar inquiry by service (product) line to establish which services are most profitable (although it must be said that the same variation in profitability may be found when the service is used by sub-profitable clients). Monitoring this situation will then indicate if one way of improving individual client profitability would be to encourage them to use those services which either yield a higher profit, or are less likely to incur the additional marketing and operational costs which occur when they use other services.

Two important figures will have emerged from the analyses: first, the value—realised and potential—of the client and, second, the cost of servicing that client. If the value and potential is low then the cost of servicing must be reduced to a minimum since there is nothing to be gained from the investment of marketing or other resources. Equally knowing what a client requires also enables an assessment to be made of the cost of meeting that requirement which, in turn, can be compared with the profit potential.

Marketing decisions will arise from the analyses—whether to increase or reduce the level of client nurturing, whether to adopt other lower cost marketing techniques than personal contact, whether to cease the service, whether to adopt or eliminate intermediaries. The financial services case referred to above illustrates this last point. Appendix 12 (page 121) identifies a number of possible approaches for profitability improvement.

Equivalency budgeting, a technique suggested by David Maister[3] is a practical and useful method in deciding just how many resources a firm can invest in pursuing an engagement. It calculates how much non-billable marketing time a firm spends to obtain a given volume of revenue. For example, the firm may discover that, on average, 30 hours are spent to obtain a £250,000 engagement. If there are prospects of obtaining a £250,000 engagement from an existing client, then the firm should be prepared to establish a marketing budget for that client which approximates to 30 hours input but probably a little less because marketing to existing clients is less costly. So, as an illustration, the firm might conclude that the situation warrants an investment of 25 to 30 hours in non-billable marketing time for the designated existing client.

Equivalency budgeting becomes a far more precise tool if the formula is augmented by a profit element; that is, in calculating how much non-billable time has been involved in obtaining engagements of given sizes if the engagement profitability is also considered, still keeping in mind the beyond profit aspect of any instruction, a further precision is added.

In considering beyond profit issues, firms should include lifetime values of individual clients where their changing needs can be met throughout their life cycle.

Experience accumulated in serving clients in the past is of considerable value in deciding on the level of service which will be justified in the future. Client value analysis is the appropriate technique for making this decision cost-effectively. It enables marketing tactics, most particularly relative to personal contact, to be decided for individual and for groups of clients sharing the same characteristics or, in the last resort, to withdraw from that market or cease to serve an unprofitable or sub-profitable client.

ACTION POINTS

- Analyse business spread across client base to establish if a Pareto effect applies
- Identify cost factors in servicing clients
- Apply cost factors to appropriate clients to establish level of profitability
- Identify reasons for higher than average costs as a ratio of business obtained
- Develop strategy to reduce cost/increase turnover (see Appendix 12)

NOTES

(1) Hirsch, R. "Getting the ratios right", *Management Today*, April (1990).
(2) Canning, G. "Do a value analysis of customer base", *Industrial Marketing Management*, Vol. 11, pp. 89–93 (1982).
(3) Maister, D.H. *Managing the Professional Service Firm*, Free Press, New York (1993).

APPENDIX 12

PROFITABILITY IMPROVEMENT TACTICS

		Rank for quick impact	Rank for permanent impact	Current perform-ance
a	Justify higher fees (specialise, innovate, add more value)			
b	Increase utilisation (billable hours per person)			
c	Find ways to use juniors more in the delivery of services			
d	Drop unprofitable services			
e	Drop unprofitable clients			
f	Improve speed of billing			
g	Improve speed of collections			
h	Use marketing to get "better" work, not just more work			
i	Invest in new (higher value) services			
j	Develop methodologies to eliminate duplication of effort on engagements			
k	Help engagement leaders improve project management skills and performance			
l	Speed up skill-building process in staff			
m	Make greater use of para-professionals			
n	Reduce space and equipment costs			
o	Reduce support staff costs			
p	Deal with under-performers (partners)			
q	Deal with under-performers (non-partners)			
r	Other (specify)			
s	Other (specify)			

You are asked to rate the items on this list in three ways. First, rank the items from 'a' to 's' according to which action will have the quickest impact on profitability. Then rank the items according to which will have the most permanent, long-lasting impact on profitability. Finally, for each item, rank your firm's performance on a scale of 1 to 5 (1 = we've really got this one under control).

Source: Maister, D.H. *Managing the Professional Service Firm.* Free Press, New York (1993).

13
Key Clients

Client value analysis, as shown in the previous chapter, is required because every firm has a small number of clients who make a disproportionate contribution to the prosperity of the organisation or its prospects. Nevertheless few firms have developed a coherent and consistent marketing policy which reflects this favourable inequality.

Even the largest practice cannot claim to have unlimited resources for marketing although it is worth quoting an ex-chairman of IBM "My marketing department has unlimited resources and it exceeds them every year". Since finance, skills and time available for marketing are highly constrained, particularly for the small and medium sized firm, it must make business sense to stratify clients in terms of the extent to which they are to be nurtured.

A key client might be defined as one where a loss or gain would have a significant impact on the service supplier's operations. This does not necessarily relate to turnover or profit generated only. Some other criteria are listed below. Each client and potential client should be studied to establish if it is, or could be promoted to key client status. Among the factors to be considered in identifying who is and who is not a key client are:

- Merits of engagements, that is, knowledge and experience that would be gained for the firm as a result of the assignment
- Profitability
- Volume of business
- Potential business

- Anti-cyclical demand
- Opportunity to develop new services
- Size of contracts
- Client's prestige
- Entry into new areas of technology, business or markets
- Quality of business let
- Full range purchasing
- Utilises otherwise under-used resources
- Procurement advantages
- Generates demand for non-core services
- Continuity of demand

Thus the first step is for firms to examine their client and potential client base and to create classifications to decide which names on the database should command disproportionate resources. A practical classification is as follows:

1 Businesses which are to be the target for major marketing activities by the enterprise because circumstances and requirements favour both the client and the supplier.
2 Those which could be considered for a major marketing effort because circumstances favour the purchaser but not necessarily the vendor, thus calling for some change in the latter's activities and their "offer".
3 Those which are easy and low cost to service but have only a low or irregular need.
4 Those which can never achieve key client status because of the type, quality, timing of their requirements, nil or low growth prospects and competition.

Obviously the most interesting actual and potential clients are in group 1; that is, organisations with a high growth in their service requirements and show profit potential where circumstances also favour the service suppliers, so that competition is more easily countered and held off.

Group 2 represents a more difficult and longer-term situation but nevertheless, is a category which has to be considered carefully. Here the client or prospect's activities and likelihood of growth make them highly suitable targets, but it is a situation in which the competition usually has some advantage, perhaps in the form of a unique facility, resource, product or skill which makes them the favoured supplier or practitioner. The task must be to identify the competition's advantages and to evaluate both the possibilities of matching and surpassing them and the profitability of so doing.

Group 3 organisations should command only the minimum amount of effort required to maintain the *status quo*. Their potential compared to key companies is small and the cost of meeting this must be kept low. Thus, although volume or value may not be great, profit as a percentage of turnover could still be in the higher quartile.

Group 4 clients have no growth potential for the service firm, competition is keen and in fact the mirror opposite situation to group 1 exists. While such users should never be arbitrarily dropped, certainly they must not command or dilute limited marketing resources. Thus key clients are likely to be drawn from groups 1 and 2.

VULNERABILITIES

The next stage is to examine the character of relationships; that is, who within the target organisation is known and by whom within the firm and the quality of that relationship. A simple exercise, perhaps using a format such as the one in Figure 13.1, is extremely valuable. The top horizontal column shows those in the organisation who interface with the client's personnel, the vertical column gives the names of those with whom they have contact. The letters are a semantic code indicating the quality of the link.

The example given in Figure 13.1 shows at once that there are two vulnerabilities. First, only one person in the service firm knows the Chairman—usually an influential if not a critical figure in the appointment of a professional practice. If the Chairman leaves the company and the Vice-Chairman takes over, the link at Chairman level is downgraded. Second, DMW has seven contacts, mostly high quality. If DMW ceased employment with the practice, the quality of the remaining contacts is much inferior. A chart such as this shows quickly and efficiently just who with the client company must be the target for marketing activities and possibly the form those activities could take.

Name and title	Our contacts				
	DMW	GBA	GP	DJ	Others
Chairman: *M.J. Harrap*	A				
Vice-Chairman: *T.C. Addison*	A		D	B	
Managing Director: *P.V. Longman*	A	B		D	
Finance Director: *W. Chambers*	B		B	A	J.B. — C
Director: *D.M. Evans*	A	D	A		
Director: *R.P. Cass*	C		A	D	
Director (non-exec): *J.J.G. Hill*					P.M.W. — B
Director (non-exec): *J.D. Wiley*		B			
Company Secretary: *A.D. Wesley*	B		A		
Major stakeholders			D		
No audit committee					

Key:
A Close relationship, partly personal
B Good relationship, but formal
C Occasional contact
D Has met but not worked with

Figure 13.1 Relationships with decision makers

The parameters of a key client having been established, as well as the quality of the links which exist, the next steps must be to consolidate and improve the relationships. To do this, all the normal marketing tools will be required. It is less their selection than their utilisation which must be considered. In the continuum of the communication process (see Figure 10.1), most of the steps will have been accomplished and the objective is to widen the appeal.

The classification, however, omits an important target group—more important for some professions than others. These are referrers, third parties in the network who introduce clients to professional service firms. For quantity surveyors, orthodontists, medical specialists and barristers, referrers are the key to obtaining new clients or patients even though there has been de-regulation or reforms in all four professions, albeit providing widely differing liberalisation. Potential referrers must also be classified in terms of the likelihood of them introducing valuable clients, the quality of the introduction and the frequency with which they occur. Obviously any referrer who sends a stream of high quality clients must be nurtured in precisely the same way as a key client and therefore in this context all that has been said about key clients applies equally to the whole referral network. Stimulating the referral system is covered in Chapter 20.

Pro-active marketing directed towards key clients requires an identification with clients' interests and a real understanding of their needs and wants, perhaps even those they are not as yet aware of themselves. Services must be offered, either free-standing or grouped, which will provide the appropriate benefits. All this implies an intensive programme of client servicing. This would include a regular check on the quality of the services delivered and how it accords with expectations, frequent *relevant* communications which might take the form of newsletters, reprints of articles and press releases and, of course, visits and telephone calls. Members of the firm must be immediately accessible and punctuality and quick responses are *sine qua non* even if it can only be achieved at the expense of reducing the service to non-key clients.

High on the list of marketing tools will be interpersonal contact and client visits to the firm. What is required is for the senior managers to set themselves a visit schedule so that contact with the decision makers and influencers can be widened and made regularly, and the perception of the practice as committed to and concerned with the development of that client clearly demonstrated.

Indiscriminate invitations with no other purpose than a chat and perhaps a meal very soon lose their attractiveness. Every invitation to visit the practice should have a very real objective. There has to be a favourable trade-off benefit for the client's investment in time. What will they learn or gain from making such a visit? Could the same effect be achieved by a telephone conversation, or a letter? In inviting clients to the service firm's offices, there should be a clear answer to these questions before any invitation is issued.

This is not to say that there is not a useful social purpose to be served but there should be no confusion between a social and a business invitation. Of course, social contacts are an important part of all professional services marketing. Indeed the golf club has always stood high on the list of social venues and the huge increase in corporate entertaining is indicative of how much weight all companies and professional service firms place on the benefits of such activities. It is obvious it would be both expensive and not particularly beneficial to use corporate entertaining for clients in groups 3 and 4 and it can only be used with discretion in groups 1 and 2. A reference to Chapter 7 will show that information on the individual's personal interests is called for. This can be used not just for interpersonal contacts but as part of a nurturing programme for key clients.

MATCHING STATUS

It is particularly important to note that there should be an equivalency in terms of matching status between buyer (or buying influence) and the service firm's personnel. There has to be some matching of rank. It is not only the Japanese who are sensitive on this point. It does not mean, however, that less senior members of the practice should not be introduced to the important decision makers. After all it is usually hoped that these practitioners will eventually emerge as senior members of the service firm. Thus the opportunity should be taken where it occurs to see that the key decision makers in the client company meet and get to know as many professionals as is practical. Client "hugging" by senior personnel is commonplace in most professions. A policy as part of a client care programme of introducing, albeit slowly, less senior members of the firm can contribute to reducing or removing the problem.

Negotiating skills are always required (and it should be said when so much of professionals' work is concerned with negotiation on behalf of their clients—lawyers, accountants, surveyors, loss assessors—how rarely they receive training in negotiating skills as part of their professional development). Key clients are usually well aware of the leverage they possess and will not hesitate to use it. Thus, in adopting a key client strategy it is important that the practitioners are skilled in negotiation techniques.

But key clients are not just the concern of the professionals. Everyone without exception, down to the lowliest members of the organisation, must be able to recognise them. They are the ones who are not kept waiting on the telephone or in reception, are not subject to pre-emptory demands for payment, do not receive non-personalised correspondence, are not asked to adjust their schedules and time to fit in with the firm's needs or convenience, and where the knowledge of their organisation and of their personal position is not superficial or non-existent. Chapter 19 deals with the role of support staff in developing a professional practice. While this role is always important, in the case of key clients it can be critical.

It is more than likely that key clients will require special back-up services which it would not be profitable to supply to every organisation the firm deals with. There are over 60 non-core services which could be supplied in order to enhance the core service.[1] Only a client value analysis (see Chapter 12) will enable the practice to decide just what it is profitable to offer and the basis for any charges which might be levied for them.

Key account marketing does not differ fundamentally from any other marketing except in its frequency, intensity and type and level of contact. However, more than a change of emphasis is needed if it is to be successful. What is also required is a change of attitude towards actual and potential key clients and towards the marketing itself.

These principal points, covered in more detail in Chapter 21, should be noted:[2]

- Closer working relationships must be developed
- Negotiating skills are needed
- Improved internal co-ordination is vital
- More and better back-up services have to be available
- Optimum follow-up is necessary
- Better intelligence means fewer missed opportunities

ACTION POINTS

- Establish criteria by which to classify a key client
- Identify by name which clients or potential clients do or can potentially fall into the key client category and which referrers to include
- Develop a vulnerability chart (see Chapter 26, pp. 337–40) for each target identified
- Devise a pro-active and on-going marketing campaign to nurture those on the key client list, most particularly programmes that encourage inter-personal links
- Ensure everyone in the firm knows the identity of key clients and those of their personnel who interface with professional and support staff

---

NOTES

(1) Wilson, A. *Marketing Audit Checklists*, List No.3 Appendix 3A, McGraw-Hill, Maidenhead (1992).
(2) Wilson, A. *New Directions in Marketing*, Kogan Page, London (1991); pages 119–30 contain a full discussion on the role of services in added value.

14
How and Why Commercial Concerns Select a Practice

The decision to appoint a professional adviser is never taken lightly, although both the method of selection and the identification of suitable firms tends to be unsystematised and in some ways arbitrary. Decisions are invariably taken at a high level and never left to relatively junior managers, as is often the case in the purchase of commercial services, or of products. There is no role for a specialised buyer function in the appointment of a professional practice. This is an important distinction between other types of purchasing by companies where there is a buying department or buying function. This arises because senior personnel whose main activities will be far outside that of selecting professional practices, if only because it occurs so rarely, cannot develop the expertise which a buyer would be expected to command and with this lack of expertise goes the lack of negotiating experience.

However arbitrary selecting professional firms may be, it is nevertheless necessary to understand the framework within which decisions are made even if it is never stated formally or if there is only an unconscious awareness of the questions invoked in deciding to appoint, change or seek additional professionals. These fall neatly into six groups:

- Is a service needed?
- Why is a service needed?

- What service is needed?
- Who needs the service?
- How should the service be rendered?
- Who should render the service?

IS A SERVICE NEEDED?

The recognition of the need for a service may come from several sources. It may be intuitive—that intangible and sometimes fleeting characteristic which distinguishes the successful entrepreneur, entrepreneurial manager and intrapreneur from others. It may stem from creative anticipation of the future; from judgement based on the consideration of both historical and current factors; from the development of a specific phenomenon in the company's operating *milieu*, from internal changes and pressures or from technological change.

Of course, the identification of a need could come from the hoary old salesman's approach of "creating the need". But *creating* a need which is not in reality a requirement is not marketing (it has been ingeniously defined as inventing a cure for which there is no known disease). The true role is better described as *identifying* clients' latent needs. Here again the practice developer must be aware of the blurred boundaries between "want", "need" and "expectations".

Identifying latent needs can be accomplished in a number of ways. A similar problem will frequently emerge in totally unrelated areas. Its solution in one area can readily lead to the application of the problem-solving technique to other areas. A question of the development of optimum price strategies in a multi-industry market for a particular service or product may indicate the existence of an identical problem, resolved or not, for other services or products in the same industries, or the same services or products in other industries. In either circumstances, it may not have occurred to other companies in the market that their price strategies also require examination and revision, perhaps because of changing conditions which initiated the requirement for a new price strategy.

A company bidding for British government contracts may not be aware that the specific circumstances relating to an offer may fall within the ambit of the Transfer of Undertakings (Protection of Employment) regulations. If it does, then the successful bidder must take over the contracts of those employees currently responsible for the work in governmental organisations. The implications are obvious and apply right across industry. Thus a human resource consultancy practice could identify employment problems their clients tendering for government work might not be aware of, such as with the Transfer of Undertakings legislation. In marketing professional services, the first task is to gain an understanding of prospective clients' businesses and to think with them and for them in the early identification of problems which match the capabilities of the service firm.

The reason why many professional organisations remain small may be less because of the dependence of the firms on a limited number of people with the right mix of skills than upon dependence on individual flair for identifying need and an inability to communicate this flair to others in the company. Such a situation is unnecessary since need identification can be formatted as a systematic and structured process. All who are involved in marketing are called upon to use their creative powers to the full. Nowhere is this more necessary than in developing a structured approach to need or want identification which can be met by professional services.

WHY IS A SERVICE NEEDED?

The "why" of service selection has important implications for the way the service is presented and the messages which are to be used. Knowing why a client has chosen to seek help from a given profession enables the marketer to concentrate on that topic and present the solution in terms of appropriate client benefit. Clients make no secret of the reason they are consulting although in some cases there may be some inhibition or reluctance to do more than present the reason in a disguised form. For example, heavy staff losses could be regarded as a reflection on recruitment or induction techniques or the corporate culture. A personnel manager would obviously prefer to suggest the reason had little or no connection with his or her own selection or induction skills.

Table 14.1 Reasons for choosing a profession

| | Examples | | | |
| | Private client | | Corporate client | |
Reason	Circumstances	Professional used	Circumstances	Professional used
Need for special skills for a specific reason or circumstance	Repetitive strain injury	Ergonomicist	Staff losses caused by poor induction techniques	Industrial psychologist
Intermittently recurring requirement or need for temporary extra capacity	Investment advice	Banker or Stockbroker	Acquisition of a property portfolio requiring structural surveying	Chartered surveyor
Nature of problem: one-off, sporadic recurrence, long term	Invention protection	Patent agent	Building extension	Architect
Need for total objectivity and/or freedom from internal pressures	Redundancy	Outplacement consultant	Pension fund management	Investment counsellor
Lack of physical resource	Polluted water supply	Chemist (and laboratory equipment)	New product development	Contract R&D
Cross-industry fertilization	Employment change	Career consultant	Diversification	Management consultant
Anonymity or confidentiality	Illness	Doctor	Company acquisition	Financial analyst
Emergency requirement	Injury to animal	Veterinary surgeon	Threat to computer system	Security specialist
Legal requirement	Conveyance	Solicitor	Audit	Accountant

WHAT SERVICE IS NEEDED?

The identification of the need for a service does not necessarily imply that the type of service required is always clear-cut. The need for differing types of services may be concurrent at several levels of activity and management. For example, if expansion of manufacturing activities is being planned, is marketing research needed to validate market size and growth hypotheses? Should any expansion be based on present plant or should new plant be built? This may be the province of consulting and production engineers as well as accountants and other financial experts. If new plant is decided on, then where should it be located for optimum results? Here, the logistic, facility management, infrastructure and planning experts may be needed. The questions are not mutually exclusive and, in fact, form a decision tree along which, at various points, different professional services may be needed to take the firm to the next decision.

Choices are arrived at in a variety of ways, but the question which is posed in such a situation is: "If management has been familiar with all the professional services available for reducing the areas of uncertainty and resolving problems, would it have used such services?" The answer almost certainly is "yes" which underlines a need for continuing communications between service providers and the clients they aspire to serve.

This raises certain important implications for marketers of services. The successful projection of an image of competence in one field may rule the service company out in another. This is how it should be if the choice were, for example, between a firm with expertise in marine insurance to the exclusion of all else, and another whose areas of activity were limited to life insurance. However, a firm with an image and a substance of capability in quantity surveying may not be considered in a situation in which negotiating capital allowances is required, because management cannot always make the transition necessary to relate quantity surveying expertise to this particular problem. The answer is again communication, but on an individual level.

It is expecting too much of human beings to assume that any provider of services will not, in the first instance at least, attempt to see a service need in terms of their own existing services. However, an ethical and professional approach will ensure that if the best "fit" is not one which the service provider can give, they will say so and even recommend alternatives. No matter how much professional service firms may know this and practise this, it may not be apparent to the seeker of services. A primary task in marketing professional services is to ensure that the potential client has faith that he or she will be advised objectively.

It is vital, therefore, that those who offer their professional services in situations where the need for a specific type of service is not unequivocal, must make their initial appraisal of the client problem on a totally open-minded basis. In circumstances of this type, an important part of the marketing task is to be sure the right service is offered, not only in terms of the company's professional expertise, but also within the full range of services (or indeed products) which may be available to meet the particular need even if the service firm itself cannot provide what is required.

Ignorance of Alternatives

Just as clients, even highly literate ones in a business sense, may not be certain a service is needed, he or she may be equally uncertain as to which service is appropriate. In any one situation, it is possible to consider perhaps four or five viable alternatives (as Figure 14.2 shows) all offering the same end result—a problem solution. The fact that, in many circumstances, viable choices do exist lends further strength to the statement that choice is destroyed if information is withheld.

WHO NEEDS THE SERVICE?

The fact that different problems requiring different services exist simultaneously at different levels of decision making has already been indicated. But given the ability to see this does not resolve the difficulty of who precisely needs the service; that is, who in the company will make the decision on: (a) which service will make a contribution, and (b) which firm will be invited to provide the service.

It is not usually the internal lawyer who needs legal services, but his or her own "internal" clients, such as the personnel manager or

Table 14.2 *Which service to choose*

Competition to:	Subject	Alternative service
Solicitors	Planning appeals	Architects Surveyors Town planning Consultants Do-it-yourself
	Probate	Banks Advice centres Do-it-yourself
	Taxation	Accountants Tax consultants Banks Insurance company Estate planners
Accountants	Corporate and financial planning	Merchant banks Consultants Do-it-yourself
	Computer development	Consultants Computer manufacturers Software services Do-it-yourself
	Taxation	Solicitors Tax consultants Banks Insurance companies Estate planning
Doctors	Healing	Acupuncturists Osteopaths Psychobiologists Faith healers Placebos and self-healing Pharmacists
	Preventive medicine	Homoeopathics Herbalists Pharmacists Diagnostic centres Para-medicals
Surveyors	Town planning	Specialist consultants Architects Do-it-yourself
	Structural surveying	Architects Specialist consultants Structural engineers
	Marketing of property	Estate agents Property shops Computer services Do-it-yourself
	Property management	Specialists Developers Local government Do-it-yourself

the contracts department. It is not the head of management services who requires an ergonomicist, but the chief design engineer. Although the personnel manager and the design engineer may claim no great knowledge of the techniques of the specialist they need, their role in the decision making on the choice of service required and the firm to render it is vital.

The decision-making unit (DMU) can be defined as a number of individuals who are participants in the decision-making process, who share common goals which the decision will help to achieve, and who also share the risks deriving from the decision. Thus, it embraces all those who influence, specify, control, and purchase. An important point which should not be overlooked is that there can well be people within a client organisation without power but with influence. These individuals can and often do occupy a lowly position in the management hierarchy. An accounts clerk reporting critically upon a bank's inefficiency, a personal assistant expressing grave reservations concerning a management consultant's knowledge or a farmhand complaining about a vet's tardiness in responding to an emergency call can all lead to the practice losing the client.

Typically three or more people will be involved in a decision to purchase a professional service, and it is not exceptional for as many as nine or ten individuals to contribute towards both the decision to purchase a service and the selection of the service firm. The inter-relationship of decision makers can be illustrated, as shown in Figure 14.1.

Since the view is stubbornly held that the person designated in any particular situation as buyer is the decision maker, not surprisingly a very large number of visits and a substantial part of all promotion have been found to be routed to non decision makers or those who only contribute to the decision. An inordinately high number of contacts are wasted as anyone involved in marketing insurance, property and architectural services will confirm.

In the same way information required by decision makers is also frequently misrouted because of the wrong identification of those involved in the purchasing decisions. Technical data is given, for example, to decision makers who are concerned only with the commercial aspects of the contract, and, of course, the reverse is also true.

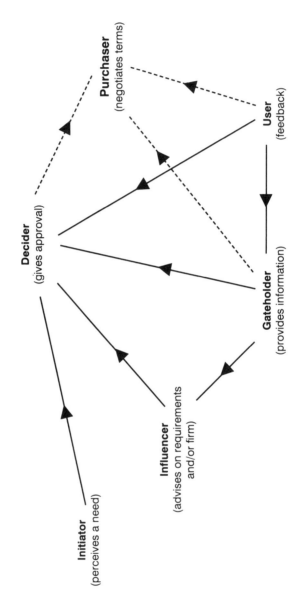

Figure 14.1 *Buying influence centres*[1]

The major questions for marketers of services are:

- Who initiates the inquiry?
- Who are the individuals involved in the decision-making process?
- On what basis will they make the decision about: (a) the service needed; and (b) who shall render the service?
- What facts do they need to arrive at these decisions?

This information will not be yielded by waiting for it to appear, but must be sought out by research; not even when the approach is from the client side will the information be available automatically. Other than the fact that the inquirer, *prima facie,* may be one of the individuals involved in the decision-making process (but equally he or she may not be), all the questions still require answers. It is true, of course, that it is relatively simple to obtain the necessary data when the initiative for inquiry comes from the client side. However, only if the answers to the questions are available does it become possible to plan and implement effective tactics to obtain the engagement.

HOW SHOULD THE SERVICE BE RENDERED?

The "how" and the "who" of services are closely interlinked. One will, to some extent, depend upon the other. But generalizations are useful at this stage. Clearly, in deciding how the service will be rendered, the purchaser is concerned not only with timing, but also with the way in which the service will affect day-to-day operations and, where applicable, how the involvement of the service personnel will impact on his or her own staff. The long-term gains of the effect of the service could be easily nullified by the immediate adverse conditions created by the use of the professional service firm. A new product search commencing with a corporate audit of strengths and weaknesses which, through tactlessness, ineptitude, or inexperience of the consultancy firm's staff, may well be interpreted by senior management as a threat to their personal positions, may result in staff losses or demotivation with disastrous results. Thus, the buyer sees the "fit" of the practice to the purchasing company to be important.

During the execution of the service, there must be constant feedback of information on progress and results to the management of the purchasing company. This provides a stable operating arrangement. Service projects will sometimes change during their execution. Without good communication and feedback, the areas of uncertainty can widen and become more intense, and expectations may move out of line with reality. This leads to disappointment and frustration at the end of the project and often the problem the service was intended to resolve is not resolved, or new problems are created.

Thus, the management of the client company will need to know the type, frequency and quality of the liaison which will be developed. This is particularly true where work on the buyer's premises is either inappropriate to the project, as in external training programmes, or intermittent, as in some types of financial advisery services.

Just as the delivery of a product is not necessarily the end of the supplier's involvement, neither is the end of a service contract the end of the service firm's involvement. The providers of professional services often have an open door through which to watch the developments stemming from the completion of their work. They rarely take advantage of this. The continued interest shown in the client's performance after the completion of an assignment clearly indicates the practice's confidence in its own work and demonstrates its commitment and sense of responsibility. It is one manifestation of its professionalism. It also provides opportunities for appraising new service needs. The "hit-and-run" service providers are a menace to themselves, their clients and their profession.

The purchaser of services needs confidence that the service will be seen through to its successful completion and interest will not die on settling the last invoice. So important is the follow-on in professional services that many such practices are now building education and training into their work, to leave the client company with a future capability for solving its own problems in the same field.

Nowhere is this better illustrated than in the introduction of corporate long-ranging planning into companies. Originally this was most frequently undertaken by management consultants who withdrew on completion of their work. Many companies which introduced corporate long-range planning systems then found that their own staffs were not sufficiently skilled or experienced to maintain them and certainly did not own the plans. They rapidly fell into disuse or were misused. Today, consultants' briefs, when involved in corporate long-range planning projects, are to assist firms to develop their own systems rather than to create and implement one for them. In the process of this in-house development, the firm's own staff receive training and exposure which ensure that the planning system is an on-going process and is not dependent upon outside aid to maintain and adjust it.

WHO SHOULD RENDER THE SERVICE?

For the service firm, this question is the key one. If need for a service has been properly revealed, the appropriateness of the service offered has been proved, the identification of the part of the organisation requiring the service and those who will decide on its implementation completed, and the method of rendering the service successfully explained, then the success of the offer should be assured. However, it is not. It is only at this last decision point that the combination of the basic concepts comes into play. In going through the choice process, the purchaser, having arrived at the moment of decision on who shall provide the service, will choose on the basis of the practice which appears to offer the greatest reduction of uncertainty, understands the problem most completely, and has demonstrated a high degree of professionalism. Thus, the correct handling of the first four questions is only to bring the professional service firm to the point at which the company is among those to be considered. Only in rare cases will all competition have eliminated itself at the first four hurdles. The main competitive battle commences at "who".

Mention has been made previously that there are few things in marketing about which it is possible to be dogmatic but three issues stand out, two of which have already been identified (every practice has a unique advantage or resource of some sort; services cannot be purchased unless the service firm is known). The third "absolute" is that when all things are equal the professional service firm already in place will almost certainly win. Clients do not change practices for an all things equal situation as there is no equivalent benefit to be gained for the risks involved in a new supplier providing precisely the same service. Chapter 8 explains how unique selling "packages" can be developed.

In order to be considered for an engagement, the marketing task of any practice entering the "who should render the service" stage has to offer something beneficially different and better than the existing supplier. This means that they have to have some knowledge not just of any other firms competing for the engagement but also of the incumbent. There is only one question to which they must provide a satisfactory answer: "Why should this client commission us?" The answer has to be objective and based on the real benefits the clients will receive. "Because we are better than the others", or, "because we have been in the business longer than anyone else", or, "because we pioneered the technique" are not answers that will deliver the client. Each has to be converted to benefits and supported by some evidence or demonstration that the firm can deliver. Combined with other checklists in the book, Table 14.3 will at the very least assist the practice developer to avoid the grosser errors.

Table 14.3   *Competitive quotations and tenders*

- All incoming requests or offers to submit proposals circulated to everyone likely to be involved and the marketing committee (if one exists) or a partner
- Decision taken if an offer is to be made (if not an acknowledgement and expression of appreciation for being included in the invitation list and a reason for not quoting is a courtesy which must be observed)
- Decision taken who within the practice will lead
- Lead professional selects personnel to develop the proposal
- Member of team deputed to prepare background material on client service and relevant experience (see Appendix 7.1 and Figure 24.1)
- Draft proposal written by team leader with inputs from other team members
- Team review background material and draft proposal and agree changes, costing, timing and roles
- Team leader and other members interview client decision makers
- Proposal refined using material gathered at client interview
- Request to prospective client for a personal presentation by team
- Presentation strategy decided
- (After decision) Team leader contacts client for reasons for being chosen or not chosen
- Feedback to firm

It is perhaps appropriate to emphasise at this point that the physical and aesthetic quality of the proposal document can be an important factor in the client's decision making. Some decision makers and influencers may have no other contact and their perceptions will be highly influenced by the documentation. This must meet the four *desiderata* of all offers—precision, finality, protection and professional appearance. References made to Terms of Business as a marketing tool in Chapter 10, pages 97–8, are equally relevant to proposal documents.

DECISION FORMING FACTORS

While the processes which have been described so far are those which commercial organisations adopt, formally or informally, to choose a practice, the reasons for choosing are much more difficult to classify. There is a considerable overlap of corporate and personal consideration which is always difficult and sometimes impossible to unravel.

Within the business *milieu* there will always be constraints but to understand the non-objective indeed emotional issues which can play a significant role in a decision it is necessary to study the decision-making unit members as individuals. The chapter which follows examines the key factors but it is emphasised here and in that chapter that the separation of the decision maker as an organisation member from him or her as an individual in their own right is, in many instances, unreal since so much is common to them in both their *personae*.

In a corporate decision the selection of one practice rather than another is an amalgam of the many things both quantitative and qualitative as Table 14.4 shows. In quantitative terms, the would-be purchaser of the professional services is looking for evidence that they will receive value for money, that the work will be completed on schedule and with the minimum of disruption. But of equal importance will be such factors as the empathy between the practitioners and the management and staff of the client firm, the service firm's reputation and track record, accessibility, and the many issues which are referred to in Chapters 16 and 17.

These decision-forming factors will, of course, vary from situation to situation, most particularly because of the significance of the decision to the purchasing firm. However, as always, there is

Table 14.4 *Examples of benefits corporate decision makers seek*[2]

Financial (for the decision maker's firm)	The service (for the decision maker's firm)	Social or political (for self)	Personal
Absolute lowest fees for comparable offers	Pre- and post-service around the central service	Enhancement of decision maker's standing with own management	Internal liking and respect as a result of the decision
Greatest cost-effectiveness	Specific features to be introduced into the service		
Operating or administrative cost reductions	Speed of completion	Creation of personal leverage with professional service firm	Compatibility of decision with decision maker's self-perceptions
Long credit	Allocation of specific personnel	Prestige derived from reputation of retained firm	
Contingency payment pricing (fee based on acts to be performed or accomplished)	Acceptance of responsibility and liability		
	Compatibility between service firm and own staff		

Buyers will not seek all types of benefits but will have priorities and combinations of benefits

Source: Bonoma, T.V. "Major sales—who really does the buying?", *Harvard Business Review,* Cambridge, Mass., May/June (1982)

the question, which in professional services can never be under-estimated, of the temperament of the decision makers. Some will be more influenced by the personality and charisma of the service presenters while others will be completely impervious to these phenomenon. Many will be swayed by a track record and the bidding firm's client base. Yet others may seek the psychological security of qualifications. The "mix" is complex and changing and so pervasive that it can overwhelm objective factors such as fees or timings. Business-to-business buying despite protests to the contrary is far from objective; professional service buying is even more influenced by non-objective factors, most particularly be-cause the purchaser is buying an expectation and has less oppor-tunity to assess the service than the buyer of a product.

Thus, while generalisations can only be interesting rather than useful, at least the verities for all situations can be identified and the marketer can ensure that these issues are adequately dealt with in offering a service.

The subjective factors which might for example surround the decision to buy in a diagnostic medical service for company personnel may be difficult to identify. It could be peace of mind, actuarial information required for pension or insurance purposes, proof of fitness for specific work, confirmation or refutation of a previous diagnosis or even stakeholder confidence. It is not until the practitioner knows the benefits which are sought that the presentation for the service can be made to emphasise those benefits.

Taking a prospective client through the five stages which lead to a decision, and which were set out in Chapter 9, can only be achieved if the benefits sought are known and the client believes they can be delivered. An assessment of the service they anticipate receiving will be based on the benefits offered, and these in turn will be weighed against the features of the service which will yield those benefits. While it is true that, in a sense, the client is not concerned with how the benefits are achieved only that they should be, the likelihood of them being convinced that they can be delivered is not great unless the necessary skills, experience and qualifications exist. These are not what is purchased but they provide a reasonably reliable surrogate for assessing an intangible service yet to be provided.[3] See also Chapter 15, pages 154–5, for an explanation of the role of evidence.

The professional must adopt a Janus-like approach. The features of the firm must be converted to benefits; the benefits sought by clients must be aligned to the features, that is the resources, skills and experience of the practitioners. Thus, what the firm offers is not necessarily what the client purchases—as Table 10.1, page 96, clearly shows.

The whole process of choosing a professional practice can be encapsulated to show the key questions everyone concerned with practice development should be able to answer in relation to the individual client. While it is appreciated that it is a great deal easier to set out the questions than to determine the answers, the difficulty of the task is not a reason for not attempting it. In this instance any information is better than no information since it would be an inconvenient rule that nothing could be done until everything could be done.

1. Who are the powerful decision makers and what are their policies?	2. What specific benefits does each important decision maker want?	3. What are the features of our offer and how do they meet benefit requirements?	4. How can we prove the features will yield the benefits?	5. How do important decision makers see us?	6. What marketing strategy and tactics do the answers imply?

Figure 14.2 *Encapsulation of key factors*

ACTION POINTS

- What steps can we take to obtain regular and timely information on the issues listed in columns 1–5 in Figure 14.2?
- How will the information be disseminated within the firm?
- How will the information be used?

NOTES

(1) This figure is based on Bonoma, T.V. "Major sales—who really does the buying?", *Harvard Business Review,* Cambridge, Mass., May/June (1982) and adapted for professional services with his permission. Relatively few practices have a negotiator or buyer but the dotted lines represent a further possible participant in the decision process.

(2) This table is also drawn from the work referred to above.

(3) The reader is referred to Wilson, A. *Practice Development for Professional Firms,* Chapter 9, McGraw-Hill, Maidenhead (1991) for an in-depth description of the process as well as an explanation of the role of evidence—human, environmental and collateral—in the client decision-making process.

15
Why People Choose a Practice: the Private Client

It may seem unnecessary to separate the private client's decision processes in choosing a practice from those of the corporate buyer of professional services. The same requirement exists to take them through the five affirmatives given in Chapter 9: a need (or want) must exist; the service fits the need; the firm can provide the service; the fee or expected fee is acceptable; and the time for the completion is satisfactory. Clients are afflicted with the same uncertainties in decision making, the taxonomy of problems does not differ and there is an overriding need for total professionalism. In fact, the private client and the members of the decision-making unit are closely similar.

The different approaches which are needed for these two segments—corporate and private—are much more questions of emphasis and attitude than messages, methods and media. The corporate purchaser of services has both an organisational and individual *personae* which are closely intertwined but which act strongly on each other. Private clients only consider their personal satisfactions and needs while members of the DMU invariably consider both.

The corporate decision making is often, indeed usually, shared between different people with different responsibilities, different personal aspirations and possibly even different corporate objectives. The corporate buyer of services is more constrained by organisational goals and policies and while not impervious to non-commercial appeals they are more objective in their choices. Added to this, corporate decision makers are usually far better informed about the services they are buying than the private client, less swayed by non-commercial aspects of the offer and, in the final analysis, must answer for the decision made to peers, superiors, stakeholders and perhaps even the electorate.

It will be seen in Chapter 19, within the context of support staff, that there are well-defined human needs, not usually overtly stated, which certainly apply across the spectrum of decision making in situations where an exchange of money occurs in return for goods and services. Moreover these needs, although less likely to be expressed overtly by the corporate client, are as applicable to them as the private client. However, it is perhaps from the work of Warren Wittreich, most particularly his seminal article,[1] that the practitioner can gain greatest benefit. Wittreich identified three phenomena that have a pervasive effect on the purchaser of professional services, which have already been touched on in Chapter 5—uncertainty, understanding problems and engaging a professional.

Uncertainty

All clients are uncertain about some aspect of a service or the practitioner. This is bound to be so when it is impossible to assess either until the service has been rendered. These uncertainties can range from transitory doubts to total apprehension. A professional service must make a direct contribution to the reduction of client uncertainty relative to their business activities or their personal situation. Substantially, patients do not visit a medical practitioner simply for medicines. A response after a medical examination, "I wouldn't bother about booking your holiday" will do nothing for the relationship since, even in the most dire circumstances, the patient is looking for reassurance and hope. Yet they are unlikely to walk into the surgery with those two words on their lips any more than issuing a demand to be greeted with dignity. This is a need, a want and an expectation combined.

There are many sources of uncertainty and the client-centred professional and all the support staff will seek to understand these and to mitigate them. Whether it is the receptionist putting a nervous or intimidated client at their ease or the professional explaining the intricacies of an issue, the result is the same—a client who feels he or she is dealing with a concerned practice. The phrase, "people do not care how much you know until they know how much you care", might be a somewhat sentimental cliché but it is close to the truth.

The attitude, "no one ever got fired for buying from…", naming the leader in the profession is one way which decision makers attempt to reduce uncertainty and with it reduce risks. For the non-leaders this aspect of uncertainty must be identified and attacked with the offer of the appropriate reassurance as to competence, resources, commitment, value for money and other aspects.

The marketer's task is to identify the sources of uncertainty and mitigate them. Taking only one aspect of choice, "which service to choose" from Table 14.2, page 136 illustrates just how wide the choices of a service are for a single problem apart from the choice of the practice itself.

Understanding Problems

The *raison d'être* of every professional firm is problem solving. No one seeks the assistance of any professional unless there is a problem to be solved. Every organisation offering know-how as their "product" are service companies or firms but not all service firms offer know-how "products". This is the difference between a professional and a commercial or consumer service. Table 9.1, page 80, provides a taxonomy of the problem matrix and illustrates the marketer's role in problem solving. From this it will have been seen that the professionals must assist the client to identify the substantive problem and then to solve it.

It is sometimes necessary for these to be re-stated if they are to be resolved. There is a real advocacy role here as clients may have to be persuaded to agree the substantive problem. Solving problems clients do not think they have wins no friends. A truly professional service must come directly to grips with the fundamental problem of the client seeking to use the service. Successfully delivering a service is wholly dependent on obtaining an understanding of the client's situation. This is not true for a wide range of products and commercial services.

Engaging a Professional

Since clients are purchasing an expectation and there is no means of establishing with certainty precisely what level of service will be received they will use a series of surrogates to assess the likelihood of the service meeting their needs and expectations. Some of the surrogates will be substantially valid—past experience, the client's own and others, reputation of the practice, track record—and many barely relevant—the appearance of the practitioners and offices. One of the factors that will be considered will be the apparent professionalism of the practice. Clients only want to work with wholly professional practices and practitioners. This is one of the surrogates they will adopt in deciding whether to appoint a practice. Unfortunately, "professional" like "quality" cannot be defined with accuracy and it is very much in the eye of the beholder. Judgement can and is made on the way the professional looks, talks and body language although none of these provide a guidance as to their technical competence. Chapters 16 and 19 go into the subject of projecting professionalism in some depth.

The interrelationship between the three dominant but unspoken client needs, wants and expectations is obvious. The more professional the practice or practitioner appears the less will be the uncertainty; the better they can obtain an understanding and agreement of the substantive problem the more professional they will appear. It is not, of course, sufficient to sense needs. It is necessary to demonstrate to clients that their real needs have been understood and that the service, both in content and manner of its delivery, will match these needs.

THE "TRAWL"

If the task of selecting and appointing a professional practice is divided into its three substantive phases then the differences and what they mean for the marketer can be identified:

- Identification of firms which are considered to be capable of providing the service which is perceived as required
- Deciding if the selected organisation has the skills and resources to be able to deliver the service for an acceptable fee
- Evaluating if an empathy exists between the would-be purchaser and the professionals

As with corporate clients, the single most important major source of information used by private clients to find suitable professional advisers is the interpersonal network. Research has shown that over 85% of new corporate client acquisitions can be traced to this source. The equivalent figure for private clients is almost certainly well over 90%.

When a need for a professional service is perceived (although the perception may not necessarily be correct), all the evidence shows that the first action taken is to use the network. "Do you know a good loss assessor?"; the most frequent source for this advice is, not surprisingly, family, friends and business associates. The reader might well consider how he or she first knew of their own professional advisers. It would be surprising if most of them were not the result of a recommendation from this group of informants. Almost in the same category comes professional, social and other organisations. This is, of course, the "golf club" link which was not just important but critical before de-regulation days.

The third most important source of information appears to be directories, most particularly classified directories (see Chapter 25, pages 320 and 323–324). While these dominate there is evidence of some use of specialised directories and lists such as will be provided by professional associations and commercial publishers of directories and year books.

The next information-generating segment is other professional advisers used by private clients. That is asking one professional, say an accountant, to recommend a solicitor. There is no very recent research on the subject but past inquiries revealed that bank managers were the most frequently consulted professional group but, given the low regard into which banks and other financial institutions have fallen in recent years, it could well be their role is not now as dominant as in the past.

Advertisements can obviously be a source for producing inquiries for professional services although, as with all advertising, it is difficult to relate new clients obtained directly to given campaigns. Nevertheless there is little doubt they are an influencing tool, particularly for financial services.

There are three groups of professionals where choice is more likely to be influenced by the factors that govern selection of retailers rather than those which apply to professional service selection. These are opticians and pharmacists and some types of financial services such as building societies and insurance brokers. The opticians and pharmacists, in particular, are highly dependent on what is termed in retailing as "foot fall"; that is the numbers and socio-economic groupings of potential customers frequenting the vicinity of the premises. For these professions window display and merchandising are critical. For the others and for professional practices with a strong private client base, a street level office with window display will build recognition and recall and thus is an influence in choice.

One other source of information potential private clients use and which can lead to ultimate business are exhibitions. These are finding increasing favour and bring in people with a definite interest in the exhibition topic. Financial institutions are usually to be found at county shows and consumer exhibitions. Recruitment fairs attract training organisations and human resource firms. Industrial product exhibitions draw technical consultancy practices (see also Chapter 25).

All this, of course, implies that typically the private client considers an array of firms in the same way as most corporate purchasers of professional services do. The reality is different for two reasons. First, in seeking a recommendation they generally only follow up one possible supplier; second, if the feeling from or ambience of the first contact is satisfactory the private client tends not to look further. This means the first contact has a huge advantage that should not be lost. The implications are that the professional practice must target influential parts of the network for their promotion as the actual clients themselves—Chapter 20 addresses this issue.

SKILL ASSESSMENT

Here, not infrequently, a client faces dual problems: first, in deciding which discipline is the most appropriate for a particular problem; and second, which firm is the most suitable to appoint. While it is true that, in many circumstances, there can be no doubt whatsoever which service to choose—litigation, auditing, insurance broking, dentistry, optical—there are a wide range of alternatives for other problems as Table 14.2, page 136, demonstrates. The corporate client is likely to have greater experience and knowledge if only through consanguinity with the problem or the profession. The private client whose needs are far more sporadic does not usually have the opportunity to build the appropriate knowledge and experience.

The second issue—which practice offers the correct level of skills?—is just as difficult to assess. While, to take an extreme example, it would hardly be practical to retain a Queen's Counsel to dispute a parking fine, it might equally be unwise to seek the services of an architectural technician to design a complex structure.

The private client for the most part has no way of checking the competence of a professional practice or practitioner, certainly not at the outset when, as explained, they purchase an expectation. In-house professionals in the same discipline as the potential service provider usually have the knowledge and experience or make a reasoned judgement of the competence of the practitioner. Such a situation would be rare for the private client. Thus of necessity the latter falls back on to the use of surrogates to decide if the level of competence and experience meet their needs.

The sort of evidence they seek comes in three forms:

1 *Human evidence.* An optician dressed as Superman or an insurance broker in a Hare Krishna attire are both likely to generate discomfort because of the dissonance between the expected and stereotypical appearance of professionals. Such appearances may well convey to a client that the practitioner is insensitive, undignified and lacking *gravitas*. Clients attempt to ascertain qualifications: associate, membership or fellow of the professional association, the appropriate degrees or diplomas although it would be assumed that if a solicitor is in business he holds a practising certificate and other professionals the appropriate membership or accreditation. If, as has been indicated in Chapter 1, legal protection is removed to some titles such as architect then one selection factor will be removed.

2 *Environmental evidence* refers to the physical aspects of the infrastructure. It takes little imagination to deduce the effect on a private patient of ancient apparatus, a less than hygienic surgery and uncomfortable examination equipment in the premises of any practitioner concerned with personal care. The effect can be just as negative in other types of professional services even where equipment and premises play no part, or a very minor part, in the delivery of the service. Lack of computers, facsimile, word processors, or a host of other office aids may well say something about the success of the practice or the attitude of the practitioners. Thus, claims regarding the possession of some physical resources such as laboratories, audio-visual equipment, information retrieval systems, and special purpose premises, may be covertly checked by the prospective client.

3 *Collateral evidence* comprises such items as stationery, print, graphics, reports and practice identity logos and symbols. While human evidence can have an immediate and pervasive effect in eliminating a firm from consideration or can even terminate a relationship, environmental and collateral evidence is not as potent, but inconsistencies can and do have a cumulative effect.

Practice development, particularly in attempting to influence the selection process, must include a definition of the desired effect of all three forms of evidence on the potential client, and activities and evidence must be adjusted and manipulated to achieve compatibility.

THE EMPATHY FACTOR

Unless totally intimidated, few private clients will retain or return to a professional where there is a positive lack of empathy. While the empathy really relates to individuals, the ambience of a practice can often have a favourable or unfavourable impact even before there is a meeting between the professional and the client.

The choice of health care professionals, however, seems to fall into a different category to most others. Patients rarely visit doctors to appraise or evaluate them. Once in the surgery it is an extremely rare occasion not to complete the consultation, although they may never return.

Given the daunting nature of many professions and professionals there is frequently a degree of apprehension in a first meeting. Dentists who have singularly failed to sell painless dentistry in fact often stimulate the fear of a visit by displaying what patients perceive as pain inducing instruments and not dampening odours associated with pain, such as the penetrating smell of the mixture of zinc oxide and oil of cloves which is so closely linked with the discomfort of cavity filling. Waiting rooms are often stark and uncomfortable, display peremptory notices and are manned by unhelpful, unconcerned staff.

Atmospherics[2] are an important aspect of ensuring potential clients are comfortable. They send silent but persuasive messages to visitors. They can be defined as the designing of buying and consuming environments in a manner calculated to produce specific cognitive and/or emotional effects on the target. This is not to say commercial clients are not influenced by atmospherics, only that the effect is more pervasive with the private individual than with a decision-making unit operating within corporate rules.

In the interplay between practitioner and client, there is one question dominant in the prospective client's mind: "Do I want to work with this firm and with this person?" The private client will contract for the service provided the practitioner has satisfied him or her that the correct service has been chosen, the best firm to deal with the issue selected, the optimum level of skills and resources will be applied, the fee level and timing will be acceptable and there is empathy between the two parties. Since empathy largely derives from contact between individuals then the skills of communication and social intercourse are paramount. Chapter 24 goes into some depth about this important issue.

It is useful to trace the "find and appoint" process since the marketers can ensure that the route is simple, trouble free and pleasant. The danger for all professionals is to become so obsessed with the problem they forget about the client. A lively appreciation of client needs, the factors which include their decisions to appoint a practice or to work with a practitioner will avoid this risk and lead to a mutually satisfying and stable relationship.

At the beginning of the previous chapter it was pointed out that it is difficult to separate the reasons behind a decision to choose a practice when corporate and personal needs are so closely entwined. The marketer therefore may find it helpful to take this and the previous chapter together recognising that the client in a personal capacity is still the same person as in their corporate role. Social scientist, Abraham Maslow did not distinguish in his *Hierarchy of Human Needs* between the two situations since it is still the one person.

Table 15.1   *Service stages*

Client searches for service supplier • •	Where, when, how to get the service. Service content.
Pre-meeting contact • • • • •	Ease and speed of telephone and postal communications. Responsive in day and timing requirements of any meeting.
Arrival • •	Location, signposting, reception, punctuality.
Contact • • • • •	Expectations and realisations; own and other peoples. Previous contact experience will influence expectations.
Termination • • • • •	Assurance purpose of meeting has been achieved. What happens next? What are service provider's tasks?
Follow-up	Checking outcome, concern. Complain resolution. Follow-up offer.

Source: Whittle, S. and Foster, F. "Customer profiling—getting into your customer's shoes", *Management Decision* 18, Vol. 27, No. 6 (1990).

ACTION POINTS

- Identify all actual and potential sources which might refer private clients and develop a contact programme
- Ensure all the "evidence" clients use to assess a practice is compatible with their requirements
- Check the "atmospherics" of the practice for equal professional and client compatibility
- Review efficiency of the service stages (Table 15.1)
- Seek client and support staff ideas for improvements

Further Action Points at the end of Chapters 16 and 20 should also be considered.

NOTES

(1) Wittreich, W.J. "How to Buy/Sell Professional Services", *Harvard Business Review,* Cambridge, Mass., March/April (1966).

(2) The concept of atmospherics as a communication tool was first propounded in Kotler, P. *Marketing for Non-profit Organisations,* pp.219–221, and *Marketing Professional Services,* pp.240–241, Prentice-Hall, Englewood Cliffs (1975 and 1984, respectively).

16
Images: the Critical Decision Factor

In recent years the professions have become more sensitive to the image of their various disciplines—more so than concern with the image of their individual practices. Perhaps this is because the majority of the professions are not now held in the same awe or approached with the same deference as in the past and, as a result, neither their advice nor their attitudes are accepted uncritically. Indeed in many countries there has been a veritable and unremitting storm of criticism levelled at the professions and some have become the butt of every cocktail party barb as watchwords for rapacity and sharp dealing—an image enhanced by opulent life styles. Lawyers, estate agents, bankers, accountants and architects have borne the brunt of public anger, vituperation and cynicism. A poll in the United States in 1993 showed that 31% of those interviewed thought lawyers were "less honest" than most people.[1] The dislike of lawyers is, of course, nothing new. "First thing we do, let's kill all the lawyers", will be found in Shakespeare's *Henry VI*. Only the veterinarians appear to have emerged from this public *auto-da-fé* unburned.

That the image of the professions generally should be such a poor one is understandable given the background explained in the early chapters of this book. However, an interesting phenomenon not often commented on by those outside the professions is that the majority of surveys into clients' and the general public's regard for almost all the professions, which tends to be negative, is most usually qualified by "but mine's different". The question then arises why does the aggregate of "but mine's different" not result in a good image for the professions as a whole?

Inevitably suspicion falls on the media for it is truly said that of them "good news is no news and bad news is good news". Thus every minor misdemeanour, every error, every negative attitude is expanded on. The solicitor who absconds with client monies, the accountants who failed to identify major malfeasance, the doctor who refused to visit a dying patient, the bank manager who overcharges for inadequate services and the architect whose building is technically and aesthetically inadequate are all held up for public vilification.

It is obvious that the individual practice has been able to separate itself from the image of the profession as a whole but the seminal question is should it? The answer must be an unequivocal "no". No matter how efficient "mine" may be, the image of the profession must have some negative effect on the individual firm. Negative or antagonistic perceptions discourage clients from seeking services if they see a way of avoiding the use of professionals. Thus the total volume of work becomes unnecessarily reduced and more often to the disadvantage of clients.

The collegial bodies have substantially failed their professions in changing their images. Nowhere is this better illustrated than in dentistry. Some 39% of the British population visit their dentist regularly. A further 11% have occasional check ups. This means that half the population avoid dentists until pain or appearance forces them to make a visit. This low visiting rate should be compared with the incidence of dental diseases—79% of dentate adults suffer with some form of periodontal condition. Dominant among the reasons for not attending regularly as was indicated in the previous chapter is the fear which dentists unwittingly engender of the pain associated with a visit. Today dentistry is substantially painless but the dental associations have failed to promote this.

The Law Society's early dismal Mr. Whatshisname image promotion is indicative of some of the unskilled efforts to change public attitude. (It must be said in fairness that later campaigns were more sophisticated but still did not produce any noticeable improvement in the image of the solicitor.) Half-hearted attempts with booklets "Why you need a Chartered Accountant" and similar publications by other associations are too feeble to make the slightest impression on the situation. Only by pressure from members and their willingness to meet the cost, can sustainable high impact campaigns be undertaken and be effective. There is some evidence that this is now occurring since, in 1993, the Law Society of Scotland appointed an advertising agency, giving them a reputed budget of £500,000.

IDENTIFYING THE "PUBLICS"

The private practices' publics and the professions' publics are inextricably woven together and such efforts as are made by individual practices concentrate on a far too narrow target—clients and non-clients. To limit image development and improvement work to these two groups is also to limit the effectiveness of any campaign and thus ultimately the success of the practice.

Table 16.1 *Target "Publics"*

	The professions' publics	The firm's publics
Clients		•
Non-clients		•
Clients' industries	•	•
Community	•	•
Staff		•
Stakeholders		•
Suppliers		•
Government	•	•
Financial community	•	•
Media	•	•
Opinion formers	•	•
Special interest groups	•	•
Educational bodies	•	•
Professional organisations (own and others)	•	•
Referrers		•

Clearly not all of these targets can be the subject of image improvement campaigns since it would be well beyond the resources of most practices. It is however perfectly possible to stratify them in accordance with their importance and then the efforts can be divided proportionately. There is little doubt the two obvious groups already mentioned—clients and potential clients—would head any such stratification, perhaps followed by referrers and staff. This last group is perhaps one of the most neglected of promotional targets and efforts and yet is one of the most critical—see Chapter 19.

The important breakdown referred to in Chapter 11, page 102, in the client and non-client categories again applies. They can be divided into six groupings all of which can and indeed will have different perceptions of the practice, and which are also relevant to the profiling technique described in Chapter 11:

1 Regular clients
2 Transactional clients—sporadic or inactive
3 One-off clients
4 Lost clients
5 Potential clients to whom proposals or offers have been made but not accepted
6 Potential clients who know of the practice but have not invited them to submit proposals or offers

To take an extreme, the likelihood of regular and lost clients having the same image of the firm is zero. ("Lost" in this context refers to clients who have ceased to use the firm because of failure of some aspect of performance or expectations not being fulfilled. It would exclude clients lost because of take-overs and mergers, and other business reasons.)

MULTIPLE IMAGE CONCEPT

To the multiplicity of targets must now be added the fact that firms do not have "an image". They have a series of images. Everything can create perceptions of the firm and the individuals—the way people dress and talk, equipment used, quality of correspondence, punctuality and myriad other aspects.

Most organisations which are concerned with their images, and most of their advisers who are supposed to know better, are rarely familiar with the discrete images so that most campaigns fail or are aborted. If a single reason could be ascribed to the massive waste of money, time and talent, it is because of incorrect perception that organisations' images are single dimensional. It is necessary therefore now to consider the multiple image concept whose practical implications will become obvious:

- The *current* image—how does the outside world see the particular subject?
- The *mirror* image—how does the firm see the particular subject?
- The *wish* image—what does the firm wish the particular subject image to be or to become?

It requires little imagination to appreciate how these three types can clash. Indeed, Burns when he wrote, "O wad some Pow'r the giftie gie us to see oursels as others see us!", well expressed the conflict situation between the *current* and *mirror* image. Not quite so obvious, however, is the conflict between them and the *wish* image, and the image which will produce the best impact—the *optimum* image; in other words, the distinction between how the firm *wishes* to be seen and how it *ought* to be seen to improve its operations.

An added complication is that different members of the practice may well, indeed probably do, have different perceptions of the firm under each heading and each perception is more likely to reflect the desire for self-esteem, or the social or emotional requirements of the different members of the firm rather than the impact on the publics it serves.

At this point it is necessary to include an important warning. Images not based on reality are easily identified and the gap between reality and what is projected will place the firm in an infinitely worse position that if it had no image at all. Image correction is far more expensive and more difficult than image creation. The multiple image concept discourages dishonesty or inaccuracy, if only because if the mirror image deviates from the current image, it creates within firms damaging internal attitudes of cynicism, self-deprecation and demoralisation and externally disbelief and distrust. For example, in an attempt to project an image of involvement and concern for clients, the firm claims that partners are involved in all matters it handles while the professional and support staff know this to be untrue. A case history from a major professional practice with a strong private client base illustrates this. Some 30 support staff of the firm with no professional staff present were interrogated by a consultant and were asked if they would recommend the practice to their friends. The vast majority of those present said "no". Further investigation revealed that it was common knowledge within the practice that unqualified staff were often used on projects and their time was billed at a qualified professional's rate. This case reveals the damaging effect of dissonance between the wish image and the current image.

A wish image might be for the firm to be seen as a young, energetic team with a special interest in commercial property. In fact, clients may well have a preference for maturity—the firm's track record and an understanding of the client's business may be considered more important than a generalised interest in commercial property. This would be the optimum image.

Thus the image development task can now be defined. The optimum image must be agreed by all the partners and managers within the practice. By internal marketing they should seek to convince all members of the firm that the optimum image is identical to the image they wish for. Thereafter ensuring reality matches the optimum profile the current image can be developed to align with the optimum image. If the four images are aligned then success is certain.

Given these vast numbers of variables: six categories of clients and non-clients; fifteen or more image targets; variable image objectives within the one organisation; and four separate images, practical and profitable image development might appear to be an impossible dream as indeed it is unless the fourth dimension—the optimum image—is understood.

An image that is "all things to all men" is, of course, most desirable, but since that is unlikely to be achieved, the objective is one that is most attractive to the firm's important publics—most particularly clients and potential clients. To establish the optimum image, tactics must be based on the image requirements for the service and co-ordinated with the practice's overall image need and the reality of the firm and its achievements.

The development of the optimum image depends on interrelationships and cross-influences. For example, the current image may perhaps be too strongly linked to a particular service or technique, some of which may carry the seeds of obsolescence, declining or changed requirements in, say, architecture. The antipathy which has arisen among the public and housing authorities alike for high rise residential buildings is an example.

There is little wonder, therefore, that with conflicting objectives and conflicting perceptions, image building is a highly inexact and sometimes unpredictable activity. Only if marketing tactics take account of the multiple image concept is there any possibility of a suitable image being built.

FIRST IMPRESSIONS

It is against this complex background that the actual image development, improvement or correction activities must be undertaken. First impressions are perhaps the most formative aspects of perceptions and once established difficult to change. It has been truly said you never get a second chance to make a first impression. It is rare for the initial point of contact to be the professional. There is usually a single or a number of gateholders between the inquirer and the professional, each one of whom is creating an impression of the firm in terms of courtesy, efficiency, empathy, accessibility. Thus switchboard, reception, secretaries and others must be friendly, interested, helpful and always courteous. Offices must be clean, tidy and well maintained and ideally its decor suitable for the types of clients served. Whether this is mahogany panelling and portraits of the founders or smoked glass partitions, a VDU on every desk and ultra modern furniture is of no consequence since opulence can be as disturbing as shabbiness. What is vital is that clients should feel comfortable in an ambience suitable to their expectations, needs and indeed life style. Some veterinary practices have different consulting hours for cats whose owners do not like to visit because of the risk of dogs in the waiting area. It is this type of sensitivity to needs which brings clients and keeps them.[2]

Other first contacts might occur through correspondence or promotion such as brochures, newsletters and media advertisements.

It ought not to be necessary to state that correspondence should be free from typing, spelling or punctuation errors with paper, enclosures, envelopes of good quality but this *desideratum* is not always achieved. All print should be clear, modern, comprehensive and memorable. Everyone must be totally professional in manner and appearance and responsive, involved, enthusiastic, sympathetic and supportive.

What might appear to be trivial matters takes on an importance of great significance during early contacts. Every effort should be made to meet client preference for the timing of meetings; the office must be open the stated hours, inquiries have to be routed efficiently and rapidly and messages passed on, received and actioned. Accurate routing of inquiries can only occur if everyone likely to receive them knows, with precision, to whom to direct them so that the inquirer is not moved around the firm, probably repeating the inquiry at each stage. (A secretary who asks a caller, "may I tell him what it is about" should ensure that "him" knows and does not ask the caller to repeat the information.) Chapter 21 touches on this issue. The one way to ensure that messages are passed on and dealt with is to make it clear throughout the organisation that the person receiving the message will be held responsible for it being actioned. This is bringing peer pressure into play which is often an infinitely better motivator than instruction.

Punctuality is a significant factor in influencing the way clients judge firms. Unpunctuality is a discourtesy and sends a message that the client is not important to the professional or the firm. At the very least, where there is a delay the client should be given the reason, kept informed and, of course, apologies must be offered. If, however, the client is late the need for them to be dealt with without delay becomes considerably greater because if they are then kept waiting, inevitably they will believe that they are being "punished" for their own tardiness.

The first impressions checklist below indicates the salient issues which should be checked and where necessary adjusted. Observation will give a guidance to how good or poor first impressions are, but gentle interrogation of visitors will give a far more accurate view—see Appendix 5, page 50.

It is not possible to over-emphasise the importance of support staff in the image which they create for the firm as Chapters 18 and 19 explain. The arithmetic is stacked heavily against the firm.

FIRST IMPRESSIONS CHECK LIST[3]

Correspondence
Acknowledged or quickly answered
Error free typing
Good quality paper and envelopes

Initial Welcome
Receptionist on hand to greet
clients
Client is made to feel welcome
Client is not loaded with paper
work

Phone Calls
Telephones are answered properly
Telephonists identify themselves
Telephonists "smile" over the phone
Knowledgeable

Meeting the Client
Visitor accompanied to office (or)
office location is easily
ascertained
Outer door is clearly marked

Arrival
Visitor has clear directions to location
Indications if parking is available
and where
Entrance clearly indicated

Staff Members
Are clean and neat
Are dressed professionally
Are friendly and helpful
Smile

Reception Area
Is clean
Is orderly
No excessive or intrusive noise
Has up-to-date decor
Has warm lighting
Has firm's literature, current magazines,
neatly stacked or displayed
Has no peremptory signs
Smells fresh
Has no barriers to receptionist
Atmosphere is warm and friendly
Professional use of display area

You
Are clean and neat
Are dressed for success
Are smiling, enthusiastic and
friendly
Appear unrushed, no interruptions
(take time with clients)

Few of its members can obtain clients, anyone can lose them. Lip service is paid to the fact that staff are one of the most valuable assets the firm possesses and then these assets are continuously treated in a cavalier fashion, not privy to the firm's plans and aspirations and are generally regarded as commercial peons. Non-fee earners are often regarded as a necessary but expensive overhead. They have relatively low status, little in the way of career prospects and are generally perceived within the typical, professional, organisational caste system as being at the bottom of the heap. Even the title "non-fee earners" has a derogatory ring to it:

> "A practice cannot be client-centred if the support staff are not client-centred. It is a rare circumstance for a client to be able to contact or meet the lawyer without there first being some intervention by a non-professional member of the firm—telephonist, receptionist, secretary, personal assistant. Equally, accounts managers and clerks also make a vital contribution to the good or poor image of the practice. The quality of this contact impacts directly on the client's perception of the practice and creates a favourable or unfavourable ambience within which the lawyer must operate."[4]

This is as true for all professions as it is for lawyers.

The emphasis has been on first impressions but what happens during the course of an assignment and at the end of it is of no less importance, particularly when it is obvious that the impressions a client takes away at the end of an engagement will be in a sense the first impressions for the next engagement. Image aspects beyond first impressions will be found particularly in Chapters 17, 18, 22 and 24.

COMPETITIVE COMPARISONS

As with most aspects of marketing, images cannot be considered in isolation. It is always necessary to obtain information on and knowledge of competitors' actual image and their strategy. If, as has been suggested, the firm's image can be a deciding factor in appointing it, then images are as much a competitive weapon as any other marketing technique. In an ideal world marketing research should be undertaken to establish the image profile of competitors but, where this is beyond the skills or means of a practice, then it is necessary to fall back on less accurate informal inquiries. While they may not yield the depth of information or have the same degree of validity, they nevertheless can make a contribution in relating the position of one firm with another. Information should be sought by informal discussions with those who have had direct experience of the firm, those who know of them by reputation only, suppliers, stakeholders, media, staff members (although much care and diplomacy is needed with this group) and their professional organisations. It is then possible to make judgements of the perceived performance of the competitors on a number of different aspects.

Figure 16.1 — Competitor comparison

Issue		Ourselves	Competitor A	Competitor B	Competitor C
Performance	Primary operating characteristics	1 x___ 5	1 ___x_ 5	1 ___x_ 5	1 ___x_ 5
Reliability	Consistency of performance, dependability and low risk of error	1 ____x5	1 ___x_ 5	1 ___x_ 5	1 ___x_ 5
Responsiveness	Willingness of employees to provide service	1 __x_ 5	1 __x_ 5	1 ___x_ 5	1 __x_ 5
Competence	Possession of the required skills	1 ___x_ 5	1 ___x_ 5	1 _x_ 5	1 ___x_ 5
Conformance	Extent to which service meets any established standards	1 __x_ 5	1 __x_ 5	1 _x_ 5	1 _x__ 5
Access	Approachability and ease of contact	1 __x_ 5	1 __x_ 5	1 _x_ 5	1 __x_ 5
Courtesy	Politeness, respect, consideration and friendliness of contact personnel	1 __x_ 5	1 __x_ 5	1 _x_ 5	1 ___x_ 5
Communication	Keeping customers informed in language they can understand	1 __x_ 5	1 _x_ 5	1 ____x5	1 __x_ 5
Credibility	Trustworthiness, believability, honesty and positioning	1 __x_ 5	1 _x_ 5	1 __x_ 5	1 __x_ 5
Security	Freedom from danger, risk or doubt	1 __x_ 5	1 _x_ 5	1 __x_ 5	1 _x__ 5
Understanding/ knowing the customers	Making the effort to understand Customer's needs	1 ___x_ 5	1 __x_ 5	1 ____x5	1 ____x5
Tangibles	Physical evidence of the service	1 _x__ 5	1 _x__ 5	1 ____x5	1 __x_ 5
Cost	Clear pricing/accurate estimation	1 x___ 5	1 ___x_ 5	1 ___x_ 5	1 __x_ 5

Key: 1=Bad 2=Poor 3=Acceptable 4=Good 5=Excellent

Figure 16.1 Competitor comparison. There is a further explanation of these issues in Table 17.1, page 178

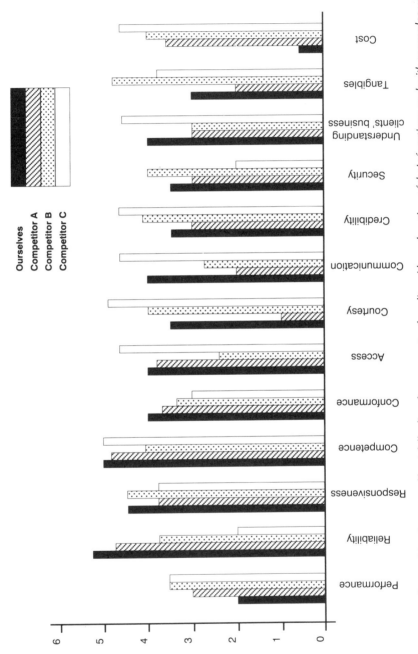

Figure 16.2 Competition image profile. A fuller list of components of quality with explanation of their functions and with examples will be found in Table 17.1, page 178

If the results are now graphed as in Figure 16.2 it is then possible to see where competitors are more highly rated and where they are weak. This then directs the strategy to either seeking to surpass competitors or to attack them at their weakest points.

However, it is necessary to apply judgement to the importance factor before deciding whether it is worthwhile attempting to outpace a competitor on it. For example, if a competitor has a particularly good reputation for "Security, freedom from danger, risk or doubt" but if these are not issues to the client then there is little point in diverting activities to achieve a better rating on these factors. The warning in the next chapter concerning rating and performance comparisons applies here also. Being better than a competitor on an image component that is of no consequence to the client does not off-set being perceived as a worse performer on one that is important. Further comment on the comparisons will be found on pages 178–80.

ACTION POINTS

- Check externally and internally on the three images (*current, wish, mirror*)
- Agree *optimum* image target and target publics
- Identify any gaps between present performance and that required to achieve the optimum image and close them
- Check first impressions
- Make competitor comparisons and act on findings

NOTES

(1) Quoted in *The Times*, 10 August, London (1993).
(2) van Tilbergh, C.A.H., van Meer, R.A. and Smets, M.R. *Van Dierenarts Practicus naar Praktisch Dierenarts*, Brocacef BV, Maarssen, The Netherlands (1987).
(3) Adapted from Stallard, R.E., Hess, K.M. and Scales, R.J. *Handbook of Dental Marketing*, pages 115–116, Penwell Books, Tulsa (1986).
(4) Pimm, G. and Wilson, A. "The Critical Role of Support Staff in Marketing", *Professional Lawyer*, London, November (1990).

17
The Quality Dimension

Since quality—real or perceived—is one for the most important factors in the formation of images and since it is totally pervasive within the organisation and in the client–professional relationship, there is much value in considering quality in detail while recognising its close link with those aspects of images which are included in the previous chapter.

The oft-repeated argument used by all the professions opposing de-regulation has been that marketing, which is equated with selling or advertising, is unnecessary: "The only advertisement we need is the quality of our service". (It is worth noting that clients or patients are usually considered insufficiently intelligent to understand the mysteries of a discipline. This does somewhat undermine the statement that the quality of a service which is not understood is its main attribute.)

If, however, the shibboleths of the past are abandoned "quality" takes on a real meaning and is now an essential part of the bundle of attributes clients purchase when they appoint a practice and is obviously one of the main factors influencing the firm's image. In future, claims for the provision of a "quality service" will have to be demonstrated by the delivery of quality or by accreditation.

The critical importance of quality is obvious enough. A reputation for poor quality, which in turn implies that value-for-money has not been delivered, will always lose clients, who will be disappointed because their expectations—wrongly or rightly based—will not be met. Replacing lost clients is not the only cost of poor quality services. A firm in such a situation will tend to spend a great deal of time and money correcting errors, will lose key referrers and will probably have a high rate of employee turnover. A reputation for poor quality will doom a firm to continually higher costs for a considerable period of time.

The elimination of scrap and waste is of constant concern to managers in manufacturing companies. Professional service firms have their own type of scrap pile—clients who do not return to the practice. If the cost of this "scrap" is measured it can be seen there is a huge advantage to be gained in eliminating it and many of the causes will relate back to failure to deliver quality. If the cost of losing a client is known, then it is not difficult to devise a trade-off against the cost of eliminating the cause of loss.

This takes the discussion round in a full circle because of the definitional problem of "quality" which is as elusive as a definition of professionalism or marketing. An *habitué* of luxury class hotels and a user of one-star hotels, both staying at a middle range hotel, will have two diametrically opposite views of the quality of that hotel. The former would regard its quality as poor having been accustomed to a very high level of service and facilities while the latter would perceive it as luxury, being normally exposed to more basic facilities and a large element of "do it yourself" in the provision of products as a substitute for service (tea-making and shoe-cleaning machines rather than room and valet services).

While there can never be any absolute measure or evaluation of quality, the problem is narrowed down by the adoption of set quality standards embodied in the British BS 5750 the International ISO 9000 series and the Australian Quality and American Baldridge Awards. While there have been some well-founded reservations made about how far these external standards can be applied to professional services[1] and, in particular, to very small practices, there is little doubt, justified or not, that their award does give sentient users of professional services more confidence in their suppliers than might otherwise be the case. For the moment at least, accreditation under any of these schemes gives a competitive advantage. It has been prognosticated that, by the end of the decade, it will be a condition of acceptability.

It would be unwise however to ignore the growing volume of criticism of the different schemes—the fact that the standards are not absolute but set by the organisations themselves, the actual methods adopted to decide whether accreditation has been earned and, strangest of all, virtually any organisation can become an accrediting body. So far as professional services are concerned accreditation does not indicate the possession of skills in providing the appropriate service. It simply indicates that a firm has reviewed its operations and written procedures to ensure a consistent and high quality (*not defined*) delivery of service. It is not without some significance that the British government has advised local authorities against making BS 5750 a requirement for tendering. Service level agreements are recommended instead.

There are further difficulties for the smaller firms that can deliver quality but cannot meet the high cost of accreditation and for some professional services where the conditions for accreditation and monitoring breach rules of confidentiality. At the moment professional practices must notify clients that independent examiners will be reviewing files. As yet the effect of clients refusing to allow this have not been spelt out. Such compromises as have already been made on this latter issue have noticeably reduced the value of the accreditation. The alternative, which has been adopted by many central and local government organisations, is to enter into a service quality agreement with clients where the level of service to be delivered is expressed in specific terms. This may well be the route for professional services.

There is a suitably fine range of clichés that can be adopted to define quality: "quality is getting it right first time every time"; the PERFECT acronym, Professional, Efficient, Reliable, Friendly, Expert, Caring, Trustworthy; "service quality is the extent to which clients' experience of the service coincides with their expectations for the service". Unfortunately the only definition that really fits all circumstances does not provide a practical guide for developing and sustaining quality. *The client defines quality* is a basic verity but then it begs the question as to what criteria the client uses to define quality.

If this concept is accepted then the first stage of establishing quality parameters has to be to obtain an understanding of what criteria the client is using. In many, if not most, instances the lay client cannot establish quality of the service content—that is, technical competence. A non-lawyer can ascribe personal injury claim lost to low quality performance of the lawyers but it could well be *force majeure*, a weak case in law, unreliable testimony and the many other factors which can sway a legal judgement. Short of a disaster, few patients are in a position to judge the quality of surgery. What they and all other clients of a professional service can judge, without exception, is the way the service is delivered; courtesy, concern, responsiveness, accessibility are just some of the criteria by which quality will be evaluated but which alone have no bearing on the quality of the core service rendered.

While practitioners, most particularly consultants who have discovered a rewarding new niche in quality, promote whole ranges of services to help firms achieve it, and while accreditation bodies have been set up, there has been little serious practical research undertaken into the fundamentals of quality and its role in marketing. Lack of basic theory has never worried marketers in the past and (from their perspective) there is no reason why it should now. It is, therefore, important to look beyond the quality hype into what it really means, how it can be achieved and then how it can be promoted.

VALUE AND QUALITY

But to begin with there has been and continues to be confusion between *value* and *quality*. Quality is an intrinsic measure and defines the product or service. It may contribute to value but it is not itself value. The use of the word quality can be misleading because it is often assumed that quality and value are synonymous or that clients can compare accurately competing services or service firms on strictly intrinsic factors. It is a long time since Peter Drucker pointed out that "value is what they [suppliers] in their business define as quality. But this is almost always the wrong definition".[2] Drucker, as is often the case, is honoured more in his reading than in the adoption of the actions he recommends.

Without further complicating the definitional problem of quality, it is important to appreciate that value itself breaks into three components.

- *Use value*—the ability of the service to accomplish its objectives (i.e. problem solution) and its reliability (punctuality, availability, flexibility)

- *Value in use*—the total cost of the service (finding and selecting a practice, briefing, adjusting to service needs)
- *Perceived value*—the value of the total offer

If properly identified as a client requirement, quality can contribute to value but, it is repeated, it is not value itself. The service providers, by definition, cannot produce value, they can only deliver the service.[3]

A systematic approach to understanding the quality dimension is clearly needed when the variables are so great and the interrelationships complex:

- Client identification of key components of the services
- Establishing their relative importance to the client (weighting)
- Establishing through data comparison how far service performance matched clients' expressed needs (realised and un-realised)

DETERMINANTS OF QUALITY

A market-focused approach to quality must commence by isolating the determinants of quality. There are many of these: certainly only a limited number will apply at one time and the final perception will be an amalgam of experience of the issues which the client regards as quality indicators. Moreover clients only become sensitive to service quality issues when they are distinguished from the norm or expectation in some positive or negative manner. A typing error in a critical document highlights lack of supervision or care whereas typing quality is not normally a significant indicator since it is expected that documents will be error free.

Without suggesting that Table 17.1 is complete or indeed ever can embrace every circumstance or service, it does provide a usable framework for considering those elements which together can project a level of service quality.

There are, however, factors surrounding service appraisal which the practice developer should be aware of. Because services are people dependent, service performance by any one person can vary over time. A deterioration can be caused by demand patterns which cannot be met and which create delays and queues, by the situation at point of delivery, by the attitude and physical condition of people with client contact. Most people become sensitive to service quality only when it is exceptional—good or bad—to the norm. While special circumstances or critical incidents have considerable significance, they are not necessarily indicative of clients' assessment of quality over time. Equally the absence of complaints does not necessarily mean service quality is good. Issues that yield client satisfaction are neither the same nor the mirror opposites as those that yield dissatisfaction. Interest and concern at the point of delivery does not necessarily generate statements of satisfaction but lack of them can easily produce intense complaints. As Chapter 23 makes clear, simply focusing on the eradication of complaints is important but it leads only to reducing dissatisfaction rather than producing satisfaction.

IMPORTANCE VERSUS PERFORMANCE

It is only the comparison of importance with performance that can accurately guide the practice to consistent quality. Moreover a highly rated performance against a low-rated importance factor will not offset poor performance against what is regarded by clients as a vital component of the offer. In the illustration in Figure 17.1 it can be seen at once that there is an outstanding performance in terms of qualified back-up but this is not a critical issue with the client. In contradistinction, progress reporting is obviously one of the firm's shortcomings yet it is of considerable moment to clients. There is, in the hard world of practice development, no trade-off between the two issues.

If a graphic representation of the results is overlain for each competitor firm it instantly emphasises differentials and will also make a contribution to developing a competitive advantage. In the previous chapter the comparative position of four firms on a number of issues were displayed in bar chart form in Figure 16.2. This figure reveals that the firm conducting the exercise surpasses the competition only in terms of reliability while for cost it is rated as the worst (highest).

Nevertheless, in looking at the general pattern, it is consistently (but not wholly) perceived as superior to the others. Competitor C is well ahead on what might be termed marketing and client

Table 17.1 Determinants of service quality

Component	Function	Examples
Performance	Primary operating characteristics	• holding, transferring and providing money products (banks) • delivering markets (advertising agencies) • property advice (surveyors)
Features	Supplementing basic functions	• counselling (life insurance) • project viability (leasing) • portfolio management
Reliability	Consistency of performance, dependability and low risk of error	• accuracy in billing • keeping records correctly • performing the service at the designated time
Responsiveness	Willingness of personnel to provide service	• mailing a transaction slip immediately • calling the client back quickly • giving prompt service
Competence	Possession of the required skills	• knowledge and skill of the contact personnel • knowledge and skill of operational support personnel • research capability of the organisation
Conformance	Extent to which service meets any established standards	• financial audit (accountants) • medical tests (doctors) • building regulation compliance (architects)
Access	Approachability and ease of contact	• service is easily accessible • lead time to receive service • convenient hours of operation • convenient location of service (mobile health services)
Durability	Length of utility or relevance	• education and training services • R&D • financial advice (pensions)
Courtesy	Politeness, respect, consideration and friendliness of contact personnel	• consideration for the client's property • clean and neat appearance
Communication	Keeping clients informed in language they can understand	• explaining the service • explaining the benefits • explaining the trade-offs between service and costs
Perceived quality	Trustworthiness, believability, honesty and positioning	• firm's reputation • service reputation • personal characteristics of the contact personnel

continued

Table 17.1 Continued

Component	Function	Examples
Security	Freedom from danger, risk or doubt	• financial security • confidentiality
Understanding/ knowing the customer	Making the effort to understand the client's needs	• learning the client's specific requirements • providing individualised attention (outplacement)
Tangibles	Physical evidence of the service	• physical facilities • equipment used to provide the service
Cost	Clear pricing or accurate estimating	• known financial commitment • no hidden extras • contingency pricing (estate agents)

Sources: This list is a compilation of the work of Garvin, D.A. "Competing on Eight Dimensions of Quality", *Harvard Business Review,* Cambridge, Mass., November/December (1987) and Haywood-Farmer, H. "A Conceptual Model of Service Quality", *International Journal of Operations and Production Management,* Vol. 18, No. 6 (1987).

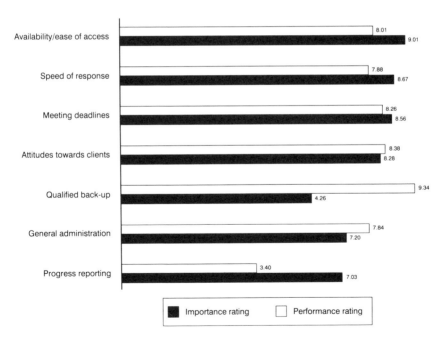

Figure 17.1 *Importance/performance comparison*

care issues, outstripping the competition on accessibility, courtesy, communication and understanding client's business—and all on a lower fee basis. However, such a profile could well lead to the jibe "their marketing is better than their work".

QUALITY SYSTEMS

Practice development and quality managers and others with marketing responsibility require practical advice rather than exhortations, the latter being available in profusion. As with most aspects of marketing, a systemisation of what needs to be done will always lead to more consistent performance provided the objectives are clearly stated.

The three elements are:

- *Organisational*—setting quality standards, strategy and tactics
- *Process*—integrating the enabling functions such as research, design, clerical, scheduling, finance, information, training
- *Point of delivery*—knowing what the firm and the clients expect of staff; receiving inputs; delivering outputs; adapting performance; empowerment v. job scripts

Organisational

The quality standards or objectives for each aspect of service must be set. While it is substantially true that what gets measured gets done, unfortunately not everything in service quality is measurable and therefore standards have to be both quantitative and qualitative. Whereas it can be easily stated that "response shall be within X hours", "progress reports every Y weeks" it is difficult to quantify courtesy or competence except by semantic scaling.

Nevertheless, and even within these severe constraints, it is feasible to set a quality level and to promulgate them through the firm. From "telephone answered within three rings" for the switchboard to "report formats to conform to those recommended by the Accounting Standards Board" embraces a wide range of issues.

It is at this point that it is usual for the ultimate objective of zero defect to be given as the *desideratum*. While it is undeniable that zero defect is achievable in some respects, in the totality it will be found that clients are not prepared to meet its cost. If getting it right 97% of the time costs x, then 98% will cost x^2, 99% by a factor of 4 and 100% perhaps by a factor of 8. The rise in costs is exponential. There is a trade-off between perfection and fee and thus between what the client wants and what the client will accept.

Zero defections are a more practical target than *zero defect*. For many clients zero defect is far too costly so the possibility of small errors is an acceptable trade-off against high fees needed to guarantee zero defect. If it is known just what attributes a client will sacrifice for lower fees, then it is more than possible to produce a quality level that is totally acceptable. While this is simple to state it is not so easy to achieve, although there are well established but sophisticated techniques that can be adopted to obtain this information such as "Price and Perceptions of Performance".[4]

Process

Quality has to be made to happen since it embraces the totality of the firm's offer and what it actually delivers. To make it happen there are enabling functions which contribute to both the corporate and individual activities and will involve many indirect functions, some obvious some almost subliminal.

Perhaps the most ubiquitous of these functions is research of different types. Between the desire for a given level of quality and its achievement are a number of roadblocks which arise from or can be removed by the enabling functions. Chief among these are what have been termed "quality management gaps" and which can be resolved by research:

- Difference between client *expectations* and management *perception* of client expectations
- Difference between management *perception* of client expectations and service quality *specification*
- Difference between service quality *specification* and service actually *delivered*

- Difference between service *delivered* and what is *communicated* to the clients about the service

Research will enable achievable quality standard objectives to set and permit a comparison to be made between the importance of a component to the client and the performance achieved as is illustrated in Figure 17.1.

The Appendix to this chapter provides inputs for a research questionnaire to establish both the firm's own profile and that of its competitors. Whether it is used for the latter or not, it should certainly be mandatory to establish clients' reaction to the appropriate issues listed and then to take whatever action is required.

Finance is another recognisable enabling function. There has to be sufficient funds to meet quality objectives. The need for these funds may be generated by the cost of employment of personnel with higher skills or qualifications, state-of-the-art equipment, library facilities, obtaining accreditation, research and development for devising innovative services or improving existing ones, testing, developing and extending professional and management training. Obviously there has to be cash flow or capital to meet these important requirements.

A third aspect of process which certainly has a strong integrational effect is training. This refers not just to continuing professional development but also to marketing and, of course, to client care. It will be seen from Chapter 21 that training is one of the techniques to achieve a higher level of inter-departmental cooperation which itself may be both a function and an outcome of a quality programme.

Point of Delivery

As has already been indicated, clients cannot for the most part assess the technical excellence or otherwise of the core service, but they can and will nevertheless judge it, the firm and the personnel by the way in which the service is delivered. Thus, the point of delivery or the individual becomes a critical factor in quality assessment. Consequently every one in a practice has to know what the firm expects of them and what the client expects of them. This leads straight back to the setting of objectives and standards referred to above.

The manner of the attendants on the airline check-in desk in no way exemplify the quality of aircraft maintenance, security, schedule punctuality and luggage handling, but an unpleasant encounter will immediately and perhaps irreversibly create an unfavourable quality image of the airline. This situation can be replicated within any service firm. The veterinary surgeon's reception area is the equivalent of the check-in counter and a demonstrable concern for the animal, use of up-to-date equipment, surgery hygiene and waiting room facilities are the equivalent of aircraft maintenance, security, punctuality and luggage handling. Thus, everyone in every service has to be quality conscious and understand the real meaning of client care.

In Chapter 18 the importance of supply chains is explained. These are not just the channels which exist between the professionals and their clients. There are supply chains within firms with individuals receiving inputs and delivering added value outputs. The quality of the services rendered in the internal supply chain governs the quality of the service finally received and both the system and those who work within it must be deeply involved in quality campaigns—a situation that is explained in detail in Chapter 19.

Because, as has been frequently emphasised, professional services are essentially people businesses, variation in performance is inevitable. It must, however, be contained by continuous monitoring of quality, most particularly at the point of delivery of the service and by identifying motivation and training.

ACTION POINTS

- Decide which determinants of quality apply to our services
- Survey clients and, if possible, competition to obtain information on importance/performance
- Set quality standards
- Identify quality management gaps and take actions to close them
- Do trade-off analysis of cost/value of formal accreditation (BS 5750, ISO 9000, Baldridge)

NOTES

(1) Pengelly, R. "Quality and the Consultant", *Professional Engineering*, February (1993) and Norman, M. "Big BS5750 is Watching You", *The Times*, London, 20 July 20 (1993).
(2) Drucker, P. *The Practice of Management*, Harper & Row, New York (1962).
(3) Reddy, N.M. "Defining Product Value in Industrial Markets", *Management Decision*, Bradford, Vol. 29, No.1 (1991).
(4) An explanation is given in Wilson, A. *New Directions in Marketing*, Chapter 2, Kogan Page, London (1991).

APPENDIX 17

SERVICE QUALITY STATEMENTS[1]

It is important that my professional service suppliers:

1 Fulfils promises made
2 Understands my personal needs
3 Are easy to contact on short notice
4 Has offices that project a good image
5 Return my messages promptly
6 Record all important details accurately
7 Has up-to-date equipment and technology
8 Points out best and worst scenarios
9 Can think strategically
10 Are courteous and polite
11 Are accurate when reporting and giving advice
12 Refer me to someone else if too busy
13 Continually keeps me informed of progress
14 Follow my instruction explicitly
15 Does "extra" things for me and the company
16 Follows up even when there is no current matter
17 Explains intentions clearly
18 Provides cost justification when billing
19 Admits expertise limitations and refers me
20 Assesses matters objectively
21 Has staff that have a good appearance

22 Has an informal and friendly manner
23 And I can relate to them
24 Understands my business needs
25 Has a good reputation in field of expertise
26 Discusses fee structure upfront
27 Writes reports that are easy to understand
28 Provides a quick turnaround time
29 Is prepared to meet me at my offices
30 Has good legal contacts (advocates, arbitrators)
31 Puts me at ease and removes any uncertainty
32 Sets high standards
33 Is dependable and consistent
34 Achieves good results
35 Provides a cross section of services
36 Is conveniently located
37 Gives clear explanations if problems arise
38 Always provides a backup contact person

NOTE

(1) Mackenzie, J. *Service Quality and Service Satisfaction*, p.44, Buys-Mackenzie, Randburg, S.A. (1992).

18
Developing and Sustaining Client Care Programmes

Most client care campaigns have three things in common; they are launched in a blaze of publicity; they exhort employees to pay attention to quality without being precise as to what they and those they serve mean by client care and quality; they all have a short-term effect and lapse. This is because organisations do not enter into the campaign with full appreciation of, and commitment to, the scale of change that is required. They concentrate on fault finding, not cause elimination. Client care is seen as the role of professionals or managers made responsible for quality control and whose job is to find fault. Failure to improve quality is perceived as a point-of-contact problem only. In short, there is no fundamental change in the way the organisations operate.

Care of the client and awareness of their needs is the major issue for the decade, most particularly for professional organisations competing for an increased share of an at best stagnant market. "Client care" like "quality" and "zero defect" are among a number of fashionable management phrases honoured more in their omission than commission. To demonstrate concern for clients a number of important and highly practical steps must be accomplished:

1 *Understanding*. Obtaining an insight into the client's needs and what they expect from the firm. This understanding is not just

at partner level or in the marketing department, but includes every employee, whether they have direct dealings with clients or not.

2 *Measuring.* Establishment methods to evaluate the standards of client care delivered.

3 *Involvement.* All staff must be involved in both setting and constantly improving standards of service quality. There has to be an acceptance at all levels that today's top quality is tomorrow's average quality.

4 *Development.* Creating systems, organisational structures and styles of management that enable people at the client interface to take client care decisions on their own initiative (empowerment).

5 *Communication.* Tying together all of these elements is the quality of the organisation's communications—internal and external, vertical and horizontal. Communication must be frequent, consistent and involve everyone in the practice.

Because client care is highly dependent on motivation at three levels—management to drive it, staff to deliver quality, clients to demand it, it is appropriate to define some of the benefits which will accrue to all three types of players—more detailed information on support staff motivation will be found in the following chapter:

- For *staff*—better perception of adding value, and therefore a better understanding that they are making a significant contribution to the team effort; increased involvement in the decision-making process and thus more opportunity to effect change where necessary; pride in being part of a successful team; less re-work.
- For *clients*—increased consistency and accuracy of work; change from adversarial attitudes to alliances; confidence in the reliability of the services; better value which in turn contributes to clients' own success; better response to clients' changing needs.
- For the *firm*—measurable performance standards; improved quality; improved use of resources; reduced error and cycle time; increased opportunity to sustain market share; higher retention of clients; attraction of better quality staff and staff

stability; reduced marketing costs which result from the implementation of world best practice which brings an enhancement of the corporate image.

IMPERATIVES OF CLIENT CARE

The method of releasing these benefits are not difficult to understand or apply. The problem lies more in maintaining than establishing standards. There are a number of imperatives which apply in introducing any client care programme if there is to be even a remote chance of success. Quality has to be driven from the top, there is no osmotic process by which it will permeate upwards. Standards of excellence have to be established and must be disseminated and accepted throughout the organisation. Everyone must know what the clients and the firm hope to receive from them. Partners and management must provide the support to enable members of the practice to achieve excellence. This means the provision of the functions which permit them to perform appropriately, for example training, research and service design.

Understanding Client Needs

Logically the starting point must be to identify the components of client care so that each can be subject to evaluation and level of performance defined. Ideally components should be measurable, but that which cannot be measured must at least be capable of evaluation. Table 17.1, page 178–179, lists, if not all, then the majority of components which are used to evaluate quality in a service.

A client satisfaction review should be conducted and this ideally will extend to past or lost clients. Table 18.1 is a starting point. Chapter 16 makes clear the perception a lost client has of a practice and that which an ongoing client holds will be widely varied and both make a contribution to identifying that which is good and that which is capable of considerable improvement.

Essentially an effective survey or inquiry falls into three headings: *technical*—the quality of the work; *service*—the way that it is

Table 18.1   *Client care indicators. For other possible facets to investigate see Appendix 17.*

• Overall client satisfaction/ evaluation	• Adherence to timetables, schedules
• Accessibility of staff	• Partner involvement and responsibility
• Attitude of all personnel	
• Number of errors, freedom from errors	• Extent of client participation in service
• Extent of repeat purchasing	• Cost of service
• Benchmark against competitors	• Efficiency of communication
• Completeness of service	• Reliability/safety measures
• Extent of waiting time, delays, lead times	• Time taken to resolve complaints
	• Number of complaints/claims /reworking

delivered; and *communication*—the success, or otherwise, of the firm in communicating, conveying or acquiring information. Needless to say, not all the items for investigation in Table 18.1 will apply to every organisation but it does provide a useful checklist or, at the very least, a starting point in considering, measuring or evaluating the level of client care being delivered and can be used to augment the quality checklist in Appendix 17.

Establishing Methods of Measuring the Standards of Client Care

The next stage must be to set the client care parameters which must be practical and achievable. Those service aspects that can be quantified must be "Response to an inquiry within 48 hours", "Completion ±1% of quoted time", "telephone answered within five rings". Those performing standards which are non-quantifiable will have to be set on a qualitative basis but this means more than a generalised statement about being "nice to clients". By way of example, with an incoming telephone call there are probably four or five points where concern, interest and helpfulness can be demonstrated. Figure 18.1 illustrates this and similar schematics can be produced for all aspects of client contact.

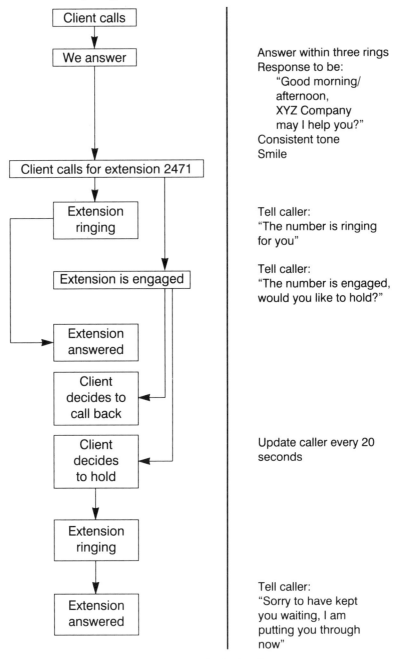

Figure 18.1 *Standard of performance*
Source: Sacker, F. and Martin, N. Customer Care, Industrial Society, London
(1987).

One American insurance company has succeeded in identifying five key standards that emphasise a knowledge of client needs: initiative; accessibility; responsiveness; enthusiasm; and team work; and they use these as the basis on which rewards are made to personnel at all managerial levels, including part-time employees. Feedback on these key issues is obtained from client surveys, discussions with line managers and others outside the department or business unit and their own assessment of individual's performance. Appendix 18 lists those activities which are used to establish quality of performance. What is important, however, and this has emerged from other studies, is that employees most frequently do not know but should know how performance is evaluated and by whom.

Involvement

No client care programme can succeed unless everyone with direct or indirect client contact is involved and are willing participants. It is obvious from the foregoing that this involvement must include the setting of standards for individuals, departments and the firm as a whole and their maintenance and improvement. Client care crosses all hierarchical and organisational boundaries. Those at the point of delivery, who are just as likely to be lower level as senior professional staff, become a critical part of the effort.

However, it is dangerous and misleading to suppose that those delivering client care are free-standing operators. They are totally dependent on others in the supply chain to enable them to deliver service. The supply chain concept is important as it states in its most simple but most persuasive form that everyone in the firm is someone else's supplier or client and therefore part of a team. The surveyor needs the research department to provide him or her with up-to-date valuations for a particular area; the surveyor's secretary depends on the surveyor delivering the draft of the report; the proof reader cannot carry out that function without the documentation; the post room requires the package in time to dispatch. If there is a break in the supply chain then the fault ultimately reaches the client. The failure might appear to them to be at the point of the delivery; in the example above, the surveyor.

There is an exact analogy to be found in the airline industry. An inquiry into an aircraft crash which is attributed to pilot error (a convenient verdict) frequently fails to ask the question as to whether the cumulative cause was other people's errors:

> "The common cause of this series of accidents is recorded as pilot error, but this explanation is correct only insofar as the pilot's action is recognised as but one side of an inevitably fated triangle. The geometry is completed by inadequate flight training, and by failure to anticipate the critical effect on the pilot's perception of the change in propulsion characteristics"[1]

Development

It is extremely difficult to deliver client care consistently. It is heavily influenced by the attitudes, motivation and training of service personnel unless the appropriate organisational structures and management styles exist. Essentially structure must comprise and integrate the enabling functions which permit client care activities to occur. Precisely what the enabling functions are depends on the type of discipline practised but, in general terms, these would be such aspects as information, training, research, service design, procurement, technical literature, marketing and promotion, clerical/secretarial, security, cleaning and maintenance, and all the plant, equipment and premises required to create and deliver the service.

All these have to be managed and linked so that they form a seamless fabric of client care. The operation has to be so good that the system is invisible. Some activities have a logical link and can sensibly and economically be grouped together. There is little problem of co-ordination in such departments. It is when activities and functions are vertical and disparate, that is in separate departments, that co-ordination is most likely to break down. Interrelationships will not occur on instruction. Positive organisation mechanisms must be created and managers motivated to ensure that these horizontal and vertical links are unambiguous and understood by everyone.[2]

The second aspect of development concentrates on the point-of-delivery (individuals). This then raises the old management technique of delegation under a new name "empowerment". This is the freedom of individuals at the point of delivery to adjust their performance to the needs of the situation and to make decisions which will satisfy both the client and the firm. The traditional approach was for service providers to work on the basis of job specifications or scripts, that is, clear instructions on how to act in any situation with no variation from the response approved or permitted. While this had the virtue of perhaps protecting the firm the result was more often that not unsatisfactory to the client. "I'm only following the rules" is a response which is the polar opposite of client care and is not calculated to improve the client's image of the organisation. The rules may say that the bank teller deals with customers in queue order but how much more sensible and customer satisfying it can be to ask if anyone in the queue objects to the teller completing a rapid transaction before a complex one at the head of the queue.

Empowerment or delegation is no more than trusting the individual to make decisions that will satisfy both the client and the firm. This can only be achieved if that individual understands the needs of both. The culture of a practice must be one of encouragement of decision making and of personnel involved knowing the limits of their skill, knowledge, and authority. It is nevertheless a dangerous two-edged weapon, given the volatility of human nature. It can only be given where there is extensive training and strong motivation to satisfy. The rewards of empowerment can be considerable. Although not a professional service, the Laura Ashley case on page 196 clearly shows this.

Communication

Because, traditionally, professional service firms have not been influenced by the market nor seen any need to cultivate it, it is barely surprising that the quality of their communications is poor. Quality applies as much to communication as technical expertise. It is a fact that in the majority of client grievances the Solicitors Complaints Bureau is called on to investigate, some 80% in 1992 derived not from neglect, delay, malfeasance or obfuscation but from the simple failure to communicate. Studies in hospitals have shown that patients who understand the procedures to be undertaken and all the aspects of therapy, recover far more quickly than those who are treated as file numbers, or "cases".

It is management's duty, and through them, to ensure those at the interface communicate in a timely and unambiguous manner. It has already been strongly emphasised that it is not the task of the client to understand, it is the job of the professional to be understandable. Thus, communication is the fifth protocol in the covenant between the professional practice and the clients.

Internal communications are essentially the sharing of goal-related information and the generation of feedback. Information sharing provides all members of the firm with the knowledge they require to achieve the objectives set. Confirmatory and corrective feedback encourages improvement in service but at the same time assists in making sure no one loses sight of their objectives.

Personnel, no matter what level they are within the practice, who are not kept informed feel cut off, lose motivation and eventually erect the barriers that are the antitheses of client care "It's not my job". It is not difficult to define what comprises good communication but it is not easy to achieve or maintain it:

- *Relevancy*—irrelevant information debases its source
- *Clarity*—the message must be self-evident and explicit
- *Accuracy*—incorrect information can only lead to errors of omission and commission
- *Timeliness*—too early or too late is not helpful
- *Availability*—it must flow easily vertically, horizontally and between all the players with an interest in the particular subject
- *Convincing*—belief in the content

If the message is checked against these important parameters it will ensure that the passage of information is totally reliable and wholly effective.

As for the communication tools, the most important will almost certainly be face-to-face contact, either formal or informal, and newsletters most particularly to highlight achievements such as the firm's successes, and about clients who have benefited from the firm's service. Effective practice manuals, posters and other display devices, internal mail, audio/visual presentations are just a few of the methods which can be used. Speed and flexibility always add to the effectiveness of communications. If a quick meeting or telephone call will resolve a situation it is better than a long memorandum.

Communication is the engine of motivation and no client care programme can be sustained unless motivation is of a high order, sustained and shared throughout the organisation. Different things motivate different people and some of them have been mentioned elsewhere in the book, for example recognition, being part of a successful team, career opportunities, the possibility of developing new skills and, for most people, some form of pecuniary award in money or benefits.

Although perhaps difficult to apply in some professional services, a technique adopted by a product company has much to recommend it in terms of maintaining interest in all aspects of quality and client care. The company sets aside a pool of money based on the cost to the firm of rectifying complaints. If the pool is not fully used then the amount left is divided between members of the firm as a bonus. This provides a strong financial incentive to avoid re-work. Obviously the pool sum has to remain reasonably constant and not reduced as a result of improved service delivery and reduced client complaints otherwise there would be no incentive to eliminate faults.

WORLD BEST

Client care campaigns, even when driven from the top, fail more frequently than they succeed, for the reasons given at the outset of this chapter. In looking at "world best" companies it is a salutary exercise to compare how many of those judged world best about a decade ago remain in that league. The seminal American study on excellence[3] identified 43 companies in 1982 as "excellent" of which only six remained in the list by 1990. A similar examination in the United Kingdom showed that of eleven top companies identified between 1979 and 1989 only five survived by 1990. Nevertheless, even with this sobering statistic it is a worthwhile exercise to attempt to establish a commonality between service companies which, on a judgemental basis, are perceived as providing excellence in quality and client care whether it be a product or service:

- *Work design and personnel role*—characterised by a good "fit" between special needs and motivations of particular employee groups and special features of the work; job enrichment

- *Career paths are explicit*—meets "what's in it for me?" query; dead-end and repetitive work de-motivates or generates a mechanical approach to clients
- *Service delivery as a performance*—encourages personnel to regard their delivery of a service as a "being on stage" (a performance)
- *Client care standards understood*—employees are fully aware how performance is evaluated and how the evaluation is conducted
- *Proprietorial attitudes understood*—a sense of "ownership" created towards unit/department clients, performance, premises and equipment used to serve them
- *Achievement at departmental level stimulated*—less significance is placed on the attainment of group-wide objectives because employees often have difficulty in relating their personal activities to the achievement of the corporate objective

Just how powerful this last issue is can be illustrated by the results of empowering staff by a manufacturing/retailing company, which even though not a professional service firm does provide an encouraging and valid comparison:

> "Sales assistants at Laura Ashley have landed windfall payments totalling thousands of pounds after being allowed to ignore highly paid merchandising and sales executives and run their own shops.
>   Staff at ten stores spent four months deciding how to market the clothes, running their own fashion shows and making subtle changes within the shops to try to improve profits. They were given a free rein by head office, which normally dictates policy, and cash incentives linked to percentage increases in the set target profits.
>   At the flagship store in Oxford Street (London), the 25 full and part-time staff were celebrating their share in £42,274 yesterday after increasing profits over four months to the end of January by 62.4 per cent.
>   Profits at the Liverpool store increase by 139 per cent. The test has been extremely successful in proving that staff react quickly and effectively when given the freedom to make commercial decisions."[4]

A great danger lies in the fact that it is always easier to turn client care, like quality, into a variable in order to meet costs or schedules and the temptation to do so is considerable. For the quality organisation, quality which embraces client care is a well defined and unvarying or improving element in the firm's operations.

As with every other aspect of practice development it is always important to be able to check progress. There is little point in pouring in time, money, skills and other resources unless there is at least some reliable indication that the objectives are being, if not achieved, at least approached. Chapter 27 explains the appropriate management and control techniques which can and should be adopted for practice development and of which benchmarking client care is a part.

INITIATING A CLIENT CARE PROGRAMME

As with most aspects of practice development, start-up is usually the most difficult part of the entire activity. Start-up in the case of client care has to be a responsibility of a senior person who has both the motivation and the power to obtain the appropriate resources and to initiate the system. This means there is a strong advocacy role involved since everyone, without exception, has to be committed to a client care programme. This commitment will only emerge in a genuine form rather than lip service if the benefits, as set out on pages 187 to 188, of such a programme can be explained or demonstrated.

Launching a campaign with intense promotional activity, followed by no visible action or change, will lead to a great deal of cynicism, demotivation and non co-operation. There should be no announcement until the campaign details are agreed and resourced. The programme should be devised for the first year of the activity. It must set out the objectives of the campaign, the responsibilities, the timing and the standards which will be adopted.

For criteria to be meaningful there should be a base line. Thus, while it is not mandatory, research into existing client view on the level of client care should be sought to identify strengths and weaknesses and even personnel delivering outstanding or poor performances. The checklists in Table 17.1 and Appendix 17 will provide a practical starting point for drawing up a questionnaire. The result of the research ought not to be regarded as internally confidential but widely available to everyone. Every member of the firm should be encouraged to contribute views on client care quality and where and how it can be improved.

The schedule should seek early victories since senior members of the firm and others will expect to see something happen and favourable changes occurring. Thus attacking the obvious and most easily rectified problem areas will be the first priority. Resources must be sufficient to enable the objectives to be met. These must include training, perhaps improvements in equipment used and the promotion of the campaign to both staff and clients.

BENCHMARKING

If quality campaigns are to be effective and to improve over time then there has to be some method of comparison that will reveal both improvements and deterioration in performance. The most effective way to do this is benchmarking. This can be defined as a continuous process of measuring service quality and systems against previous performance and against the performance of firms which are recognised as competitors or are leaders in their own professional areas. All the components of quality given in Table 17.1 will yield quantitative or qualitative data through research, formal and informal, and this will form the basis of any benchmarking criteria.

Four elements are involved:

- Clients identify the key components of the service in technical delivery and communication terms
- These are then weighted to show their relative importance to the client; the significance of this becomes obvious when the issue of "importance against performance" is considered
- Evaluating the organisations performance (actual and perceived)
- Establishing by approximate data comparison how far service performance matched client's expressed and non-expressed needs

If the process is then repeated after set periods of time, there will then be an actual basis against which comparisons can be made.

Because benchmarking benefits everyone within a profession, there is a strong case for sharing data in an aggregated form in the manner in which the interfirm comparisons were and are conducted. This is, perhaps, a role for the professional associations since they can most easily organise and disseminate the information while remaining detached and independent and can ensure confidentiality.

The most suitable activities for benchmarking are those which can be quantified as the comparisons can be exact both internally and externally, but this does not avoid the need and benefit for at least evaluating the changes in non-quantifiable activities. The process set out schematically in Figure 18.1 illustrates one type of activity and performance which can be benchmarked for both the firm on its own and compared to competitors. The checklist in Table 18.2 identifies the issues and activities to be examined but such an inquiry if conducted among competitors can and should only be undertaken by independent researchers. Contacts who may have experience of, and been exposed to, competitive firms can also provide an indication on the quality of their performance but this approach is so informal as to be hit and miss. Unless the information is treated with great care it could be misleading.

The bar chart used to illustrate image profiles in Figure 16.2 once produced forms the basis for both competitive and on-going internal changes and illustrates where they have occurred in the clearest possible form.

INFRASTRUCTURE AND CULTURE

It has been observed, however, that external as opposed to internal benchmarking had hardly achieved acceptance when its imperfections and possible dangers for some firms became apparent. An international study of nearly 600 services and manufacturing businesses showed that benchmarking against the world-class performers is only helpful to companies that are already performing at a high level of efficiency and delivering quality.[5] The problem identified by one commentator suggests that "low performers do not have the quality infrastructure ready to support the organisation-wide changes necessary to emulate the best."[6] It is suggested that low-performing firms should focus on nurturing cross-functional teams, training and empowering personnel, especially those who interface with the actual user of the services (or product).

Table 18.2 *Survey of competitor telephone technique*

Firm...	Did the professional give his/her
Address..	name?..
....	Did he/she ask your name, address,
Tel/Fax No..	telephone?...
How long before the telephone was	If you gave it to the telephonist, did
answered?...	you say so or did you repeat it?...........
What was the manner of the person	....
answering?...	Were you questioned on details of the
....	inquiry?..
Were you asked your name/telephone	Were you asked if there were any
number?..	special problems/needs?.....................
Were you connected directly to the	Was a visit to the office or to you
appropriate professional?..................	suggested?..
If not how many other conversations	How difficult was it to agree a
did you have and with whom, e.g.	date/time?...
secretary, before you spoke to the	....
correct person?.................................	Did the professional appear
Did you have to repeat your inquiry	concerned to meet your date/time
after each or any of the abortive	requirements?.....................................
contacts?..	If an immediate answer could not be
How long did it take from the	given was there an offer to call
telephonist answering your call until	back?...
you spoke to the correct	If an offer to call back was made, did
professional?......................................	they, and after how long?....................
If there was a delay, were you kept	Did you ask for a quotation or cost
informed of progress?......................	indication?..
What was your first impression of the	Were you satisfied with the
professional's answering method?..	response?..
....	If not, why not?..................................

(Note: the term "professional" is used as a generic for the appropriate person for the service
needed, e.g. surveyor, solicitor, etc., and should be substituted)

A structure of a client care programme, however effective, is in the final analysis unlikely to succeed unless the culture of that firm is one in which clients are truly appreciated. A client orientated culture is necessary throughout the firm.

The IBM philosophy for making customer care work can be summed up even if the company's performance in the early 1990s would seem to indicate they did not follow their own precepts:[7]

- Don't rest on your laurels—a long heritage of superior service does not guarantee future success
- Segment your market—different clients have different needs
- Measure yourself against the best—client satisfaction does not exist in a vacuum
- Make client satisfaction part of the reward system—a variable compensation programme based on customer satisfaction can be a powerful incentive
- World class quality is the basis for improving client satisfaction

---

ACTION POINTS

- Appoint a senior person with complete authority to devise, initiate, operate and monitor a client care system
- Involve everyone in the design of the system so they "own" it
- Do not set a commencement date until everything is ready and staff is trained and motivated
- Be sure everyone understands what the firm, colleagues and clients expect of them
- Empower staff to maximum extent possible
- Use benchmarking techniques to check compliance and progress

---

NOTES

(1) Allen, J. "The Designers View", in R. Hurst (ed) *Pilot Error*, Crosby Lockwood, London (1986).
(2) Guidance on structures to achieve inter-relationships although not specific to client care, will be found in Porter, M.E. *Competitive Advantage*, Free Press, New York (1985).
(3) Peters, T.J. and Waterman, R.H. *In Search of Excellence*, Harper & Row, New York (1982).
(4) *The Times*, London, 28 February, 1992.
(5) *Best Practices Report*, Ernst & Young, The American Quality Foundation, New York (1992).

(6) Hequet, M. "The Limitations of Benchmarking", *Training*, Minneapolis, USA, February (1993).

(7) Etherington, W. "Putting Customer Satisfaction to Work", *Business Quarterly*, London, Ontario, Summer (1992).

APPENDIX 18

QUALITATIVE STANDARDS[1]

• The employee exhibits knowledge of the customer and his or her needs, anticipates these needs and does not wait for the customer to ask to find out that something was missed, and takes initiative in following up to ensure that all aspects of the product or service are in place.

• The employee exhibits concern for others and their opinions, cultivates good speaking and listening skills even under pressure, and maintains optimism and enthusiasm about his or her work no matter how difficult the task. The bottom line is that the customer enjoys working with the employee.

• The employee is accessible to customers. This involves scheduling workday activities (e.g. meetings, lunch) whenever possible, so as not to interfere with the customer's needs.

• The employee is responsive to customers, whether they have a serious problem or routine inquiry, and communicates in a manner that lets customers know they are important and valued. Even if there is no resolution, the employee lets the customer know the problem is being worked on. The customer should never need to follow up to find out the status of a project.

• The employee ensures that work is completed according to schedule, documents are free of errors and files are appropriately organised. Work and delivery quality are critical to effective service and a professional image because they affect the customer's perception of the business unit.

• The employee understands and encourages team work; is willing to take the initiative, through cross-training and self-study, to learn more than just his or her own job; and assists fellow employees with their jobs, because the success of the unit depends on this team-work. Where appropriate, he or she fills in for others, offers counsel and advice, and shares work knowledge.

NOTE

(1) Burns, K.C. "A Bonus Plan that Promotes Customer Services", *Compensation and Benefits Review,* New York, October (1992).

19
The Critical Role of Support Staff in Marketing[(1)]

The foundation of every client-driven firm is person-to-person contact with the client. But this is all too frequently eroded, not just by those charged with the task of marketing the practice's offering, but by others in the organisation who interface with the client but unfortunately do not regard client care as their responsibility. The not inconsiderable efforts that have been made in consumer markets to inculcate the principles, activities and motivation involved have not been wholly effective but few professional organisations have attempted to apply them at all, and where they have it has been substantially at practitioner level. But support staff are a vital part of every practice's resources and have to be seen and treated as part of the marketing team. They represent a potential fund of goodwill and of talent albeit of a non-technical and non-marketing nature, which can be effectively used to improve client relations, the image of the enterprise and very much enhance the volume, quality and regularity of engagements received.

The reason many rank and file members of a firm abrogate any marketing responsibility reflects, in part, a far from uncommon attitude which regards support staff as a necessary and expensive overhead. The problem has already been set out in Chapter 16 in relating the firm's image to the attitude and activities of staff who are held in very little regard and who receive relatively poor rewards for their contribution. Yet everyone within a practice, no matter what their work may be, contributes to profits. The difference between the rank and file and others is that the latter usually have their performance quantified in the form of billable hours and the former do not. But the question must always be asked even though the answer is obvious: "How much less revenue and profit would there be without support staff?"

Since achievement of a consistently high standard in any marketing effort requires the enthusiastic involvement of everyone who interacts with the client (not necessarily face-to-face), practice managers and other professionals need to master the skills necessary to ensure that all personnel are committed to marketing and to clients. The image of the firm has a pervasive effect on its marketing success and everything and everyone conveys an image as is demonstrated in Chapter 16. It has been well expressed that excellent organisations treat the rank and file as the root source of quality and productivity. This axiom applies to all enterprises.

Every practice would like to earn the compliment "a nice firm to do business with". This cannot happen unless all personnel with whom the client has contact, whether by telephone or correspondence or in a face-to-face meeting, are client centred. In this context the marketing input of support staff is highly significant. After all, as stated in Chapter 16, the arithmetic is simple—very few members of any organisation can obtain clients but anyone can lose them. It is a rare circumstance for a client to be able to contact or meet a practitioner without there first being some intervention by a support staff member of the firm—telephonist, receptionist, secretary, personal assistant, clerk or other personnel. Indeed, some of these people may be the only member of the practice the client meets or speaks to regularly. Accounts managers and clerks and others who never see the client also make a contribution to the good or poor image of the practice. The quality of the contact impacts directly on the client's perception of the firm and creates a favourable or unfavourable ambience within which practice development must operate. When the strategic position of support staff is appreciated, their importance as a marketing resource will certainly lead to a re-evaluation of their role in and contribution to marketing.

However, the support staff, apart from being one of the most valuable marketing resources a company possesses, are also one of the most costly. Because this asset is both important and expensive, the skills needed to guide and motivate support staff are of paramount importance for the success of any enterprise. Professionals charged with the marketing of the practice's services and skills continuously assess the needs of the clients and their organisations: they formulate their mission statements, plan their major aims and set goals, gathering resources to enable them to execute their plans. All this is how it should be. Nevertheless, they leave themselves unnecessarily vulnerable by not ensuring that the department rank and file (as well as others in the organisation who have client contact), if not incorporated into the marketing effort, are at least made sensitive to the importance of their role in ensuring the firm is indeed client driven. So how are support staff motivated and how is commitment gained in helping to market the offerings of the firm?

MOTIVATION

A person's view of work is influenced by many factors, some which are outside the control of partners and managers, for example, family life, previous jobs and past experience. Influences, which are to a greater or lesser extent within the control of management, include current job content, education and training. Promising employees can be motivated by giving them the opportunity to acquire additional skills, training and further education with a view to increasing their career prospects. Others will look only for a monetary reward. A discussion on pay is a subject that needs separate attention because how staff are rewarded for the work done and any additional effort they contribute is, of course, a very significant motivator but is not the only one. The way people are managed is of equal importance. This is among the many skills not taught in professional training.

   With one exception, there is little merit in discussing the theories of motivation and behavioural patterns and their validity other than to note that the generally recognised motivating forces which govern human behaviour are as applicable in a professional, or commercial, *milieu* as in society generally. The only difference in human behaviour within the context of any business activity is that it is constrained by organisational goals and policies. Whether professional or support staff, individuals do not leave their psychological needs at home when they attend their place of business: their unwavering search for personal and financial safety and security; their desire to be part of, and accepted by, a group of individuals with, if not similar then, acceptable likes, dislikes, activities and ambitions; their needs (just like those of clients) for recognition and the opportunity to develop their potential and, thus, self esteem.

It is not difficult to deduce that unless the professional service firm can satisfy these very basic requirements of their support staff they are not very likely to be successful in meeting clients' verbalised and non-verbalised needs. If these needs are transmuted into a commercial ambience the relationship becomes clear. Physiological needs can be related to the requirement for services to be efficient and cost effective, for example that banks honour cheques; safety needs relate to reliability and accessibility such as emergency or hot-line advisery services; "belonging" transmutes to partnership with professional advisers and their understanding of client requirements; self-esteem requirements are met by the professional service firm committing their resources to the clients and demonstrating their importance to the service provider; self-fulfilment comes from strategic alliances where the service provider is an open participant in the long-term conduct of the client's affairs.[2]

Within an organisational context, partner, practitioners and managers have an influence on the needs of support staff and, if total commitment to marketing and to the clients is to be gained to meet set goals, firms must respond to these. It is a form of trade-off. If support personnel are to share the partner's vision and culture of a client-centred, client-sensitive organisation then the firm must also be an employee-oriented organisation. This means meeting employees' legitimate needs relating to the human side of the enterprise—setting aside time for subordinates and involving them.

MOTIVATING PEOPLE: LEADERSHIP STYLE

All organisations, no matter what professional services they are offering, must demonstrate, to their clients and potential clients, the benefits of purchasing their services. Equally, it is necessary for all staff to perceive the benefits they will receive in return for their inputs and enthusiastic involvement. If motivation is about meeting people's needs in order to gain their total commitment to the corporate aims and objective of the firm, it is also about pride—pride in being part of a successful team, pride in the contribution they make and pride in their personal achievements.

The importance of mission statements which drives the organisation was emphasised in Chapter 6. Support staff should also be included in a mission statement—what is the organisation going to do for them in return for their input? They will expect to receive a fair reward but, bearing in mind that the rank and file are ambassadors for the company all of the time, they will expect more, even if it is only just knowing that senior members of the department or practice will always listen to them and that they are part of a team which takes account of their opinions.

There are many skills required from those who manage, whether they are involved with marketing or any other aspect of the organisation's activities. Four central ones for marketing are: *communication; mentoring; supporting;* and *delegating.*

The Leader as a Communicator

Because in client-driven enterprises there will always be problems, the leader, in the case of professional services usually a senior partner or departmental head, must be able to communicate. What distinguishes client-driven organisations from others is the way that partners and management and the rank and file deal with communication problems. The essence of their approach and attitude is to understand its impact on the client and try and solve it to the client's satisfaction. At the same time, they learn from the experience as a step towards the ideal of zero defect and zero defections.

The first message support staff need is an explanation of what marketing involves and their role (and importance) in carrying out the strategy. Skilled practice development managers involve all staff in marketing training and customer care, the latter being more than a bolt on smile and "have a good day". But messages, to be effective, need efficient communication channels. Whatever the mode of communication chosen, it is essential that its effectiveness is monitored. "Effective" in this context was set out in the previous chapter as relevant, clear, accurate, timely, available and convincing.

The method of communicating information must be controllable. Cascading information down through the various levels of the organisation, making it the responsibility of each stratum of authority to ensure that the message gets through, is one technique of ensuring control. However, to avoid the "Chinese whispers" effect, it is necessary to formalise the system through in-house marketing meetings or weekly team briefings at each level or each grouping, for example departmental. If the latter is chosen, then there must also be some lateral links so that the opportunities of widening the offerings to clients who are not buying across the service range or using all the appropriate facilities, skills and experience within the company are not lost. Everyone should be involved and accountable. Chapter 21 is particularly concerned with this aspect.

The marketing message will also permeate through the practice by a bottom-up technique, that is, encouraging support staff to seek information, to participate, to be involved. Those who have no information can take no responsibility; those who have information have no choice but to take responsibility.

The way people are managed is the key to their motivation, which is critical for achieving and maintaining quality in external contacts which is the essence of marketing. Partners and managers must listen to employees' concerns and provide perspective and praise progress. Involving them in the decision-making process as much as possible is how commitments and loyalties are built.

The Leader as a Mentor

Each member of staff consciously or unconsciously will have a personal agenda—goals they wish to attain. Through their work, they will seek to achieve these one way or another whether it be a career or paying the mortgage. Whatever it is, it is the job of every professional in the firm to help them to succeed. It is here that most care is needed because such a career agenda may not, as with the professionals themselves, include marketing as part of their personal development, most particularly if a conflict exists between the image of marketing and its concomitant selling, and self-image. Such an attitude, which is not uncommon, may well reflect the disdain that many people hold for marketing. Marketing has to be marketed to everyone who is involved in marketing.

In the difficult times which have afflicted all professions since the end of the expansive 1980s, there has been a clearly discernible trend for partners and senior managers to move from a mentoring role to one where control and the discipline of numbers dominate. But mentoring should combine both direction and support. The leaders of a practice should be participants in small-group practice areas which include both practitioners and support staff and should act as a creative resource, available to answer questions and to offer ideas about practice and practice development issues. It is important to ensure that the staff are involved in setting the goals they are expected to achieve. People are less motivated and less involved with goals that they perceive as being imposed on them, even if such goals are accepted as appropriate. Subordinates must be taught how to evaluate their own work; failure can be a valuable lesson learned. Achievements, however small, should always be recognised. Providing direction is not enough; support and encouragement also have to be given.

The Leader as a Delegator

Once support staff know what is expected of them and they know the part they have to play in the marketing of the enterprise's offering, it is possible to move on to delegation and empowerment. However, they need to know what good performance looks like—to recognise a client-centred, client-oriented, highly professional organisation.

Delegation means passing responsibility for day-to-day decision-making and problem solving to subordinates. Before delegating, it is necessary to ensure that those who are to be empowered have the skills, experience and confidence to handle the task. Most people if they believe that they have a measure of control over their future will persist in tasks and do better at them. However, this does not mean that monitoring their performance ceases. The rule must be to delegate not abdicate. Empowerment is what delegation implies.

The Leader's Supporting Role

It has already been emphasised that the rank and file must be supported in their efforts in order to build their confidence and motivation. Respect for and encouragement of their contribution is necessary because they provide important marketing inputs. They must be listened to and treated as competent members of the team. A supportive atmosphere in directing them towards clearly stated organisational and personal goals must be provided and, equally, they must know the criteria by which their performance will be judged. It is a truism, but nevertheless worth stating, that every member of the team, no matter how lowly, must know what they are being asked to commit themselves to. This is particularly important in marketing. The part they have to play in building and maintaining excellence in client relations while the practice grows into an expanding and high-profile firm must be explained.

Leadership Style: Clarity and Consistency

Being consistent does not mean treating everyone the same, since the needs of people differ. It has been said that there is nothing so unequal as the equal treatment of unequals. Partners and managers should not be afraid of changing style and adopting one appropriate to the situation and the needs of subordinates. Lack of consistency leads to confusion and ultimately abrogation. However, there should be no confusion between consistency and obstinacy. Adjustments to changed circumstance but within the mainstream of policy shows quite clearly that the practice is both aware and responsive. However, adjustments should not only be promulgated but should also be explained and justified. Instructions must be understandable and understood—clarity is everything.

LOYALTY

A litmus test of the extent to which support staff see themselves as part of and loyal to the organisation should be made but using an independent facilitator or else non-identifiable internal questionnaires. Every member of the staff (and it could do no harm to extend this to non-partner professionals) should be asked if they would recommend the services of the firm to their friends and relations. In one recorded instance of this inquiry (referred to in Chapter 16) being made almost 100% of support staff gave a negative response. When employees have no confidence in the firm's services there is an urgent need to probe and rectify the reasons. In the case quoted the reason was because support staff were aware that non-qualified staff were used on assignments but charged out at professional rates. This led to a total reconsideration of fee setting methods and ultimately to a "blended rate" charging approach (see Chapter 22, page 253) which was found to be acceptable to clients and seen as fair by the staff.

Managing people is all about relationships and getting things done by others. Motivation is all about achieving personal goals and being involved. Support staff have to know what part they must play in marketing the company's offerings. Leadership in marketing must come from the top and the most senior members of the firm have to demonstrate, in a most obvious way, their commitment to the marketing effort.

ACTION POINTS

- Train to develop leadership skills
- Ensure job design and roles are characterised by a good "fit" between special needs and motivations of particular employee groups and special features of their work and responsibilities
- Make career paths explicit to meet the "what's in it for me?" query; avoid dead end or repetitive jobs which are de-motivating and generate a mechanical approach to clients
- Encourage personnel to regard their delivery of a service as "being on the stage" (a performance)
- Encourage proprietorial attitudes and create a sense of ownership towards the department's or the firm's clients, performance, premises and equipment used to serve them

NOTES

(1) This chapter is based substantially on the work of Gina Pimm and adapted with her permission from "The Critical Role of Support Staff in Marketing", *Professional Lawyer*, London, November (1990).
(2) Harrington, M. "What does a Customer Want?", *Across the Board*, New York, April (1993).

20
Networking: Stimulating Referrals

The referral system or, in line with marketing's urgent need to make old methods look like new techniques, "networking", is the single most important practice development tool and as such it warrants very close study. Apart from its extremely low cost and high yield in marketing terms, it is claimed, and empiric evidence seems to support this, that clients obtained through personal referral tend to be more loyal than those who retain a practice through other marketing techniques. Stimulating the referral network should be deliberate, not fortuitous or reactive. The steps to be taken by each practice are simple and represent no more than an ordered methodology which avoids the mistakes of omission and commission.

Even the most rigid professions have never condemned networking as a technique since its use has been hallowed by time and by the very discreet way that it has been conducted. It must be said that for a technique that has the approval of all professional bodies, the support of practitioners and the accolade of success, it is astonishing that the workings of the interpersonal network are not really understood and certainly not utilised to their full potential.

It is, unfortunately, a fact of business life that there is usually an asymmetry in referral activities and that it most usually works to the advantage of one party. That is, the cross-flow of referrals is not equal. In many areas of commercial activity this can be compensated for by a balancing "finder's fee" or commission arrangement. In some professions, however, the sharing of fees with non-members of that profession is specifically banned and in others it would offend the culture of the professional relationship. When the flow is substantially one way, there are nevertheless methods which can be adopted to mitigate if not overcome the disadvantages where compensation cannot be offered in the form of fees.

In terms of obtaining new clients, professionals have two targets that only overlap slightly—potential clients and those who can introduce clients but are not necessarily themselves clients. The equation is a simple one. A client provides a single source of business, a referrer can generate many leads and new clients and thus a referrer is as important a target for promoting the practice as any user of the firm's services.

The significance of networking is further illustrated by the fact that surveys on how business was obtained by professional firms before and after de-regulation reveals that referrals continue to be a most important single source of new clients and, across all the professions, probably continue to exceed 85% of all new business introductions.

Before looking more closely at networking it is as well to note that the referral system can work both ways. It can, and it is, used frequently to deter people from approaching a particular practice. Not every inquirer asks in a neutral form "can you recommend a good dentist?" Some say "what do you think of Ambridge Dental Centre?" The latter question as formulated encourages comment which may be qualified, the former yields only a name.

SOURCES OF REFERRALS

Research shows that, overwhelmingly, the major sources of referrals come from five clearly defined groups:

1   Existing clients both recommending other companies or individuals and, within corporate organisations, other non-users of the service within the client firm.

2   Interprofessional referrers.
3   Intraprofessional referrers.
4   Business and communal involvements.
5   Internal cross-referrals.

Existing Clients

From observation and research it is clear that the greatest number of referrals come through existing clients. There is an often-repeated statement by professional firms that "a satisfied client is the only requirement for a successful practice". "Only" is a simplification, nevertheless it is substantially true but it does require the qualification that clients have to declare their satisfaction to other firms and individuals seeking professional advisers. In other words, referrals depend not just on "satisfactions" but on statements of "satisfactions" either sought or volunteered. This last statement links directly with methods that can be adopted and can be used to encourage clients to express satisfaction: these are dealt with below.

For most professions conducting both commercial and private business there is always a group of potential new clients with whom they have direct or indirect contact. Within commercial organisations these are individual employees with personal needs for professional services; private clients are most frequently in employment and their employers represent a potential business source. There is no reason why a satisfied commercial client cannot make it clear to their own employees that, for example, the firm's solicitor or accountants would be willing to assist staff members with personal professional service requirements. There are advantages for all the parties involved. For the individuals the fact that they are using the company's adviser gives them a leverage far greater than the value of their personal business might secure and also an insurance policy in that the weight of the company as a client stands between them and the professional in the event of any dissatisfaction. For the company, making available to staff a professional facility adds to the value of the total business this generates for the professional practice and thus creates a useful countervailing power. In addition, it demonstrates an interest in, and care for, individual members of the company and assists good personnel relations and staff welfare. For the professional practice, a new client catchment is created which within it has further strong possibilities for a sub-system of referrals by the individuals served.

The converse is not as likely to occur but nevertheless not without value. It is always possible that a private client is in a position to give a professional practice or practitioner with whom he or she has a satisfactory relationship the necessary "visibility" at a time when the client's employers or other business contacts are considering appointing a new or additional professional adviser.

Interprofessional Referrers

In addition to the firm's direct referrers, there are also generic bodies of individuals and organisations which may well be referral generators and should be included in any promotional targeting effort. Research has shown that, depending upon the discipline, recommendations for professional advisers will typically come from providers of complementary professional services: venture capital firms sometimes refer their clients to executive search firms recognising a need for skills as well as finance; doctors recommend specific hospitals to patients; architects introduce quantity surveyors. In addition, referrals could well come from governmental advisery services, court officials and police, Inland Revenue and Customs and Excise.

The extent to which clients are interchanged in financial services can be seen from a study conducted by the University of Liverpool in the mid 1980s and illustrated in Table 20.1. The complexity and density of the network relating to the property market is illustrated in Figure 20.1. Nevertheless, in terms of delivering customer satisfaction, the diagram conceals how the referral system can create resentment, particularly in financial services. Clients may object to building societies designating insurance companies and the independent financial adviser recommending policies which yield the greatest commission for the seller.

Table 20.1 Types of business passed to others

	Passed on	To	Keep
Stockbrokers	Annuities Pensions Non-linked Unit linked	Insurance brokers	Pooled investment products
Accountants	Pooled investment products (and bits of everything else *except* pensions)	Insurance brokers Stockbrokers	Pensions
Solicitors	Pooled investment products Unit linked	Insurance brokers Stockbrokers Insurance/UT Companies	Pensions Annuities

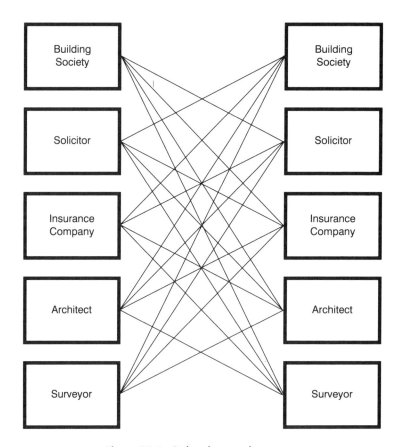

Figure 20.1 *Referral network: property*

Intraprofessional Referrers

These can stem from overload (or under capacity), lack of exper-tise or experience in a particular area of activity, inconvenient location, clash of interests* and even personal preferences. Larger organisations sometimes prefer not to undertake smaller assign-ments which they may pass on to smaller practices. It is not at all uncommon in accountancy, property related professional services and law not to deal with private clients.

There can be, of course, a reluctance to introduce clients to actual or direct competitors for a particular engagement or matter since the client may well prefer to remain with the firm introduced and to conduct all their relevant business needs with them in the future. This is indeed a difficult situation and, needless to say, a danger that must be considered. The problem is particularly relevant to situations where professional organisations establish foreign or, in some circumstances, even national geographic links. "Correspondents", "associate offices", "agents" and other nomenclatures which cover association arrangements are particu-larly prone to "client rustling", but clearly there are only short-term gains to be made by such unprofessional actions. While it is not too difficult to police such arrangements and the proscriptions can be severe, where the client, without any inducement from the beneficiary firm, expresses a preference for the latter there is little that can be done.

There is, however, a special group of practitioners, where it is mandatory or usual to go through another practitioner. At the present time it is impossible for a member of the general public to retain a barrister without the intervention of a solicitor and a medical specialist will only see a patient recommended by that patient's general practitioner. It is usual, but not compulsory, for an orthodontist's patients to be introduced by a general dental surgeon and even an animal behaviourist cannot be consulted

---

* A major not wholly uncommon dilemma illustrates this. Two long-standing clients of one of the largest legal practices in the City of London were in contention over a resisted take-over bid. To act for one of them would have indicated without room for doubt the firm's preference and would certainly have ended in the loss of the rejected client and probably both clients if the bid was successful. The decision was taken to act for neither and as events turned out the bid failed and both clients returned to the firm. Such integrity and diplomacy does not, however, always have so satisfactory an ending.

Table 20.2 Professional intermediaries

Profession	Intermediary/referrers	
Barrister	Solicitor	
Quantity surveyor	Architect	
Consulting engineer	Developer/contractor	
Medical specialist	GP	Client/patient
Animal behaviourist	Veterinary surgeon	
Orthodontist	General dental practitioner	

without the intervention of a veterinary surgeon. It is obvious that for these niche professions the successful cultivation of the intermediary is critical.

Business and Communal Involvements

Another very important source of referrals is through communal and business involvement. Once again this is a new business source which has never been criticised by any disciplinary body. Such involvement often enables practitioners to combine real personal interests with obtaining new clients. However an important warning enunciated many years ago by an American lawyer is well worth repeating. Time has not eroded the essential verities of the statement:

"Can you get clients from social, civic or charitable organizations? The answer to the question is simultaneously 'yes' and 'no'. If you join an organization solely to get clients, you will be wasting your time and money. The other members will see through you, and you won't get anything from them. On the other hand, if you belong to an organization because you sincerely believe in its purposes and you work hard for the organization, the other members will be impressed...and they will come to you with their legal work."[1]

Apart from anything else the image gain from participation is considerable, most particularly in smaller communities where it is relatively simple to achieve high visibility. But, like all techniques for stimulating the network, there is also a downside. Involvement with controversial causes and activities will produce antagonisms as well as support.

A medium-sized legal practice's audit of contacts revealed members of the firms belonged to parent–teacher associations, a local operatic society, a cricket club, a squash club, a model railway club, and activities in two charities. Business involvements were Rotary, local Chamber of Commerce, Institute of Directors, local Law Society and Young Farmers Club. Over the years most of these, one way and another, had generated clients.

Pro bono publico work, apart from the personal satisfaction which can be engendered, can itself generate network contacts and make a considerable contribution to the image of the practice. In considering stimulating the referral system, *pro bono publico* work should have a high priority for its intrinsic value for networking and for its contribution to the community.

Internal Cross-Referrals

For the larger organisations, most particularly those where there are departmental barriers, referring clients from one department to another represents a highly practical low cost method and yet all too frequently this does not occur. The reasons are many but the barriers are not insuperable. The next chapter examines this potential business source in depth.

In reviewing the areas which can yield new clients and new business through networking, their importance is further enhanced when it is appreciated that these same new clients frequently return to their professional advisers so that the cumulative value of referrals becomes even more significant. The issue to be addressed now is how these sources of new business referrals can best be cultivated.

IDENTIFYING THE REFERRER

The first important step is to establish precisely who the referrer was. It should not be assumed that a referred potential client will always identify the person or organisation who made the reference nor that the referrers will themselves indicate a referral has been made. Every new approach to the practice should be investigated to establish how the person involved knows the firm and how they came to contact it. This will provide information on the referrer for incorporation into the database. It will also reveal whether other techniques such as media advertising or direct mail are working. Many firms already obtain this information on an informal basis. It should be brought together and the list treated as an important information contribution for practice development.

ACKNOWLEDGING THE REFERRER

Having established the source of any referral, which is a necessary pre-condition for stimulating the network, the next stages are equally simple and effective. The first of these is acknowledgement which breaches neither rules nor professional conventions. It is unfortunately all too frequent that introducers are not acknowledged. It is an act of common courtesy, if nothing else, to express appreciation for contacts. This simple response has a value out of all proportion to the act itself. There are, if any, few individuals who do not enjoy recognition, most particularly where they are the facilitating party in an introduction. "The greatest pleasure I know is to do a good action by stealth, and to have it found out by accident", wrote Charles Lamb. He spoke for everyone. It is a very natural and basic human emotion to enjoy recognition whether from a waiter in a restaurant or a person of fame and repute in his or her own calling.

In acknowledging introductions which have been given it will never come amiss to suggest that it will merit particular care in servicing the client and, if appropriate, that the person making the acknowledgment will personally deal with the client assuming their rank represents an apparent "benefit". Originators of contacts like to feel that their introduction is of special value and that the person or organisation referred will benefit because of the role and importance of the introducer.

Research has shown that there are two overriding reasons why people recommend their own advisers which leads to the obvious conclusion that referrers' action must be acknowledged:

- An introduction reinforces their referrer's wisdom in selecting the practice in the first place

- Referrers want their advisers to succeed and are willing to help them do so

This being so, it is a critical task in the process of stimulating the network to ensure that the referrer is aware that the firm has received the inquiry and is appreciative of the contact. Acknowledgement can range from a simple "thank you" to something far more elaborate such as entertaining the referrer or where it is not expressly forbidden, as in law where a solicitor cannot share a fee with a non-solicitor, a remuneration or a gift. Everything which has been written in Chapter 13 on nurturing key clients will apply with equal if not more force to key referrers, that is, those who send a series of high quality potential clients to the practice.

A word of warning is necessary here. It should not always be assumed that because a client has been referred they would necessarily want the introducer to know the contact has been taken up. There are many professions where this apparent anomaly can occur. The request for a professional contact may have been disguised by stating that the inquiry was "on behalf of a friend" or "in case I should ever need it". If there is any doubt then, before the acknowledgement is made, client clearance should be sought.

As has already been inferred, there is no better method of stimulating inter and intraprofessional referrals than reciprocation. Unfortunately, reciprocation is unlikely to occur immediately except by coincidence and luck and moreover it may not be appropriate. The fact that an architect recommended a quantity surveyor does not necessarily mean that when the surveyor has an opportunity to recommend an architect the one who generated the referral would be most appropriate. An architectural practice specialising or with special expertise in educational establishments is not likely to be very appropriate for a private client seeking to convert a windmill into a dwelling house. The criteria for reciprocation must include suitability.

None of this rules out at least expressing an intention to cross-refer when the opportunity arises. To add some verisimilitude to this expression of intent, details of the referrer's practice or activity should always be sought and entered into the central database so everyone has access to it. Reciprocal introductions and thus the encouragement of the referring party are more likely to occur if everyone in the firm knows: (i) who refers; (ii) the appropriateness of their services or products to the receiving firm's clients; and (iii) when a cross-referral is appropriate. The larger the organisation the less likely it is that an important referral source for one department will be known and used by the others. Thus, the centralised information should be available and its use encouraged but with clear guidelines as to its use.

INTELLIGENCE GATHERING

This process of acknowledgement must also include the important function of intelligence gathering on referrers and, as appropriate, their organisation. In many professional activities it is virtually mandatory to obtain certain intelligence often even before a meeting is arranged. Stockbroking and banking are two activities where introductions are either necessary or carry great weight and thus the source of the introduction will always be probed in a first effort to establish the status and probity of the would-be client. The client database format in Appendix 7 includes an entry for referrers.

Part of the information-gathering process on introducers should also be directed to the reasons they have recommended the firm. It may well be a strength the firm have not themselves identified, an area of unique competence, facility or resource. The differential advantage which every firm possesses distinguishes it favourably from all competing practices, as explained in Chapter 6. It is not always easy for professionals to isolate their differential advantage because they are too close to the practice, the individuals within it and the profession itself. Moreover it is difficult to ask clients directly for the reasons they made an introduction (and likely to produce a somewhat facetious answer). Indeed even asking why a client chose a practice suggests an element of immodesty, the seeking of compliments or a sense of insecurity or disbelief in the practice itself. Asking a third party why they referred is not so difficult and the answer is likely to be less biased as a self-analysis of the situation.

Once it is known why introducers recommend the practice (the reasons will almost certainly be different for different situations, referrers, referrents, disciplines and clients), these are practice strengths that should be built on, communicated and explained both to referrers and potential clients.

All information on referrers should be consolidated so that those concerned with practice development can identify the important third party targets. Centralisation of the referral source is needed because the value of any particular source or individual may be disguised by the fact that new clients they have introduced have been dispersed through the practice and among different professionals. Apart from details of the referrer and their organisation if appropriate, some indication of the type of introductions they have given will also be advantageous in building up a picture of the importance of each third party contact—the type and numbers of clients introduced; the value, quality and frequency of business which develops; and details of the receiving practice's contacts with the referrer—all this will be of value in focusing marketing efforts to encourage referrals.

From this it will rapidly be seen who in the network are important. It will also reveal gaps and weaknesses in the structure. For example introductions from building society managers, but not from insurance brokers might indicate that more effort was needed to cultivate the latter. The patterning of the information is of the utmost consequence if the network is to be made to work effectively.

PRO-ACTIVE MARKETING

In order to activate the system all the techniques for marketing the practice to potential clients are appropriate. The same communication methods can be used but of course direct messages will be different. Sending referrers copies of articles, inviting them to meetings, keeping them updated on the firm's progress and new appointments, brochures, press releases, newsletters and other publications are all appropriate. Important referrers, that is those who can or do send a stream of high quality contacts, should be placed firmly in the key client category (see Chapter 13) and nurtured in exactly the same way.

As with normal practice development, personal contact is the critical tool but asking referrers directly to recommend clients or to provide contacts does not come easily to professionals nor is it always advisable. This can best be done when the opportunities occur. For example, a new member of the firm with some specialisation can be the vehicle for introducing the subject and asking if any of the referrer's contacts use or could use such specialisations. This is a great deal less difficult than seeking general introductions.

Nothing must be done to make the referrer feel uncomfortable, which can occur if they have to turn down a direct request for contacts or introductions. It is very much a question of ensuring that the skills, resources, specialisations and other features of the practice are known so that the referrer can relate this information to their own networks. Business clients, perhaps more than private clients, do understand the importance of cultivating referral sources and they will help if the approach is appropriate and has no element of importuning.

A method suggested by the American Bar Association[2] provides a generalised approach and is well worth considering:

> "Satisfied clients usually will give their attorneys names to potential clients. If you're brave and feel your client is willing to give you referrals if asked, go ahead and ask.
>
> But even so, there are ways of doing this acceptably. Do not ask the client to refer you (defined) potential clients for example (middle-size business, those in need of estate planning), otherwise it might seem that you want him to find someone in need of your firm's services—a tough request. The client will not give you referrals instantly. It takes time for him or her to generate thoughts about names; hence, you may have to schedule a second meeting to generate actual names of referrals. Initially, you could make a date for lunch, then drop the client a letter telling what you have in mind. This can also begin to stimulate the client's thoughts about referrals.
>
> Since it takes a while to jog the memory of clients, it often is productive to follow up any requests you make for referrals by asking questions about various civic contacts, social acquaintances, or even neighbours. This will stimulate your client's thoughts on the matter."

PROGRESS REPORTING

In some instances it may be possible and permissible to keep the referrer informed of progress, with the client's consent, even if it is only as innocuous a statement as "we have had some limited success so far". This type of contact maintains communication with the referrer and, again, is a reminder of the practice and its service. A progress report is another indication to the referrer that the role played in the introduction and the value placed on it continues to be recognised—again meeting a basic human desire.

Even when a consultation does not end with an engagement or the result desired by the client, a progress report is still of considerable value. If the client is displeased and has expressed his or her displeasure to the referrer, the professional at least has the opportunity of explaining to the third party, possibly in technical terms, what happened and why it happened. Successful litigation can leave a client substantially out of pocket and critical of the competence of the solicitor assigned to the case because of the outcome. The reality might be that the solicitor advised the client not to proceed with the litigation and explained the consequences of both winning and losing. The client nevertheless chose to go ahead, despite the fact that even if successful, costs could not be recovered. This is a powerful defence for the solicitor against an actual or implied criticism.

A similar situation might be found in medicine where the practitioner recommends a course of treatment which the patient fails to follow—the negative outcome is then attributed to the doctor's failure. Thus the progress report, whether negative or positive, is a valuable instrument in the effective use of the interpersonal network.

"MARRIAGE BROKING"

Another technique for stimulating the referral network is what is termed "marriage broking". That is, the referrer brings together two individuals or organisations which might benefit from the introduction while the referrer gathers the goodwill of the participants and the possibility they may be encouraged to pass contacts to him or her. Thus an insurance broker with both a design consultant and a printer as clients might well have occasion to effect an introduction to the benefit of both parties.

"Marriage broking" can create a substantial amount of goodwill but like real marriage it has its dangers. If the parties to the marriage subsequently find they are not compatible it is not unusual for the broker to get the blame. Thus, in introducing clients to each other in the hope of tripartite benefits, the downside risks should be considered. The referrer database will yield information on client interests, activities, problems, culture, or even personality and opportunities and it is truly creative marketing to identify any consanguinity which would make "marriage broking" a suitable technique to adopt.

The referral system or interpersonal network is the single most important practice development tool available to most professions and as such it warrants very close study. Its use should be deliberate not fortuitous or reactive. The steps to be taken by each practice are simple and represent no more than an ordered methodology which avoids the mistakes of omission and commission.

ACTION POINTS

- Set up mandatory system for identifying referral sources
- Ensure all recommendations are (with client's permission) acknowledged
- Establish reasons for referrals
- Build dossiers on referrers and develop a centralised list
- Offer all referrers reciprocation where appropriate
- Check on use and by whom of central listing of referrers
- Where permissible give progress reports to referrers
- If feasible and appropriate set up a "marriage broking" system

---

NOTES

(1) Foonberg, J.G. *How to Start and Build a Law Practice*, p.33, Law Students Division of the American Bar Association, Chicago (1976).
(2) Brenna, F. *Focusing on Clients*, p.83, American Bar Association, Chicago (1990).

21
The Collaborative Firm: Cross Referrals and Internal Marketing

Two of the most neglected aspects of many firms' operations are the failure to maximise the potential locked up in the client base, that is seeking to increase engagements with existing clients, and to market services within the firm.

Only in financial services does there appear to have been a consistent and successful attempt to expand business by offering additional "products" to existing customers. Banks have widened their portfolios with services such as payroll and computerised cash management systems usually, if not invariably, sold to existing customers using other banking facilities. Because, as has already been quoted, it costs between five and seven times as much to obtain a client as to retain one this fact alone should make the marketing of extended service ranges to existing clients a high priority in all professions. Similarly the opportunity to market internal service departments to other parts of the organisation is also neglected and this, too, opens up possibilities both for increased business for the internal department and reduced costs for the organisation. Both these issues are the subject of this chapter.

Multi-service, and multi-departmental firms all too frequently fail to exploit their most valuable asset—clients. Asking the very simple question, "What services do our clients use or be shown to need that they do not purchase from us but which we could profitably supply?", not only leads to new service development at a very low cost, but also reveals where the supplying practice already has an offer which will meet a client need. Summarising the situation one noted author commented:

> "The tension between individual groups and the needs of the firm are frequently revealed when individual profit centres forego activities (such as market research on a particular industry) whose benefit to the firm as a whole is large enough to warrant the cost, but whose benefit to the individual profit center is not sufficient to warrant them engaging in that activity. Even if the profit center (or individual) is assured that contribution to overall firm success will (through some judgmental process) be recognized and rewarded, such rewards are often seen as more uncertain and risky than the 'hard' evidence of an individual profit center's profitability or individual revenue generation."[1]

It can be shown that there are very real barriers to cross referrals. First among these is a lack of trust. Those involved in servicing clients may, indeed usually have, in-built reservations about exposing them to other parts of the firm which may not perform to a sufficiently high standard and thus possibly even lose the client for the practice. This leads to "client hugging" and protection of territory in terms of clients, business sectors or geographical areas. There is usually little or no reward for the individual or team in cross-selling. Their first priority is to meet their own quotas and budgets not someone else's and to service their own clients to the highest possible standard.

The problems can be generalised as a failure to share clients through the firm; marketing resources are not properly identified and thus not used. Organisational and administrative systems create unintentional barriers, and there is no coherent or consistent attempt to cross refer pro-actively.

BARRIERS

Defining the problem does not provide an answer to the difficulties. However, no solution can ever be achieved unless the reasons why the problems exist are also understood. These can be encapsulated as protection of the practitioner's "territory" in terms of clients or business sectors or geographical areas served, competition between professionals working within the same organisation for recognition and career advancement and, the commonest reason of all, poor chemistry between individuals although this in part is the outcome of the competition.

The barriers which stand between the problem and its cause and the resolution of the situation are easily described. As so often occurs in professional services, a very considerable one is a dislike of, and disdain for, marketing, most particularly of selling. But this reluctance to market other services or departments is also generated by a failure to answer, or to answer convincingly a simple but critical question, "What's in it for me?" Even where firms do have a developed marketing function, cross referrals still can be obtained without difficulty by individual practitioners who may well lack both marketing and inter-personal skills.

When the attempt is made to jump the barriers to successful cross referrals the first fatal mistake is a failure to appreciate that departments do not co-operate—people do. It is precisely the same situation as in an industrial *milieu* in the purchaser/vendor relationship—businesses do not buy products or services, people do. Lip service is paid too often to professional services being a "people business" but the thinking is rarely extended to developing systems and attitudes which reflect this fact. Professionals still attempt to create as wide a gap as possible between themselves and their clients while the opposite is what is required. This phenomenon also applies to internal clients.

Internal referrers have to be perceived and treated as clients, moreover as key clients who, as Chapter 13 illustrates, require special treatment. Images are a vital component of decision making. Just because the supplier is in-house does not make the need to achieve an internally acceptable image any less important than when seeking external customers.

Under the pressures generated by difficult business conditions there has been a notable diminution in the loyalty of practitioners as a reaction to practice management which has led to redundancies, concentration on achieving individual targets and cost cutting. For cross selling to succeed, loyalties must be generated and loyalty is a two-way requirement.

These and other barriers illustrate the difficulty of building an effective cross selling structure but they are all surmountable by internal marketing.

FRAMEWORK FOR CROSS SELLING

A pre-condition for successful cross selling has to be an audit of the firm's resources along with a client audit to see if a match can be made between what is available (or could be made available) and what the client needs (or could be shown to need).

High among the resources, but not often viewed that way, will be the range of services the firm can offer clients and potential clients. Absurd as it may seem, it is far from uncommon for practitioners not to know the full range of services and skills available to clients. The larger the organisation the more likely this situation is to apply. The rule has to be *know yourself*. If it cannot be said with absolute certainty that everyone in the firm with client contact knows every service, every skill and every resource it possesses, then the first task must be to ensure the situation is rectified. This can be done by internal meetings and publications such as brochures and newsletters but any system has to incorporate a constant monitoring and updating to ensure new members of the firm are fully informed, older members reminded and any new developments are communicated to everyone.

The second rule is *know your client*. Just as it is unusual for everyone with client contact to be wholly familiar with all their organisation's services, skills and resources, it is equally unlikely that all clients' needs (verbalised and non-verbalised), policies, perceptions, problems, opportunities and aspirations are known. The need to get close to clients is paramount if there is to be a full exploitation of the potential locked into the client base. Information on clients is often already within the firm either on the client database or held by individuals, whether recorded formally or not. These are data that must be shared because from this it is possible to decide how the firm's offering can be augmented or adjusted to meet client needs.

As can be seen, internal marketing, of which key client nurturing is very much a part, is more than a change of emphasis, it is a substantial change of attitude. New criteria are emerging for assessing professional practitioners' performance which were never previously part of the job specification. Professionals who pride themselves on the skills with which they practise their individual disciplines—law, architecture, finance, research, surveying, accountancy, health care and many others—now have to add marketing skills and, more important and much more difficult to achieve, marketing motivation.

The requirement in Chapter 13, page 128 can be applied equally to internal clients' referrers. This is to achieve close working relationships which are based on a genuine mutual interest. Adversarial patterns of the past have to be broken. Negotiating skills are badly needed, something few professionals have been taught. Improved co-ordination is required and the in-built assumption that both internal and external clients' needs are known removed. Internal co-ordination involves more than the personnel actually delivering the service. It extends to the most junior members of the organisation. Everyone has to be internal and external client centred. This means delivering high quality services in a satisfactory way—being responsive, competent, accessible and courteous and providing reliability, security, having an understanding of internal clients' problems and generating communication methods and messages that are concise, comprehensible and unqualified.

DEMOLISHING THE BARRIERS

It was Robert Frost who wrote, "Good fences make good neighbours" but, perhaps sensing they also lead to isolation, goes on to say, "Before I built a wall I'd ask to know what I was walling in and walling out". In practice development what is being walled out is the considerable potential locked up in the client base. But given that there are fences and very real ones between departments and services it is important to understand why they exist and to adopt methods which will either remove or reduce them. High among the successful techniques for turning the firm from a number of often independent groups or individuals with tensions and antipathies between them into an integrated organism are:

- *Cross staffing.* Seconding professionals and support staff from different departments to other departments to gain an appreciation of their work and their problems. This applies to both bids (presentations) and engagements.
- *Joint training.* Much can be done at the training or induction stage of new staff to give them exposure to wider areas of

activity of the firm than the section to which they are to be attached.

- *Inter-departmental committees.* This is an obvious way in which views, opportunities and activities can be discussed. This often occurs informally but it is far more effective if such a committee and work is structured and its decisions scheduled and allocated.
- *Database to facilitate access to expertise.* This refers to both content which is relevant to different departments and to its accessibility. However, for databases to really contribute they have to be used pro-actively, that is the information must be circulated and its use monitored.
- *Generating integrated client business.* Developing client relevant "packages" which brings different departments together as a necessity.
- *Optimal internal transfer fees.* Adoption of an agreed policy on the basis of fee charging where one department or service uses the skills and resources of another.
- *Cross boundary client relationship partner or professional.* This responsibility is to liaise on all a client's business and to seek opportunities to provide the client with a range of services; such appointments are common place and successful in the advertising business.
- *Compensation systems.* These should reward cross referrals. This might be achieved by making the collaborating departments *joint* profit centres, scaled commission payment related to the extent of activity involved in successful cross referral activity. Even the simple act of recognition can be a reward.
- *Circulating client profiles.* This contributes to the "know your client" requirement. They should be circulated throughout the firm, most particularly for new clients, and different departments invited to indicate what services they could provide for that particular client. This should be on-going so that changes in the client company, its market or a private client's position which might open opportunities are also made known to other internal departments.
- *Inter-departmental "getting to know you" meetings.* Problems of and barriers to collaboration can be discussed and resolved. Internal image studies conducted independently can make a large contribution here.

- *Firm level funding of collaborative activities.* This provides a "free" resource to encourage joint activities. This funding could support and encourage presentation, research, marketing, client visits and new service development.
- *Physical arrangements.* Change in working/office structures facilitates inter-personal contacts and exchange of experiences and activities. The physical lay-out of an office can be an encouragement for people to meet and discuss client matters and interests. Physical separation encourages "them" and "us" attitudes.
- *Reorganising around people who want to collaborate.* Such teams, which are already well motivated, will pro-actively seek out opportunities to market their combined skills (Chapter 24 provides information on the formation and use of small teams).
- *Internal newsletters and brochures.* These inform and remind other departments of the skills available and the client base.
- *Promoting success.* Firm-wide circulation of information on successful cross referrals acts as a motivator for others to combine their efforts.
- *Social involvements.* These frequently lead to productive discussions of interests and clients and a flow of information. Such events are a value far beyond that of mere entertainment.[2]

If, as is suggested in Chapter 6, a mission statement has been prepared and is "owned" by all members of the firm, this itself will facilitate the removal or reduction of barriers since one of its purposes is to create a unanimity of purpose, to develop a culture and to act as a focal point with which an individual can identify.

In seeking to exploit the client base by cross referrals, it should be recognised that collaboration only occurs when those involved see that it is in their interests to co-operate. However, the facts of life are that the opportunities for co-operation rarely coincide. The possibility always exists that the flow of introductions and cross referrals could be perceived as largely one way. Thus any motivation devices that are adopted must have both short and long term benefits and, moreover, the benefits should, wherever possible, be quantifiable. Devising such a system is a challenge to the firm that the would-be collaborative firm must meet.

INTERNAL USERS AND IN-HOUSE MARKETING

The preceding comments have all been directed to the purpose of obtaining more engagements from existing clients by ensuring that all the appropriate departmental services the client could usefully adopt are marketed. The second dimension is the marketing of internal services internally—the legal department to the financial department, the architectural department to the property department, the personnel department to the R&D department. The list is limitless.

There is a very strong trend in central and local government, parastatal bodies and business to close down or spin off all types of in-house service departments. The new wave is now to make what remains of internal service facilities either self-supporting or profit centres, or simply to improve the volume and quality of work of the existing departments to achieve a higher level of efficiency. The concomitant of this has been de-regulation of client departments, permitting them to seek outside suppliers so that competitive forces will ensure internal departments are not cushioned in their efforts to market and provide services. The removal of corporate protection in the sense that internal clients had to use the internal service or, at the very least, give every opportunity to compete with external suppliers as occurs in many organisations, most particularly local and central government, to a situation in which, in many cases, the internal client does not even have to short list the internal supply has been cathartic.

There is no great distinction in terms of marketing technique between marketing to external or internal customers. What changes is the strength and type of the very different forces at work.

The Targets

Obviously internal users of the in-house service are the objective. Marketing to them has to be pro-active and, like all marketing, it is very necessary to understand the client in both a corporate and personal sense. The fact that the target prospect operates within the same organisational *milieu* can lead to the totally erroneous assumption that the client is known and understood. An enhanced ability is needed to recognise their needs, even those they cannot or do not choose to verbalise. Then the task is to convince them that the supplying department can deliver what it promises.

While political issues are never absent in marketing, their influence is far more pervasive with internal markets where managers compete with each other within the same organisational structure. Buying is most usually, but decreasingly so, adversarial. Buyer and seller each manoeuvre and negotiate to obtain the best possible deal to enhance their opportunities for promotion, recognition and wider authority. The success of the buyer (or vice versa) in out-negotiating the seller (or vice versa) can, over time have a pervasive effect on the career development of the individuals involved. They may even compete for the same promotion. There is no equivalent in the open market of this competitive situation between the internal buyer of the service and the internal seller.

The Incentives

It would be foolish to ignore the competitive advantage of external suppliers in terms of what might be euphemistically called "below-the-line" incentives. An area manager of a major retailer, when asked why he preferred to use external architects rather than the company's own department, said, "You don't get Christmas presents from our architects".

But incentives, not of a material type, are available internally; security, self-esteem and self-fulfilment, and recognition, used creatively, are stronger incentives than the hospitality tent at a major sporting event. If the internal supplier can deliver a better performance than the external supplier, this enhances the user's own position. A better performance can derive from the fact that an in-house supplier has a far greater familiarity with the company's situation, aspirations, resources and constraints. This, in turn, can lead to both cost and time saving. More importantly such knowledge can deliver security or peace of mind.

The Skills

Few in-house departments have the necessary marketing skills, since under the conventional system there was no need to market. The time-honoured approach of, "this is what the department offers—take it or leave it", did not even require diplomacy let alone persuasion. Internal marketing is more than persuasive communication; it also encompasses the development of new services and packages which clients can be shown to need. The pro-active approach requires both an understanding of the client's activities and the creative ability to design and deliver service offerings which will fill needs. Superimposed on the pressure for internal marketing in an increasing number of cases, there is the requirement to offer services in the open market which brings the internal department into head-on competition with commercial practices. Clearly, the disciplines to be acquired have to be those that will bring the department to at least parity with the commercial competition. There is no way it is going to compete profitably unless it can achieve this.

Motivation

"I did not train and qualify as a personnel manager just to become a salesman", was the comment of one internal department head when instructed to sell the department's skills—recruitment, appraisal and career counselling—internally. The low regard for marketing never manifests itself more blatantly than when service department managers and staff who previously made a service available are called upon to market them pro-actively. It is here that the internal department attempting to sell its services is at the greatest disadvantage because commercial competitors do not employ representatives who do not want to sell. The greatest challenge is to demonstrate to service departmental managers that "selling" is not to be equated with the worst excesses of the double glazing, second-hand car and time share markets but, as has been emphasised earlier, can be conducted with the same elegance and sophistication as they practice in their own disciplines.

Organisational policy changes referred to earlier have led to the establishment of new criteria for assessing the in-house professional's performance related to activities that were never previously part of their job specifications. Professionals who pride themselves on the skills with which they practise their individual disciplines—law, medicine, architecture, finance, research, surveying, accountancy, and many others—now have to add marketing skills and, more important and much more difficult to achieve, marketing motivation. If the use of a service department is compulsory, then fees, quality, punctuality or the way the service is delivered are quite irrelevant in terms of retaining the client. This can lead to a deep seated "don't care" as opposed to "client care" attitude, total lack or responsiveness, accessibility and a degree of arrogance only a monopoly supplier could sustain.

The new task for internal departments competing for internal clients with outside practices must be to achieve a high level of collaboration based on genuine mutual personal, departmental and corporate interests. The reference earlier to "inter-departmental getting-to-know-you meetings" is particularly apposite for internal suppliers and clients and should be adopted on an ongoing basis.

The internal department must be perceived, and this perception must be based on reality, as responsive, accessible, courteous and competent in resolving client problems cost effectively and communicating comprehensive but concise and unambiguous messages. Supervening all this has to be a breaking down of the belief that all the internal client's needs are known. Such a state of knowledge is as unlikely as it is uncommon.

This chapter has been concerned with cross selling within an organisation. There is another type of cross selling as between different non-competing professional organisations. This is described in Chapter 25, pages 307–8.

ACTION POINTS

- Ensure that everyone with client contact knows the full range of services available and every client, internal and external
- Build client dossiers
- Design and implement a cross selling tactical plan
- Select methods to achieve greater co-operation and cross departmental knowledge of internal services, skills and resources
- Devise reward systems
- Publicise successes
- Probe internal client attitudes to the use of internal service suppliers and adjust to client needs

NOTES

(1) Maister, D. *Managing the Professional Service Firm*, Free Press, New York (1993).
(2) This list is substantially based on a compilation by David Maister, Chapter 30 "Creating the Collaborative Firm" in *Managing the Professional Service Firm*, Free Press, New York (1933), and is reproduced with his permission.

22
Fees and Value for Money

Nowhere is the clash between what is perceived as professionalism and commercialism greater than in the consideration of fees. One of the frequently quoted definitions of professionalism is that practitioners put their clients' interest above their own. This implies that payment for services rendered is of secondary importance to the service itself. The reality in most countries and for most clients suggests otherwise. Few people have noticed any reticence on the part of any professional to charge the highest fees the market will bear. Rather, there is a reluctance to discuss or explain them. The vestigial pocket in a barrister's gown into which the instructing solicitor dropped the fee is indicative of the attitude which, to some extent, still pervades.

Any consideration of the economic basis of professional practice starts with anomalies. A fee is the price that the client pays for the service and yet the word "price" is rarely used by professionals or practitioners. Some 15 different ways can be identified of describing price in the service sector of the economy. These range from the barrister's honorarium to the consultant's retainer. To some extent the nomenclatures used for price give an insight into a profession's own conception of its services while, in other circumstances, it is no more than a cosmetic embellishment to hide the reality of what in the final analysis is a commercial transaction.

It is specious to claim, as is often done, that prices gives a value of worth and a fee is a compensation for a professional service rendered. The latter is said to be an expense for the client. In contradiction, price defines a value or worth—the distinction made in Chapter 17, pages 175–6, between use, value in use and perceived value, is also relevant in this context. While it is true that it would be unusual to refer to a fee for a product, there is no reason why there cannot be a price for a service. Certainly many low technology consumer services such as dry cleaning, vehicle servicing and household repairs all quote a price for the service.

The semantics can create a communication problem but, as with many aspects of practice development, it is really a question of using terminologies with which clients are comfortable. For the foreseeable future they will expect professionals to talk in terms of fees. Nevertheless, in the present ethos there is a danger in professionals failing to regard a fee as an exchange of money for defined values delivered rather than as compensation for the skill and time involved in providing the service. If this trap is not avoided then the attempt to demonstrate value for money must fail.

Competition continues to be limited by strict regulations governing the level and setting of fees in some countries. In Germany, there is a Federal law which sets lawyers' fee-scales and another which determines the basic rates for the calculation of doctors' fees. In Italy, compulsory minimum and maximum rates drawn up by the professional association are subject to the approval of the Minister with responsibility for the professional sector concerned. The anti-trust authorities in Italy in 1991 found that the tariff rules and the disciplinary code of the National Association of Auditors infringed the competition rules and did not qualify for an exemption. In the Netherlands, fees for the medical and legal professions are, to a certain extent, laid down by law. France already has considerable experience of applying its competition rules to the professions. Several professional organisations and even some individual practitioners (medical, dental) have been found guilty of establishing and disseminating scales of fees or devising concerted practices for collectively setting such scales. Fines have often been imposed. Professions which have been forced to abandon such practices, whose fees by agreement with the government are unregulated, include pharmacists, barristers, architects, surveyors and valuers, medical biologists and doctors.

One of the fundamental principles underlying the application of competition rules to the professions, which has been promulgated by the Commission of European Union by the Directorate General for Competition (DGIV), is that the collective fixing of prices is one of the most serious infringements of the competition rules of the Treaty of Rome. For the professions, it is regarded as particularly oppressive when membership of a professional body is compulsory in order to practise or where it increases the partitioning of national markets. The professions in those countries where fees continue to be fixed by agreement will find themselves under increasing pressure to abandon or replace such agreements.

While there has been a total reversal of policy so far as some Associations are concerned, in relation to competitive pricing there is still a legacy of ambivalence. In 1988 the Institute of Chartered Accountants stated:[1] "The fact that the member may charge a lower fee than another for undertaking the same or similar work is not *improper* [author's italics] provided the client is not misled". The statement continues:

> "If, in the course of an investigation into allegations of unsatisfactory work on the part of a member there is evidence of the work having been obtained or retained through quoting a fee that is not economic in terms of the time needed and quality of staff necessary to perform that work to a satisfactory professional standard, that factor is likely to be taken into account in considering the member's conduct having regard to the obligations placed upon the member under Fundamental Principle 2 of the Guide to Professional Ethics."

But in 1992, perhaps after some second thoughts and to reiterate the position, the Joint Ethics Committee in cases of suspected predatory pricing placed the onus firmly on the member to justify their fee level. Such a procedure is likely to be lengthy and painful.

Except under well defined circumstances the professionals, for the moment at least, continue to be barred from operating on a results basis, and members are not permitted to make comparisons between their fees and those of other practices.

The professions in those countries where de-regulation has occurred do not need to be told that conditions today and in the foreseeable future cannot be compared to the past when fee scales were fixed and non-negotiable. There is no question but that the freedom and willingness of some professional practices to negotiate fees has led to re-consideration of charges. When scale fees for conveyancing were abolished in the United Kingdom, combined with a reduction in property values there were very considerable reductions in charges in real terms and they are now significantly lower than the scales that applied a decade ago would have yielded.

The ultimate heresy, so far as the professions are concerned, is public pressure for practices to publish their profits. This, it is claimed, would provide an objective guide to the reasonableness of fees while at the same time revealing whether the argument that competition is depressing fees is borne out by the facts.

Today, billing clients for services is not a simple matter, if only because what was traditionally a sellers' market has become a highly competitive and fee sensitive buyers' market. The pressures which clients experience in their own markets are transferred into their suppliers, be they for goods or services. Billing for value will become of increasing importance. It has been suggested that value, like quality, can be de-composed into a number of single issues which influence the client's view as to whether value has been or is likely to be received.[2] However, like quality, value is in the eyes of the beholders. Moreover it is far from constant. What is considered good value at one moment is regarded less favourably at another. Value, as was pointed out in Chapter 17, to buyers of professional services has three components—*use value, value in use* and *perceived value* even though they may not express value in so sophisticated a way.

Beyond this, it is possible to isolate the components of value within all three dimensions:

- Risk reduction
- Client support and involvement
- Acceptance of responsibility
- Availability
- Punctuality
- Risk sharing
- Innovative approach
- Maturity of judgement
- Dependability
- Prompt clear communication
- Problem solution
- Unique skills

It is the elements of value, as perceived by the client, that determine either what the client is willing to pay or whether he or she considers the bill excessive or, in other words, poor value for money.

The development of logical and consistent fee structures is necessary for three totally valid reasons:

1   To manage the costs of producing and delivering the service.
2   To enhance revenue/profit without loss of volume.
3   To respond to competitive threats.

MANAGING COSTS

Cost information must be detailed and timely. The basis for effective fee level decisions is totally dependent on knowing the nature and extent of costs. If the use of fee strategies in professional services is virtually non-existent, it is in part due to the inadequacies of most costing methods for services which still operate on a "faith, hope and 100%" basis. The vagaries of costing the output of practitioners' activities have caused many of them or their managements to adopt empirical and "ad hoc" approaches. One result is that, while professional service firms can usually determine the profitability of the practice as a whole, frequently they cannot calculate the profit or loss contribution of individual assignments, clients, individual professionals or services. This, in turn, means that the development of a fee strategy is virtually useless because the components which enable a strategy to be designated cannot be accurately identified. Chapter 12 deals at some length with both the value of, and technique for, conducting such investigations.

Service firms' managements cannot be in full control of their operations unless they *do* develop a reliable system of "service" or project cost accounting. Accountants and management consultants throw up their hands in horror when they find that their clients do not know with exactitude the cost of the products they are selling. Nevertheless, these and other professional service providers have often either neglected or ignored this problem in relation to themselves, relying on the total profitability of their operations to ensure continuing activity. *Sartor Resartus.* The image of the professional service providers is not enhanced. This situation is as inefficient as it is unnecessary, since a professional service firm can and should be able to identify costs. The reasons for the neglect are numerous and require study as a first step to rectifying the position.

Service firms continue to use conventional product costing techniques that are inappropriate when it is appreciated that the "product" of the service firm is usually difficult to describe and measure. Costs are primarily "people" costs which will typically account for 70% to 80% of total operating costs and perhaps 50% to 70% of gross income. Other costs are people related (e.g. premises, travel, telecommunications, entertaining). The output of personnel is both difficult to measure and highly variable in amount and quality and not just from day to day but from hour to hour and, because the client participates in production, the professional's output may be inhibited or extended by the quality of the client's input.

Unlike products, there are few if any economies of scale or indeed of scope. That is, employing the same asset to produce different products spreads the cost of the asset and shortens the time in which the investment is recovered. Using the same people to provide different services makes no contribution to cost reduction although there may be some minor savings to be made in the application of equipment over different services. The only real contribution to cost reduction is that which might derive from learning curve benefits, but even these are qualified in that there can be large variations in cost in repeated performances. Because services are, for the most part, produced and consumed simultaneously, they cannot be inventoried. So, unlike a manufacturer who can use slack time to make stock, the professional service firm is exactly akin to empty theatres and airlines where unfilled seats are capacity lost for ever.

A new development has been the more recent attempts to apply activity-based costing to professional services which is producing a much more realistic assessment of costs. Activity-based costing is the collection of financial and operational performance information dealing with significant activities of the firm. The traditional system of costing, based as it is on chargeable hours plus expenses plus a profit margin, yields after-the-fact accounting about variances that highlight past discrepancies but can no longer be corrected.[3]

On this last point it has been suggested a multiplier of 2.5 on the hourly rate will give an adequate margin. The figure has been tested on a number of professional practices and appears defensible if not probable. A possibly safe approach is break-even. What does it cost to operate the firm, overheads, fixed and variable costs? This is the figure which would allow it to remain in business, but nothing else. The profit required can then be added to the daily costs of operation and this sets the basic daily rate.

This is not to suggest that a practice could or would want to operate on a break-even situation for any length of time, only that it ensures the firm is not making a loss.

This, of course, deals with the totality of the firm's operations. To narrow the issue down to marketing the most relevant approach to costs is one which first divides them between chosen activities designed to increase awareness of the firm and its services and to create favourable images, and then those incurred in presentations and negotiations with individual clients. These costs can be evaluated at several levels:

• Marketing costs invoked by a practitioner with a full work load devoting time to non-billable activities plus any expenses involved
• Marketing costs invoked by a practitioner with a less than full work load devoting time to non-billable activities plus any expenses involved
• Infrastructure costs related to non-billable activities
• Direct marketing costs

The significance of these factors within the context of fee strategy is simply that no fee can be set or adjusted with any certainty of it successfully achieving whatever the objective may be unless the cost of the inputs to the service itself is known. The development of a fee strategy which has any real meaning is out of the question without basic knowledge of the nature of the firm's costs.

ENHANCING REVENUE/PROFIT

Every organisation or individual attempting to set a price or beyond profit fee level cannot escape from the formula:

high price/fee = low chance of success = opportunity for high profit
low price/fee = high chance of success = risk of low profit or even loss

Pitching a fee at the level which will maximise the opportunity for success with the opportunity for profit is however more than a financial calculation. Fees carry with them important image connotations which can both enhance or reduce the likelihood of success.

Research has shown that potential clients place more emphasis on fees after a service has been received than before. This might seem paradoxical unless it is recalled that at the outset the client buys an expectation. When the service has been delivered the opportunity arises to make an assessment of value for money and the delivery of the expectations. Many non-technical purchasers of service depend on fee levels quoted to indicate the likely level of quality. (In this context it is as easy to be too cheap as too dear.) Following from this, purchasers of services may prefer a professional with higher fees over one with low fees where the buyer perceives a high risk. Thus high fees will be tolerated for professionals with strong positive reputations in their particular field of expertise. Again, rising from the delivery of a service rather than purchase of an expectation, fees can well be a more important decision factor in returning to a practice than in the initial decision. When the need for a service arises urgently or unpredictably, fees are either only a minor consideration or are not considered at all. As was pointed out in Chapter 9, it is difficult to imagine a patient experiencing a heart attack engaging in fee negotiations with the doctor. Finally, as will be obvious, where insurance covers the professional fee it is not a pivotal factor in the purchasing decision.

An emphasis on profit must not disguise a beyond-profit element which can exist in every client situation referred to in Chapter 13. That is, the merits of the assignment may well ultimately yield a profit not directly linked to the project being quoted for.

A client may have a value which exceeds the profit they contribute now:

- Key client status warrants special fee arrangements
- Growth—a client with an increasing need for services has a value in excess of profits they currently generate

- Sophistication—a sophisticated client can provide insights for future development
- Industry leadership—a client who is among industrial leaders has value as a referral source or "demonstration" plant
- Share of client volume—a client who allocates a high share of their total requirements to a firm may have more (and certainly a different type of) value from one who only gives a small share

Beyond-profit elements could be the opportunity to acquire a new client, to enter a new market segment or niche, to yield a first project of the type for an existing client, to provide added value to the practice's existing know-how, to open up future potential, and there could be an image gain. Thus, in seeking to establish the appropriate profit level, the beyond-profit element also requires consideration.

RESPONDING TO COMPETITIVE THREATS

Since it's always easier and quicker to change a fee than to change a service, the temptation to respond to a competitive threat by reducing the fee is considerable and under most circumstances should be and can be resisted. It should be appreciated that, in serving different clients commissioning different services at different times, fee competition need not lead to wholesale reduction across the complete service range or client base. It can be confined to the actual point where competition is concentrated. Fee competition rarely if ever affects a whole practice simultaneously. Thus a practice should look to the relative advantages and disadvantages a competitor commands. Identification of those clients where the firm is competitively threatened and distinguishing them in fee quotations from those where their position is secure must be the tactic to adopt.

One of the pitfalls of using product pricing techniques is the adoption of a single price/fee for a service whether it's based on time, value or per capita. The "Goldilocks" principle applies—for some potential clients the price is too high so they remain potential clients, for others it is lower than it need be and they would pay more and for a few it is just right. A more sophisticated approach would permit the firm to realise higher fees from clients willing to pay more while offering lower fees from those who will not purchase at the higher levels. This is done by using a technique known as "price and perception of performance", previously mentioned in Chapter 17, which isolates service attributes, tangible and intangible and establishes the value the client places on them.[4]

ARRIVING AT THE FEE

Fee setting has a pivotal role in every practice's marketing strategy and is closely linked to segmentation and the services. It is, in fact, one more variable in the marketing mix which is developed to attract particular types of client to the practice to use particular services and to deliver an acceptable profit to the firm.

Substantially, fees are not an inducement to use a professional service, only in choosing one service firm rather than another. It is true it is possible to expand markets by identifying unsatisfied wants or needs, but a decision to engage a service is not in itself usually price sensitive. Conversely reducing the fee will not increase demand. No matter at what bargain level a problem solving service is offered, there are no takers if would-be buyers do not believe they have a problem or that it cannot be solved. There are few comparable situations to the product market where, frequently, customers would like a product if they could afford it. Since few clients could satisfy their own needs on a d.i.y. basis and very often consultation cannot be postponed, fees are substantially a competitive issue, not one in which market demand is affected significantly.

The moment the firm or practitioner looks at the techniques which enable it to devise and operate a fee strategy it finds itself faced with a dichotomy. These are the approaches offered by theorists engaged in developing a simplified model that helps to understand complicated reality and the approaches of marketing specialists discussing pricing on a descriptive level explaining what businessmen do, or say they do. Neither procedure is satisfactory. Any model is limited in use by psychological aspects, that is, the psychology of service provider as well as the client. Either concepts or techniques alone are insufficient and probably misleading. A combination and balance is needed, but difficult to achieve. This situation should be recognised in considering the strategies suggested. Fortunately some commentators on pricing and fees have been sensitive to the needs of service businesses, so that the service provider does not find himself or herself having to translate from tangible product to intangible service.

In developing fee strategies, it is necessary to think in terms of establishing the right fee by using the correct methodology to arrive at it. This is perhaps an even more crucial exercise in a service business than in most other enterprises because of the economic structure of the service businesses. Employing, as they do, relatively little capital implies that fee setting and time utilisation are the primary elements of leverage in achieving profitability.

Thirteen basic methods of arriving at fees can be identified: these are described in Table 22.1. A suggested fee setting procedure for service firms, while having much to commend it, still calls for more information than most organisations could generate.

SUGGESTED FEE SETTING PROCEDURES[5]

1 Identify client target, location, size, motivations.
2 Select an image for the firm that is compatible with the image of the target. All practice policies should reinforce the practice's image.
3 Collect data about the range of fees that clients are willing to pay for the service:
   (a) Ascertain key benefits desired by clients;
   (b) Determine client-preferred points for service differentiation and the value clients place on each;
   (c) Estimate joint and variable (or unique) costs of all services;
   (d) Develop a position for each service that fits with the organisation's image;
   (e) Establish price levels clients are willing to pay for each service at higher and lower costs.
4 Multiply the hourly rate by a multiple—for example, 2.5—in order to arrive at an appropriate price quotation. The multiple will allow for downtime, overheads and profit.

The deficiency of all the methods other than contingency-based fees is that the mechanistic approach ignores what is perhaps the

Table 22.1 Methods of setting fees

Title	Description	Effect
Offset	Low fee for core service but recouping on "add ons".	Psychologically favourable at the quotation stage, but can easily lead to difficulties on implementation. Advantages in some cases of client being able to control extent of commitment.
Inducement	Fee charged produces sub-standard profit or loss but attracts new clients or helps retain existing clients, used on the basis it will be possible to recoup fees on later transactions.	Successful with unsophisticated clients but tends to give a fee ceiling which is difficult to penetrate later.
Divisionary	Low basic fees on selected services to develop image of value for money which transfers to other services and total practice.	Generally effective so long as clients do not feel obligated or that they have been persuaded to use more realistically costed elements in the total service offer.
Discrete	Fee level brings the decision into an area of authority of a DMU favouring the firm. A lower fee may take decision to lower management; a high fee to the board. This tactic necessarily requires an intimate knowledge of the prospect firm.	While the decision can be moved into the DMU responsibility area better able to appreciate the offer, all fee adjustments upwards or downwards have associated risks.
Discount	Quotation subject to discounts on a predetermined basis, e.g. time schedule, extent of commitment, magnitude of transaction.	Positive encouragement to client to structure transactions on mutually favourable basis.

Guarantee	Fee includes an undertaking to achieve certain results— the undertaking surpassing that of competitors.	Moves competition from consideration of fees, consideration of values and places high quality service in most favourable position to compete with lower quality services.
Service flexibility	Quality of service hence cost varied to enable fees to remain unchanged.	Removes fee as major negotiating point, substituting the service, but note effect above for "diversionary" fees.
Conditional	Fee is conditional on the purchase of other services.	Tied in service has to be attractive in itself or else potential of the basic service is reduced. This method is illegal in some countries.
Predatory	Fee set well below competition as means of removing them. Realistic or premium fees applied later.	Requires accurate assessment of competitive resources and policies. Can be self-destructive and also illegal.
Skimming	Fee set high when demand is inelastic or capacity short and gradually reduced as situation becomes competitive.	Gives extra profitability and a hedge against later sub-standard profit. Enables the firm to keep an edge over competitive firms so long as the original high fee has been maintained long enough.
Blended	Flat rate fee based on merging different rates for different professionals or fee based on locations or office location.	Provides lower fees on a "swings and roundabouts" basis.
Contingency	Fee is contingent on a certain act being performed or accomplished.	Costs irrecoverable if act not accomplished. Encourages spurious inquiries.
Referential (for tendering)	Ensures lowest fee is quoted and enhances chances of receiving contract.	No fail-safe mechanism unless limits placed on lowest level. Depends on open tendering procedures.

most pervasive factor in client decisions relative to fees, that is their perception of the expectation being purchased. It is impossible to discuss fees without considering the psychology of the client. The fee setter must never forget that, especially in the absence of previous experience, the potential client will frequently decide in favour of the higher quotation and will certainly not accept the lowest quotation unless they are convinced the benefits required will be delivered. In a post-project situation clients will certainly not accept a low fee as an excuse for inadequate work. As is indicated in Chapter 17, zero defect may well be too expensive but too many defects in a service also makes it too expensive. Given little or no knowledge of the service, the firm or practitioner and the difficulty of competitive comparability, the client will use the fee level as a guide to expected quality and efficiency, however inadequate such an indicator may be. As with products, services perceived as under-priced are viewed with suspicion and the client will seek the safety of the middle to top range.

Although constrained to a certain extent by professional rules and by the nature of the markets, there can nevertheless be considerable flexibility in setting fees and devising fee structures. Although change is under consideration, solicitors in England and Wales are currently forbidden to accept a contingency fee (payment by results). However, in Scotland and, of course, in the USA there is a long tradition of the lawyer acting on a speculative basis.[6]

Professional services, despite, or perhaps because of, the knowledge gap between practitioner and client, are in many instances far more "value sensitive" than "fee sensitive". Fees, over an extremely wide range of services, are only occasionally on their own a critical factor in deciding to appoint a professional firm or practitioner. Research has shown that most would-be customers of consumer commercial and industrial services have a price range in mind, probably based on their past or other people's knowledge or experience and they will not buy if the fee or price is outside this notional bracket unless there is an urgent need. The same has not been found to apply to professional service markets. It is true that many house buyers have a realistic idea of what a conveyance would cost but few would be able to put a figure on litigation, what an executive search fee would be but not a restructuring of management grades, what an audit might be charged at but not an investigation and quantification of losses.

There should always be some room for fee flexibility and, with client and competitor knowledge and negotiating skills, the practice can arrive at a fee level that satisfies both parties.[7]

BIDDING

Bidding has been rightly described as a monumentally inefficient way of obtaining value for money, most particularly for services which cannot be compared like-for-like as with a standard product or even a standard consumer service. One effect of bidding is to immediately remove any possibility of an innovative and perhaps cost-saving approach to a problem solution. Giving the invited tenderers a tight specification which details what they are expected to do and with perhaps service level quality agreements only leaves the bidder to put a figure to the document. Stating the problem and asking the firm to offer their own approach to how it can be resolved may not produce the lowest tender fee but it will yield the most cost effective answer. The London Ambulance Service disaster in 1992 is an example of one type of situation that blind bidding can perpetrate. A totally inadequate computer system, purchased on the basis of the lowest price, failed and allegedly cost some 16 lives and an enormous amount of distress.[8]

Nevertheless, faced with a call for a bid, practices have to work within the specification set by the potential purchaser: there are guidelines if not rules to assist the bidder. Competitive bidding, it has been pointed out, is an art as well as a science. Fee setting takes place under circumstances of imperfect competition in that knowledge of the market is far from complete—who is competing, the nature of their offer, and, of course, fees quoted. There are many other non-quantifiable variables such as: competitors' attitudes towards a contract; their use of strategies based more on preventing a particular firm from getting the contract than on the bidder's desire to obtain it for themselves; or the individual firm's and competitor's need for the contract. A close approximation of such variables as these must be considered an art. Any system devised to maximise the chances of success by tendering firms in competitive bidding in order to succeed must nevertheless integrate them with the quantifiable factors, particularly time inputs and rates, out-of-pocket expenses and marketing costs.

The technique developed in industries, where competitive bidding is endemic or standard routine, usually depends on historical knowledge of successful bid prices in order to arrive at a range of prices for future bids. This information is frequently available in the public sector and among some other purchasing groups, but it is not always obtainable in professional service markets. This is partly because the professional service marketers very often feels that it is neither tactful nor in keeping with their image to discuss competitive fees and thereby to reduce the whole process to the level of a Levantine market-place. Successful competitive bidding, like any form of fee setting, requires good historical information bases. Ideally, the strategy in a competitive bid should be based on:

- Estimate of direct cost
- Amount of past bids which were successful (where relevant)
- Average of all bids received
- Identification of the bidders
- Amount of each individual bid
- Each bid as percentage of own direct cost estimate
- Estimate of each bidder's workload

By developing a dossier on each competitor, allowing that some inputs must be judgemental, it is possible to narrow the fee band within which any individual quotation may be made. It may prove possible to develop a correlation between fees and some of the factors listed. Because some professional services have standard or generally accepted cost rates (usually on a daily basis), the effort of building up competitors' cost data is made simpler. However, the problem of the allocation of indirect costs is no less for the service firm than for the manufacturer.

The creation of a model of the bid situation provides considerable guidance in deciding the bid price. This model comprises the mathematical relationships which describe, to a sufficient degree of approximation, the behaviour of the system, client and competition. Its function is nothing more than the evaluation and interpretation of the inputs and their interactions. In basic terms, the model will provide a rational evaluation of the potential profit resulting from the acquisition of the contract and the potential loss resulting from failure to obtain it. The evaluation is made against the background of uncertainty caused by imperfect knowledge of the client's and competitors' behaviour. The model permits pay-off to be evaluated against risk, while recognising that the achievement of the pay-off is subject to uncertainty. The size of the pay-off and the expectation of obtaining it are both dependent on the bid price, while the size of the risk is quite independent of the bid price.

While the approaches which have been briefly outlined are well worth further study, they do not solve the problem of fees in a competitive bid situation. However, they make the assessments which are so necessary in these situations that much easier to apply. No amount of scientific analysis will replace these judgements, because the bid fee in the end is the result of weighing up both the judgements and the quantifiable factors, and making yet another judgement on the implications of the balance struck in terms of the fee it is finally decided to quote and the profit it will yield if it is successful.

There is one final issue which is often not considered by firms invited to tender. This is the simple step of asking if the inquirer will accept non-compliant bids. While such a request will almost certainly be turned down for any standard product or service, it is frequently accepted where know-how is a major factor in success. If the firm does not wish merely to place a fee on a specification then it is always worth inquiring and making some advocacy for a non-compliant bid. The clear advantage is the opportunity for the bidding firm to show its creative and innovative approach to a problem solution. The downside is that it may reveal the inadequacies of those responsible for issuing the bid. Given a "to bid or not to bid" situation, the danger is worth encompassing. An insurance policy in these circumstances is to offer both a compliant and non-compliant bid.

Bidding can impose significant, not directly recoverable, costs on professional service firms. This is particularly true for architecture and design practices although they are frequently significant for accountants, management consultants and, increasingly, lawyers. There is, however, no such thing as a free lunch and failed quotation costs are inevitably recouped on successful offers. This is inefficient for both the bidder and those calling for bids. A sensible arrangement, which has worked well in the past in non-professional disciplines such as market research, is for the potential client to first limit the number of quotations called for and second to contribute towards the cost of the failed bids—the latter greatly encouraging the former. In the Netherlands, through the lobbying of the electrical contractors association (VEVA), a royal decree permits what might normally be perceived as a cartel arrangement to add a figure to their prices submitted to cover the cost of the preparation of drawings, cost calculations and other expenses involved in tendering. A similar situation exists in Denmark. This approach is also approved by the EU for the construction industry with very specific rules:

> "' The number of firms invited to tender' essentially provides as follows:
> • The number must be small enough to ensure that such firms do not incur the costs of unsuccessful bids, but large enough to ensure a satisfactory degree of competitiveness: between three and five firms for highly technical work and five to ten in other cases;
> • The number must be stated in the invitation to tender;
> • Where the main contractor consults more than the maximum number of firms or where the study costs incurred by each of the subcontractors are equal to or in excess of 1% of the work which could be allocated to them, the invitation to tender must provide for the indemnification of unsuccessful valid tenders."[9]

There is much to be said for this approach being adopted in the generality and most particularly in the United Kingdom where some £1.5 billion of government services, many of them professional, will be put out to tender in 1993/4 and probably increasing sums into the end of the millennium. Lobbying for a similar arrangement could be a useful activity and role for professional associations who, in the past, overtly or covertly justified their existence by their price fixing activities which are now largely illegal.

ESTIMATING

There are very considerable marketing advantages to be gained by providing estimates of the likely level of charges a client will have to meet. While this is a mandatory requirement in many invitations to submit a proposal, there remain some situations where estimating is difficult to accomplish. Perhaps the most notable examples are in law, accountancy and some financial services types of work. The costs of litigation, tax investigations, disputed take-overs, for example can easily defy accurate prediction.

Where it is possible, information on charges should be made available to the client giving perhaps hourly/daily billing rates for different levels of practitioners along with disbursements and time estimates. Even in the difficult-to-predict situations such as those listed above, it may be possible to provide a "not more than" or comparative estimate for similar circumstances.

One thing the practitioner can be sure of is that clients *do* want to discuss fees. The professional's reluctance to deal with this issue can be sometimes matched by the clients. The onus is on the professional to open up the subject. A non-confrontational opening which gives the practitioner an opportunity both to re-present the benefits and begin the closing procedures (see Chapter 24) could be along these lines: "I am sure that as a business person you will want to know what this engagement is going to cost you" (or "is likely to cost you"). For a private client perhaps, "Most people want me to explain how we set our fees and I make it a practice to discuss them at the outset".

For some professions there is either a mandatory requirement to estimate or quote fee rates while in others, although not compulsory, it is strongly advised as one way of reducing the number of client complaints made to regulating bodies:

> "If reference is made in promotional material to fees, the basis on which fees are calculated, or to hourly or other charging rates, the greatest care should be taken to ensure that such reference does not mislead as to the precise range of services and time commitment that the reference is intended to cover".[10]

About 10% of all clients contacting the Solicitors Complaints Bureau are concerned with fees and one of the major elements in these disputes is failure to adhere to the original estimate. The others, as might be expected, relate to the client's perception of value for money or, put another way, overcharging. Given that nearly a third of all such adjudications led to a reduction in solicitors' fees, it would seem some clients have a sound basis for their disagreements.

An estimate, once accepted, removes any possibility of dispute on fee level but not, of course, on the quality of the work or punctuality in its delivery. Far from being reluctant to discuss fees, all professionals should open up the subject and be prepared to provide estimates as an insurance policy against later claims or dissatisfactions.

Where it is truly impossible to even approximate a final fee, there is always the option of setting a given sum of money and for the arrangement to include the professional returning to the client when it is nearly exhausted and suggesting what further sums should be agreed. This at least gives clients the option of deciding if they want to proceed further. It also gives the practitioner the opportunity to give an account of how the monies have been expended to date and what has been achieved.

Some considerations for preparing estimates are as follows:

- Outline the billing schedule and ask the client if another schedule is desired
- State which people in the firm will be working on the matter
- Give hourly rate of each person and the number of hours expected for each person
- Consider offering the client a "blended" rate instead of separate hourly rates (essentially, this amounts to a single hourly rate for every hour put in on a matter without regard to who puts it in)
- Suggest that the client, or in the case of corporations its personnel, may want to accomplish certain tasks themselves under the practitioner's supervision: even if the client declines they will appreciate being given the option
- If the bottom line and the estimate closely accord then one possible major area of disagreement with, and dissatisfaction of, the client is removed
- Tell clients what kind of work description is normally provided in your bills and give them the option of indicating preference for a different format

UNDERSTANDING THE BILL

In many professional services billing is virtually a mechanistic process and requires no particular format. The veterinary surgeons', "To professional services", will often suffice. Where that service included surgical procedures, drugs, nursing, then a detailed bill is far more likely to satisfy the client. Like so much else in marketing the only way to decide the balance between extremes is to know the client and, knowing the client, enable the bill to be presented in a form they will understand. The verisimilitude of the bill is enhanced by detailing the cost item, for example, "telephone conference with…", "preparation of…", "travel". Items such as these would be both timed and costed where appropriate. Disbursements should always be validated by receipts.

Over-detailed bills can be just as much a source of irritation and suspicion about exaggerating the work as under-detailed bills where the reaction might be a perceived lack of input into the assignment. Add to this the resentment some types of cost items cause and it can be seen the actual bill is as much a marketing document, encouraging or discouraging the next engagement as anything else in the communication mix. For a start, clients dislike paying for telephone calls. "All I did was phone up and ask a simple question about acceptance of pharmacists' qualifications in the EU. That didn't take any work". A letter giving the client the information is far more acceptable as a justification for a fee. In the words of one American commentator, "Sell your clients stationery".

In those professions where disbursement can form a considerable part of a bill, medicine and law are two examples, it is always better to separate them from the fee so that the client can clearly appreciate what the firm is charging and what others have charged the firm. Although the practitioner may not have responsibility for the charges of an external supplier nevertheless, unfair as this is, they will be held responsible for the bill. Thus disbursements must be seen as justified, authorised and reasonable. Similarly where any tax is involved it is advisable to make this impost absolutely clear. A summary statement drawing together all charges will show the amount owing, but the bill itself for the services rendered should only contain those items which relate strictly to the fulfilling of that part of any contract the firm is responsible for.

It is always psychologically advantageous to have an account ready at the end of a project and present it. This is particularly true where the client's objectives have been fully met. Gratitude has a very short half life. An amusing diagram showed how, in a product liability litigation, the client moved from despair at the outset, to elation at the settlement, to antagonism when the bill was presented. The gap between success and demand for payment was long enough for the client to forget the intensive effort and skill which went into reaching an agreed settlement.[11] This is also closely linked with most clients' desire to see activity occurring as was explained in Chapter 5.

Where the bill is of any magnitude it is better to bill in tranches or as each stage of the work is completed rather than present a consolidated bill at the end of the project. However, interim bills, while perhaps not requiring as much detail as final accounts, still require justification.

It is a useful technique to invite the client to visit the office to discuss the *draft* bill with the professional. The emphasis is on the word *draft*. This meeting enables the client to query anything that is not clear or has not been agreed and for the professional to re-emphasise the service delivered. Moreover, when an adjustment is conceded there is no loss of face nor is it necessary to enter into a Levantine bargaining routine. The benefit of discussing a bill with a client is the opportunity it gives of making sure that he or she is satisfied they have indeed received value for money. In recommending the use of satisfaction audits in Chapter 5, it was stated on page 48 and is reiterated here that if the client is not happy the firm should be the first to know not the last. Given that a dissatisfied client tells many more people than a satisfied client it is obviously important to make sure that fees are seen as value for money. The client questionnaire in Appendix 5 identified this situation in question 12. Again, repeated from this chapter, if the practitioner is unwilling to ask that question it indicates clearly that the answer is feared and that they have reservations in their own mind about whether value for money has been received. By getting client agreement on the bill in the draft stage, it not only ensures that any disquiet is dealt with but it demonstrates to the client that the firm, far from losing interest at the end of an assignment, continues to be concerned with ensuring client satisfaction.

It is increasingly commonplace for professionals working with private clients, and even with some commercial clients, to accept credit cards. There are neither ethical nor substantial commercial reasons for not doing this. While the credit card companies' discounts are not to be ignored, the advantages are considerable.

Reasonably prompt payment is certain thus enhancing cash flow, credit risk is virtually nil, dispute on non-payment or delayed payment is between the credit card company and the card holder not the card holder and the professional. Credit card acceptance removes what, for some practices' support staff, is the unpleasant task of chivvying clients for payment or even threatening or instituting proceedings to recover the debt.

Where "overdues" have to be pursued, it is usually better to do so by telephone rather than in writing. Clients often see threats in written communications on this subject when they are never intended. This is particularly true of legal practices. Provided the "chaser" has a good telephone manner, reminders can be made with tact and good humour and without damaging the relationship.

Of course, when credit status is dubious pre- or part-payment should be insisted on. It is, after all, better to lose a client than to lose money. Seeking pre-payment is perhaps more difficult than seeking interim payment when work completed to date provides a valid reason. Again, with diplomacy it is possible to present a request for pre-payment without, at the same time, suggesting that the client is not to be trusted. A tactful way of seeking advance payment is to ask for it as part payment against costs to cover fees and disbursements that will be incurred in the early part of the assignment. Further requests which then become interim payments can be requested against work to be done with the added benefit that payments already made will have been justified to the client.

THE ROLE OF FEES IN MARKETING

The problems and rewards of effective techniques for setting fees or devising fee structures as a vital part of the total practice development plan have been treated only superficially. It is more an introduction to the subject than a detailed explanation of its mechanics. The purpose has been to ensure that the question of fees is not allowed to occupy a less important place and command less consideration within the practice development plan than its all pervasive impact on results justifies. All professional firms should examine their policies (or lack of policies) to ensure that methods of setting fees which have been used in the past are still relevant in today's conditions and will remain so in the foreseeable future.

Fee setting at the correct level is of considerable consequence both for the individual and for the survival of the firm. Fees are a weapon, or a tool, to obtain and retain clients as well as to ensure the profitable continuance of the firm. The two objectives are interrelated and lend themselves to a variety of strategies for their successful achievement. Those concerned with practice development, faced with increasing professionalism in marketing professional services, need an understanding of fee-setting techniques if they are to have any chance of success.

ACTION POINTS

- Check if costing system is appropriate, efficient and timely
- Choose the appropriate fee strategy and maintain it
- Make estimating mandatory where it is possible
- Explain billing policies to clients
- Set standards for rapid and clear billing

NOTES

(1)   Institute of Chartered Accountants, *Guide to Professional Ethics*, p.12, London (1988).

(2)   Reed, R.C. (ed) *Win–Win Billing Strategies*, American Bar Association, Chicago (1992). Although concentrated on the situation in the United States, this is perhaps the most thorough and useful book on fee setting and presentation available.

(3)   Ray, M.R. and Gupta, P.P. "Activity Based Costing", *Internal Auditor*, Altamonte Springs, USA (1992).

(4)   The methodology is explained in Wilson, A. *New Directions in Marketing*, Chapter 2, Kogan Page, London (1991).

(5)   Schlissel, M.R. and Chasin, J. "Pricing of Services", *The Service Industries Journal*, Cass, London, July (1991).

(6) Lord Chancellor's Department, *Contingency Fees*, Cm 571, HMSO, London (1989).

(7) Useful tactics, although product related, for negotiating profitable fees (prices) will be found in Winkler, J. *Winning Sales and Marketing Tactics*, part 3, Heinemann, London (1989).

(8) LAS Inquiry Report, South West Regional Health Authority, Communications Director, London (1993).

(9) *Official Journal of the European Communities*, No.C52/2, CEC, Brussels (1989).

(10) Institute of Chartered Accountants, *Membership Handbook*, p.49, London (1991).

(11) The diagram is reproduced in Wilson, A. *Practice Development for Professional Firms*, p.24, McGraw-Hill, Maidenhead (1984).

23
Lost Business Analysis: a Tool for Retaining Clients

The cheerful interrogative, "what did we do right?", is far more frequently invoked than the condemnatory, "what did we do wrong?" Yet within the answers to the latter rests all the material that is needed to improve performance on a consistent basis. Inquests, provided they are not destructive, can yield highly accurate guidance on correcting a situation, on withdrawing from a particular sector of the market or providing a particular service.

It should be mandatory that, where a practice either loses a client or a bid, they should be asked to give the reasons but not to provide material for an argument to dispute the decision. It must be made clear in seeking this information from a client or prospect that the firm is neither attacking the decision, seeking to reverse it nor will the information be used to "punish" the individual or the failed team. If a lost bid is to be investigated properly there has to be an assurance that any information sought be kept confidential and sometimes non-attributable.

In any event it will be obvious from the explanation of internal supply chain in Chapter 18, pages 191 to 192 that failure at point of delivery of the proposal, tender or presentation may well stem from failures higher up the supply chain.

The second danger to watch for is that all embracing explanation for rejection—fee level. While this may indeed be the reason, it is as often as not used as an excuse since a bid which is said to be non-competitive on financial grounds does not need any supporting reason for rejection.

Although little evidence is advanced to confirm the figures already quoted, there is little doubt the order of magnitude is right when it is stated that research has shown that a dissatisfied client will tell four or five other people, while a satisfied client is only likely to tell one or two. The arithmetic clearly indicates the need to keep dissatisfied clients to a minimum. If to this formula is added another unverifiable one which empirically feels correct—it costs five to seven times as much to obtain a client than to keep one—the case of investigating the cause of lost business is overwhelming. The practice must, of course, be prepared to do something about the situation. Again information must not just be interesting, it must be usable.

It is, perhaps, significant that none of the major works on marketing, product or service, contain any substantial comments on the use of lost business and customer complaint analysis (not the handling of complaints which is a different issue) as providing important, sometimes critically important, information input in devising marketing strategy and tactics. Obvious as it may sound, the very first step is to ensure that a client is indeed lost. Not all clients have an ongoing need for services and may return to the firm after many years' gap.

For most private clients it is not a regular occurrence to purchase a new residence so that their need for an architect, surveyor or solicitor may occur only at long intervals. An accountancy practice will know quickly enough if it has lost an audit client, but may not know if it has lost a private client who has sought advice on a specific tax situation. Where a practitioner provides a regular service—doctors' and dentists' regular check ups, vets' annual injections—it is easy to ascertain if a patient or owner has been lost. However, where services are used for one-off or sporadic purposes, their loss cannot be known nor indeed is it likely to be noticed unless a system exists for tracing old clients.

The problem again arises of how much marketing resource can be devoted to establishing who are lost and who are dormant clients. If the client has been important or has the potential to be important then obviously any loss of contact should be investigated. In short, if a client's business is worth having it's worth monitoring.

Lost business falls into three categories:

- Clients who will not return to the firm for whatever reason
- Quotations or offers which have been made but rejected
- Failure to be invited to tender or quote

Each circumstance requires careful analysis.

LOST CLIENTS

There are numerous reasons why a client ceases to use a professional service. Many will be obvious but others can be difficult to identify. Some will, of course, not require investigation and cannot be changed by anything the service organisation does. Failure of a business client, alteration in client activities which removes the need for the service, a physical move to an area where the firm cannot service the client, death or retirement are all obvious ones. Aside from the definitive nature of this last cause, it would be a sheer waste of time and money to try and retrieve any of these clients.

All reasons of a non-immutable nature can and should be probed. Useful as they are, lost business analyses are difficult to achieve because everyone is defensive and even objective observers may be reluctant to comment critically on their superiors, peers and subordinates. It can only be done by persuading the clients to give the substantive reason and, where a fee is quoted as the reason, to probe behind the answer.

That the fee level is of very great importance is not disputed but it is by no means the dominant issue in a decision to appoint a practice. Clients buy more than the fee as Chapter 10 will have shown. The package of benefits will include security, peace of mind, problem solutions, risk reduction, assumption of responsibility and many other aspects which will all be traded off against the fee level.

One of the most obvious sources of lost business is the client's perception that the specified service has not been received—in other words expectations have not been met. Whether the perception stems from an unrealistic expectation or from a real failure is of no consequence. If expectations were higher than the situation justified, the firm has only itself to blame for allowing them to move out of line with reality. Thus the fault may rest not in the service itself but in the way it was presented to the client.

Where there has been real failure, such as a mistake in design, calculation, interpretation, timing or the myriad other things that can go wrong in any advisory situation, then it is not difficult to decide what steps to take to rectify the position, assuming it can be rectified. Services are the most unforgiving sector of the whole economy and a failed service provider, whether restaurateur or researcher, will have the greatest difficulty in turning the situation round if the error is perceived as having a pervasive effect on the objectives of the assignment. That is not to say that the attempt should not be made. Given the potency of the interpersonal network then, at the very least, the client should feel that all that could possibly be done was done and as graciously as possible in the attempt to rectify the situation. It is worth noting, however, in this context that making fee refunds, while it may be necessary, rarely satisfies the client as much as an obvious effort to make good the error or damage.

Increasingly, organisations are adopting vendor evaluation techniques and this does provide a framework for checking out performance against the issues on which professional service suppliers are evaluated. Clients who adopt a vendor rating system are far more likely to be open about the reasons for changing or choosing a supplier than those who do not.

A typical vendor rating list might comprise:

- Relevant experience
- Qualifications
- Understanding of the client firm and its business
- Understanding of the specific problem
- Reliability and commitment
- Capability
- Schedule
- Flexibility
- Asset base
- Quality (see Chapter 17 for a checklist)

Within such a framework, to which must always be added the chemistry between the practice personnel and the client's personnel, it is possible to narrow down the cause of loss.

FAILED QUOTATIONS

The one certain factor which emerges from a failed quotation is that the practice is certainly "visible" to the potential client although, of course, there may well be misunderstanding of what the practice is and does. This factor does at least eliminate one cause of failure.

Potential clients, as opposed to actual clients, are usually less constrained in giving reasons for not awarding a contract since there is no need for actual or implied criticism of past performance or fee. Thus, there is less apparent blame or criticism of individuals.

One of the major reasons for a failed quotation is a failure to understand the problem. A proposal or offer will invariably contain the methods it is proposed to adopt to resolve it. Obviously solving a problem a client does not think they have is not likely to be crowned with success. Table 9.1, page 80, shows clearly where such a situation can arise. Even if the firm has identified the substantive problem but the client does not agree, then failure is certain. If the practice cannot convince the client as to the real problem then it is better to withdraw from the offer completely because, even if the assignment is completed successfully, if the client continues to believe the wrong problem has been solved there will remain an area of dissatisfaction.

If it is the intention not to deal with the stated problem or to undertake the assignment in a way not specified then the practice should seek permission to enter non-compliant or parallel bids (see page 257 in the previous chapter). Except in the most bureaucratic of organisations or where the call for bids is made by low level personnel without authority, most organisations will be willing, if only out of curiosity, to accept a non-compliant bid. Making one without prior agreement is however a certain path to rejection.

The image and perceptions of the firm and its members are fairly common reasons for failure. One firm of surveyors, with an enviable track record of being highly effective in their rating and valuation work, nevertheless developed an image of arrogance and inflexibility in insisting that they knew best. Indeed they did but the poor presentation and lack of interpersonal skills created an unsatisfactory image.

Another reason for losing assignments is not complying with the submission requirements: timing; correct number of copies of the offer documents; insufficient information; terms of business; inappropriate team or team qualifications; lack of track record. These can eliminate a firm at the early stages but, having passed through the barriers, there remains, and this is a strongly intensifying trend, the personal presentation of the proposal and the team or the much feared "beauty parade".

In the past, such presentations were rarely used by the professions, outside architecture and some aspects of design. They are now commonplace in accountancy, increasingly used in law, various branches of consulting, some types of financial services, and in personnel recruitment, outplacement and training. All too frequently an excellent offer is made which, because of poor presentation techniques and materials, is lost. As is obvious from the many comments elsewhere in this book, in professional services the individuals are as much what the client purchases as the firm.

Presentation skills should be a vital part of all training programmes for everyone who is likely to be called upon to undertake such a task. There may well be natural presenters but, for the less-gifted majority, training and rehearsal are the key words. Chapter 24 contains important checklists for presentations.

NON-INVITATIONS TO QUOTE

Substantially there are only three reasons why a practice is not invited to quote for an assignment. These are that the practice is not known or that is not considered suitable or is less suitable than those who are invited.

The problem of "visibility" was illustrated in Figure 10.1. It is one of only three absolutes in marketing to state that nothing can happen until a firm is known. If there was awareness that invitations to tender had been issued, and the practice was not invited because it was thought they were not known to the potential client, then future marketing messages and activity are obvious. However, it is important to distinguish between not being known and not being known for the particular service required. Either way there is a communication task.

It is also necessary to make a distinction between total invisibility and partial invisibility. This is the difference between being known or of being recalled immediately as being providers of a particular service or experts in a particular discipline and achieving that awareness after a reminder. In marketing jargon, this is the difference between unaided and prompted recall. There is a clear association between some goods and some services and with their suppliers or brands; earthmoving equipment and JCB or "Cat", IBM with computers, wood preservation services with Rentokil. In the professions the names of top accountancy, law and surveying firms come easily to mind. The ideal situation is one in which, when an appointment is being considered, the name of the practice will at least be on the table. This is instant unaided recall. However, at the very least, if a search is made or others consulted and the name is offered there should be recognition by those involved in the decision whom to invite to quote.

The second circumstance is where a firm is incorrectly thought to be unsuitable for the engagement. This requires careful probing for the reasons to see just how valid they may be: asset base not large enough to support the project; geographical coverage inadequate; staff not sufficiently experienced; equipment not state-of-the-art; lack of appropriate back up. Where the assumptions are valid, the practice is then faced with the options of acquiring and promoting the particular attribute or ceasing to regard the purchasing company or individual as a prospective client. If, however, the assumptions are incorrect and the firm meets the criteria then the marketing message has to be changed to emphasise the appropriateness of the service and, as with all marketing messages, demonstrate benefits, and that the service can be delivered on time and in budget. The task is essentially one of realigning the perceptions of the prospective client.

USING THE INFORMATION

There is no point in undertaking detailed research into reasons for lost business or for not being invited to quote unless the firm is prepared to do something about the situation. In the first instance it is important to establish if the reasons for rejection are of a repetitive nature; that is, a high number of failures for a particular service, an inability to obtain or retain business by an individual or team or, indeed, fee level or terms of business. Whatever the reason the firm can always make a decision to change, augment or remove the apparent blockage to business. Needless to say, repetitive reasons for failure are quite the most easy to rectify.

A useful check, if the information can be obtained, is to study which competitors were invited to quote and which one won the assignment. This information will first indicate if the client was comparing like with like and, second, whether the decision actually followed the reason for rejection. If it was stated that the decision was based on the winning offer including a multi-disciplinary team but the assignment called for the specialist skills for one discipline it would be reasonable to deduce that the explanation was less a reason than excuse. Table 14.1, page 133, may provide a useful starting point for developing a competitive analysis.

One pervasive reason which is not often researched is a failure in communication. This can take many forms: failure to identify benefits; failure to convince which benefits will be yielded; failure to reach the correct person in the decision-making unit; mistiming of communications; and others. A study of the three dimensions in corporate decision making, that is the composition of the buying unit, the incremental steps towards a decision and the decision-forming factors,[1] will reveal that different influencers and decision makers are involved at different stages of the buying decision and are considering different factors. While total information on these three aspects is unlikely to be available, any information at all will make a contribution to ensuring on future occasions that information targets are reached at the right time and with the correct message.

Few professions can give absolute guarantees but another useful source of lost business analysis is to examine reasons for issuing credit notes or refunds. These might reveal a repetitive pattern. If clients' formal and informal complaints and criticisms are documented, this too will provide a dossier on performance related to the actual service, specific clients or groups of clients and individual practitioners.

MANAGING CLIENT DISSATISFACTIONS

It is unreal to concentrate, as the chapter has done up to now, on pursuing the reasons for lost clients or lost bids, and to ignore clients' dissatisfactions which do not lead to an attributable loss of business but could contribute to a later decision to change advisers, or which simply sour the relationship between the practice and the client. Chapter 17 has already warned that to assume lack of complaints implies satisfaction is dangerous to an extreme. An unhappy client has, in fact, four courses of action:

- Change suppliers or cease to use the service at all without complaining or expressing their dissatisfaction
- Expressing the dissatisfaction to others rather than the supplier (network)
- Complain directly
- Seek redress through other bodies (e.g. insurance or banking ombudsman, Solicitors Complaints Bureau, Consumers Association, Trading Standards Officers)

The problem of the unheard client who has not expressed his or her dissatisfaction is a very real one. Very often, and this is sometimes a national characteristic, clients prefer not to make any sort of fuss and simply withdraw their business. There is no chance of resolving any difficulty if it is not known or has not been expressed. This is an appropriate place to re-emphasise that issues which yield satisfaction are neither the same nor the mirror opposite of those that yield dissatisfaction, and that absence of complaints does not imply satisfaction. Practices should always conduct a post-project inquest with clients, not seeking compliments, but attempting to find out what gave the clients the greatest and the least satisfaction, whether the outcome met their expectations, how the service could be improved, how satisfactory was the attitude of all personnel with whom they had contact. The questionnaire in Appendix 5, page 50, and Appendix 17, page 184, will provide a substantial starting point for seeking any areas where the possibility of a hidden client dissatisfaction may occur.

The actions which stem from the first two situations listed above are, of course, related first to establishing that dissatisfaction exists and then taking steps to rectify it. It may seem to be deliberately looking for trouble to probe issues which could engender complaints or dissatisfactions and which the client was not overtly aware of, or did not consider of sufficient moment to be worth the effort of formally registering a complaint. Every practice needs to look at their complaints procedures, that is, just how easy or difficult it is for clients to initiate the procedures for redressing the problem. Client dissatisfactions can only be managed if they voice their complaints.

A well researched USA study[2] among bank customers showed that some 77% of the sample had criticisms of their banks, 28% had changed banks as a result of complaints and 38% had voiced their criticism to third parties. Whether the 23% who made no complaints had no reason for dissatisfaction, or whether they did not register their dissatisfaction, is not known but the results suggest there were some silent sufferers. To be meaningful the research did relate the numbers and direction of complaints to the intensity of the dissatisfaction. Clearly a dissatisfaction which was perceived as well founded and of considerable consequence is far more likely to trigger a client loss than one which is a mere irritant and would engender negative word of mouth comments.

A formal system for receiving complaints should be instituted and such a system should be on a fail-safe basis, that is, it must be so structured that no complaint or critical client comment can be overlooked or deliberately concealed. It is never possible to ensure that all client dissatisfactions are revealed but a client questionnaire similar to the one in Appendix 5 will quickly reveal any serious matters and will also enable a patterning to be perceived.

Another useful approach, if it is practical, is to ensure that clients have direct access to senior personnel, particularly partners, to whom complaints can be voiced directly. It is usual in both business and government to exhaust the "usual channels" before taking a complaint to a higher authority. Eschewing such bureaucratic conventions provides the opportunity for a client-centred firm to demonstrate concern and the realities of their client-care programmes by making access to a senior person the preferred route. In the Xerox Corporation top executives spend a mandatory one day a month dealing with customer complaints. The magnitude of this effort is not replicated in the professions but the principle has much to commend it. A "hot line" approach, most particularly if it is a direct contact with personnel with sufficient authority to order investigation, rectification or compensation, is another practical and usually appreciated approach.

A few American financial institutions have taken the issue so seriously they have established client recovery units charged with the task of identifying lost clients, rectifying the cause of their defection and then persuading them to return to the firm. They are also concerned in identifying clients who are unhappy and therefore likely to change suppliers and to recoup this situation.[3]

Complaint handling can make or break a practice with a particular client. The indefensible should not be defended but obviously where there is room for doubt in the apportioning of blame a reasoned but non-threatening defence can and should be mounted. It is true you can never win an argument with a client but the purpose of complaint resolution must be to reach a solution that is acceptable to both sides. However, if the client is to be retained, no matter how punitive the service firm may think the resolution of the problem, it should be accepted with grace and the required actions undertaken promptly, efficiently and without rancour.

While achieving agreement on removing client dissatisfaction may not always be easy, just as in any form of dispute resolution or negotiation, there are skills involved as well as empathy. By offering options which lead to mutual benefits a satisfactory solution is most likely to be found. In addition it is always advisable to separate people from problems and deal with both without intertwining them.

The only measure of success in the use of lost business information for marketing is whether losses diminish and, as important, if clients who have had reason to be dissatisfied are retained. Both manifestations of success will indicate with great clarity if the effort of studying lost business pays off.

ACTION POINTS

- Differentiate between lost and inactive clients
- Compile a list of lost clients, lost quotations and non-invitations to quote and analyse for any repetitive reason for losses and adjust policy or approach accordingly (the profiling technique described in Chapter 11 can also be applied for this purpose)
- Check where clients have vendor rating systems and compare the firm or the offers with the rating factors
- Devise a system to ensure all complaints are identified and resolved
- Offer clients direct contact to senior personnel

NOTES

(1) For a full description of the buying process and the decision making matrix, see Wilson, A. *Practice Development for Professional Firms,* Chapter 8 and, in particular, Figures 8–10, McGraw-Hill, Maidenhead (1984).
(2) Singh, J. and Pandya, S. "Exploring the Effects of Consumers' Dissatisfaction Level on Complaint Behaviour", *European Journal of Marketing,* MCB University Press, Bradford, Vol. 25, No.9 (1991).
(3) Reichheld, F.F. "Loyalty-based management systems" *Harvard Business Review,* Cambridge, Mass., March/April (1993).

24
Interpersonal Skills

The most important single method of developing a practice is through personal contact. The decisions on the use of a service or a particular practice are made substantially on the basis of the client's reaction to the practitioner and his or her support personnel, perhaps combined with the source and strength of any recommendation. Because, without exception, the professions are people not machine based no matter how far the mechanisation of services may go, people will always be involved in their provision. The manufacturers for the most part have little direct contact with the ultimate users of their products, whereas professional services always involve the client and indeed the prospective client in their production. This presents opportunities, not available to anything like the same extent to the manufacturers of goods, to develop and strengthen loyalties through the use of personal contacts which are necessarily part of the production of the service itself.

It is rare for a professional practice to be appointed without some personal contact occurring between the practitioners and the potential client. In a sense the whole thrust of marketing in professional services is to identify potential clients and open the way for a meeting. It is only from such an encounter any engagement will occur. In Chapter 9 it was shown that the path to a favourable decision consists of reaching an agreement with the potential client on five issues. They are:

- A need (or want) exists
- The service will meet the need

- The firm is believed to be capable of delivering the service as specified
- The fee (or anticipation of the fee) is acceptable
- The work can be completed on a time scale that fits the clients requirements

Examples were given demonstrating that, for many products, the decision on all five issues is virtually instantaneous. There is not, for example, a great deal of consideration on whether to buy a newspaper, take a taxi or fill a car tank with petrol. In contradistinction what are termed "big ticket items" in the consumer goods field—purchases which are financially significant—are subject to examination at each stage. The purchase of a house, a car or a holiday will undergo consideration at every level and this is equally true for professional services of all types. Taking a prospective client through the five stages is facilitated by a number of marketing tools, but a final decision will be an amalgam of many things dominant among which will be the empathy the prospective client develops for the firm and its representatives.

Personal contact is, for professional services, the most important single marketing technique, but it is also the most expensive since, in the majority of professions, it involves the allocation of billable time to non-billable activities. Thus, the use of personal contact has to be carefully targeted and only adopted where no other cost-effective tool can achieve the same results. Personal contact has clear advantages over many other techniques.

Personal contact	Other marketing tools
Total flexibility—the message can be tailored precisely to the client's needs and their level of technical and commercial sophistication	Messages are difficult to adjust once set (advertising, brochures, direct mail etc)
Comprehensive—complexities can be communicated and explained	Number of 'appeals' limited to two or three (media advertising, direct mail, posters, etc)
Attention getting—personal contact maintains a high level of attention	Impersonal, one way communication difficult to disassociate from general background clutter (Media advertising, PR, brochures etc)

ROLES

To ensure personal contact is used most effectively there has to be an appreciation that its purpose is to obtain and retain clients. The presenter of the service has five distinct roles:

- *Information provider*—helping clients to make good decisions
- *Consultant*—offering objective advice
- *Problem solving*—assisting clients to define the substantive problem
- *Professional partner*—creating long term mutually profitable alliances
- *Negotiator*—obtaining the best deal for both parties

To be an *information provider* the practitioner must possess the information *and* to be able to communicate it. This means it has to be given at a level that is compatible with the level of knowledge of the listener. This obviously affects the form and content of the presentation. The less familiar the listener is with the subject matter, the greater the uncertainty he or she will experience although not necessarily exhibit.

The *consultant's role* is one of offering advice but this cannot be done unless there is some knowledge of the client's business, reasons for seeking the service, objectives and the ideal outcome. In the case of private clients then, information is needed on their personal circumstances. Depending on the service sought this could mean, for example, medical, financial, domestic, occupational situations. To obtain this information the practice representative in the consultant's role must be capable of asking relevant questions and, above all, to be skilled in listening.

As has been shown earlier, not all clients are willing or capable of expressing their needs or explaining their situation. To overcome this reluctance the consultant has to offer reassurance and build confidence. The strange dichotomy exists that, while many users of problem solving services like to feel their problem is unique, they equally want re-assurance that their anxieties are not. The potential user of the service, whether he or she is a personal inquirer or a corporate one, has to be reassured that their anxieties are experienced by others and that they are not without foundation. If clients can be encouraged to verbalise their uncertainties it makes a powerful contribution to the consultancy element in the interpersonal relationship. Knowledge of the client permits the service representative in the consultant's role to offer sensible and objective advice.

The *problem solving role* is obvious enough. Clients do not necessarily have an accurate conception of the problem on which they are consulting. This has been touched on in Chapter 5 and dealt with at greater length in Chapter 9. To understand client problems the dual task is to ask the right questions and to listen to the answers. Problem solving, as with the consulting element, calls for active listening, without interruption except to encourage further information, questioning, to fill gaps in the account and background and to remove any ambiguities, summing up, to obtain client agreement, offering a plan of action and explaining the follow up.

The *professional partner role*. Professional partnerships only exist when the client perceives the practitioner not just as an external resource but, for the private client, as an extension of his or her own network or, for the corporate client, as part of the internal team. To achieve this, there has to be a demonstration by the professional of knowledge of the client's personal position or operations, opportunities and threats. Appendix 7 gave a format for client information. These data can make an important contribution in any client meeting but most will be of a general nature. What is now needed is a checklist which enables a practice representative to be specific about the issues to be discussed. The checklist below provides such a list but is intended only as a basis to be individualised to fit each profession, subject and client.

The *negotiator's role* is one in which professionals seek to obtain a result which is most satisfying to their clients or, at worst, least dissatisfying. Whether it is a lawyer plea bargaining, an accountant disputing a tax assessment, an architect seeking planning permission or any other discipline in which agreement must be reached between a client and other parties, the professional has to be able to offer and exercise skills in negotiation. This will be perceived as an important part of any service which provides advice.

A major problem every professional practice faces is the reluctance of its personnel to become involved in anything which they perceive as "selling" and which they regard as something between

PREPARATION CHECKLIST FOR A CLIENT BRIEFING

1.0 Client's Profile

Enquirer
Recipient
Decision Maker
- position in company
- professional qualifications
- compatibility with our contact
  – conservative
  – cautious
  – progressive
  – adventurous

Contact Requirements
- languages
- social
- educational
- experience

2.0 Client Company/Firm

small ⎫
medium ⎬ company/firm
large ⎭

2.1 Importance
- in market (sector)
- technological
- in industry/field of operation
- financial status (risk spectrum)

2.2 Company Known to us
- previous enquiries/proposals
- previous assignments

2.3 New Company
- potential for future assignments
- our knowledge of company/firm

3.0 Client's Brief

3.1 Briefing Method
- verbal/personal
- telephone
- letter/fax
- telex
- formal brief

3.2 Briefing Details
- background
  – complete
  – requiring further research by us
  – requiring revision
  – objectives
  – well defined
  – generalised
  – vague

3.3 Timing
- proposal/presentation
  – critical
  – strict
  – flexible

3.4 Briefing Discussions/Queries:
- verbal-telephone
- meeting at client
- meeting at our office

continues

4.0 Merits of Assignment to us
4.1 General Merits
- value of assignment
- acquisition of new client
- first project of the type for an existing client

4.2 "Added Value" Merits for us
- knowledge
- experience
- market
- products
- problems
- techniques
- image

} new "enhanced"
  pioneering

4.3 Future Potential Assessment
- same client
- other clients (Home/abroad)

4.4 Our Prestige
- compatibility with image objective

5.0 Our Previous Experience
5.1 Check Relevance of
- subject/substance
- industry/industry sector
- market/market structure
- substantive problem

5.2 Check Changes Since Date of Previous Experience of Assignment
- validity of data
  – time lapse
  – technology
  – state of art
  – legal/social/political situation
  –
- condition of market
  – dynamics
  – economics
  – politics

5.3 Check Confidentiality of our Data and Information

5.4 Define Changes and Modifications Required in Approach to Problems in Hand
- business methods
  – acceptability
  – climate of competition
  – general business morality

6.0 Background
Background – *Exposition*
Introduction – *Review*
Preface – *Discussion*
Market (market sector)
- overview
- characteristics
- recent developments
- influences
  – economic
  – political
  – other
- Industry (industry sector)
  – state of art
  – trends
  – client's position
  – competition
- Brief/briefing synopsis

7.0 Objectives (Scope/Parameters)

7.1 Examine Validity of Objectives as Defined in Brief
- client's internal material
- our previous experience, data, information

7.2 Check Rationality of Client's Perception of
- market/market structure
- technological aspects
- project/matter/scope/parameters
- legal situation

7.3 Identify Options for Achieving Objectives with
- our effort requirements
- client's expected benefits
- optimum assignment yield
- budgetary restraints
- time restraints

7.4 Explore Alternative Objectives and Check
- compatibility with client's ultimate aim
- likelihood of acceptance by client
- influence on changes for securing assignment

7.5 Examine Practicality of
- re-discussion of brief
- pilot, trial, test-survey/investigation
- (Note client's internal conflicts [enquirer–decision maker], indecision, rivalry; related to method, scope; attitude to us and our competitors)

8.0 Method

8.1 Check Soundness of Method, its Elements and Programme in Relation to
- assignment activity category
- definition of objectives
- problem solving capacity
- client's capabilities
- business sector characteristics
- access to source of information
  —material
  —human
- need for preliminary investigation

8.2 Emphasise the Rationale of *What* the Method is, Avoid too explicit details of *How* it is conducted

8.3 Avoid use of Over-sophisticated Techniques for Solving Simple Problems

9.0 Assignment Yield (Written Report Outline)

9.1 Introduction
- justification of method used
- achievement of objectives
- (proof of our competence)

9.2 Conclusions, Recommendations
- essential — enabling ⎫ aims of assignment
- subsidiary — assisting ⎬ solution of problem
- marginal ⎭

9.3 Suggestions for Further Activity

9.4 Offer of Assistance in Implementation

mendicancy and mendacity. If the five roles which comprise interpersonal skills are understood it is much easier to achieve the appropriate degree of motivation.

When the primary emphasis of the service organisation is on coming to grips with a problem, it attempts to show its capability by concentrating on the five roles and obtaining an understanding of the problem in depth. This generates both confidence and interest of the client to have further discussions. The service firm can then offer a first appraisal of the client situation with a verbal presentation or with detailed memorandum or project designs which reinforce initial confidence.

PERSUASION METHODS

These five roles represent the ideal position, but they can only be adopted if the client is willing to provide the information required. Too often, at the outset of an inquiry, the client merely asks the firm to present itself and what it can do for the inquirer without stating what is wanted. If it is not possible to persuade the potential client to provide the information, then the practitioner has no alternative but to adopt an *extrinsic* approach which, in essence, is a generalised procedure for meeting the client need or problem. It concentrates heavily on the characteristics, resources and experience of the firm. Within this approach, three platforms can be used:

1 Persuading by emphasising the *firm's attributes*. For example, the availability of a full range or "one-stop" services or, in contradistinction, specialisations, niche or boutique offerings. Another attribute can be the extent of relevant experience of the issues involved, the geographical coverage the firm can offer or the methods which are used to resolve problems.

2 Persuasion by *personal attributes*. This refers to offering the benefits which may be yielded by the reputation of individuals within the firm or by their qualifications which are perceived of value to the prospective client.

3 Persuasion by *track record*. There is little doubt that in most (but not all) circumstances an excellent track record in the problem area, industry or technique is very persuasive as indeed is the

client list. However, resting on success stories or clients does have its downside. Clients can be cynical and doubt the extent of success or perhaps feel success was due more to luck than intention. Similarly a list of "blue chip" clients can easily deter a smaller firm while a list of small clients is largely meaningless.

The presenter of the service must try to work towards a position where the client will provide the necessary information which will enable a fully *intrinsic* presentation to be made. To achieve this they must be prepared to respond to the potential client's request for information on the practice and the service but by judicious questioning seek to obtain information on the problem to be solved and finally to relate the firm's skills, resources and experience to it.

MAKING CONTACT

The activity which most practitioners find most difficult is that of opening up the contact to obtain a meeting. "Cold calling" is both intensely disliked and offends just about every professional instinct and culture and, in some disciplines, practice rules too. Indeed, even professional salesmen do not like cold calling so there is every reason to sympathise with the attitude of those whose major task and skills are not selling when they react against any such approach.

There are, however, a number of methods that can be adopted which avoid any suggestion of solicitation or intrusiveness. If the practitioner keeps in mind that the prospective client must see a benefit in devoting any time to a meeting then the message is obvious. The issue is what benefits would such a meeting deliver:

- Offering a new service or new approach for an established service
- Referring to a specific problem it is known the potential client may be experiencing or is likely to experience and indicating that the firm may have an approach to solve it
- The ability to deliver a major benefit which is not available from competitors

- By referring to successful work undertaken for others in the same business or geographical area
- By seeking the answer to a question related to a potential client's field of activity which links with the firm's services
- By mailing an article, containing technical or other material, likely to be of relevance to the client stating that they will be called at a later date to see if the material merits a meeting to discuss it (in this context, the information does not have to be generated by the practice but can be a news item from any source)

This list only summarises the approaches which can be used to make cold calling less unacceptable and to make meeting non-clients a more comfortable process for the professionals than would otherwise be the case.[1]

As can be seen, the approaches suggested are a mix of both the extrinsic and intrinsic. By using the interview to elicit information from the prospective client it is possible to move on to a substantially intrinsic approach.

THE INTERVIEW

All meetings that have a business objective irrespective of the issues or personalities involved and should follow well-defined rules. They must be undertaken with a sense of their functional unity, they must have definite objectives, be well organised, and the results lend themselves to accurate interpretation and the application of judgement. The skills of interviewing clients must include all these things.

In any interaction where there is a wide knowledge gap there is inevitably the risk of paternalism or patronisation. Given the nature of all professional training and perhaps the personality of those who practise a profession, the temptation to regard the client as intellectually inferior is considerable and resisted only weakly. The first interview between professional and client is the critical point and, if the practitioner is retained, it is also the foundation for the ongoing relationship.

As inappropriate as it may seem, the ways of developing an empathy between the professional and the would-be private client are very close to those of the salesman and buyer. The skills needed to develop good interpersonal relationships are not difficult to acquire; the motivation to do so and the personality changes required are far greater and more difficult obstacles to surmount.

For the interview itself there are four stages which should be followed:

1 *Social.* Meeting and greeting. This is the first "gate". Where it occurs on the premises of the practice, it goes from the general tone and attentiveness of the receptionist and should or could include being met by the practitioner or the practitioner's secretary or assistant to be taken to the room where the meeting is to take place. Certainly standing to meet a visitor is maybe an old-fashioned courtesy but it never goes amiss. Taking coats, seating, offer of refreshment all are relaxants at a time when the reduction of tension and uncertainty is an important contributor to what follows.

The proficient practice developer must be capable of quickly creating a friendly atmosphere. The best atmosphere can be described as "cordial" since over-emphasis rapidly produces a reaction in the prospective client and being too friendly can be almost as disastrous as being aggressive. An atmosphere cordial to one respondent may be regarded as over-familiar by another and formal by the third. Thus, part of the skills involved in the opening gambits of an interview are to decide just what level of "friendliness" will achieve the correct effect. "First name terms in five minutes" may be suitable for some clients but may not be regarded as acceptable with older individuals.

If the meeting with the prospective client has occurred through an introduction it is useful and helpful to talk for a few minutes about the mutual acquaintance or to find any other common ground from the weather to a news item. (It is better for obvious reasons to avoid controversial issues.) Common ground makes a great contribution to reducing any stress the potential client and indeed even the practitioner may be feeling.

2 *Listening.* The substantive conversation has to be initiated by the client. Until the problem or reason for the contact is known, the meeting cannot be progressed. This stage of the discussion is characterised by the client describing and explaining the

situation or issue. The practitioner is listening and probably note taking. Either way, both by action and body language, he or she must demonstrate they are concentrating on the client to the exclusion of all else. "His listening is the equal to other men's advocacy" was the praise of Dr Johnson and sets a standard to be sought.

3 *Questioning*. Here the interplay between practitioner and client begins. Details, clarification, objectives, extent of commitment and other issues are fully explored. The way in which the questions are asked can have a significant effect on the client. Staccato questions phrased in different ways, qualified and at the same time indicating the questioner's views are difficult to follow, difficult to answer and increase the sense of uncertainty. Questioning should confine itself to single subjects at a time and the client given time to consider and answer. Silence, however, needs careful manipulation. It can be threatening.

4 *Responding, advising* or *counselling*. Here the practitioner may well be setting out a course of action to be considered and its implications. Possibly a plan might be suggested or an *interregnum* while the practitioner makes further inquiries, undertakes research, consults or considers the next steps. A suggested checklist for a first interview has been devised and it will be found to be applicable in most private client/practitioner situations,[2] even though it was designed for lawyers.

The sequence of any face-to-face meeting in which an engagement is sought is a logical series of steps. They presuppose the practitioner is listening actively throughout to what the client is saying and is not saying:

1 Locate the real needs of the clients or potential clients.
2 For corporate clients identify who the powerful decision makers are, but do not forget that there are always influential people who do not actually make decisions (see Chapter 14, page 137).
3 Gain attention by asking questions.
4 Arouse interest—the client's problems or needs are central.
5 Present the benefits.
6 Note and observe their reaction and objections.

7   Welcome objections, this shows real interest.
8   Overcome the objections.
9   Ask for the decision.

FIRST INTERVIEW CHECKLIST			
Listening	1	Greet, seat and introduce.	Note taking
	2	Elicit story with opening question etc.	
	3	Listen carefully to basic outline of personalities and case from client's own unhindered words.	
Questioning	4	Question on facts for gaps, depth, background, ambiguities and relevance.	
	5	Sum up and recount lawyer's view of facts, *and* check for client's agreement or amend.	
Advising	6	State advice and/or plan of action and deal with question of funds.	
	7	Repeat advice/plan of action *and* check for client's agreement or amend.	
	8	Recount follow-up work to be done by client.	
	9	Recount follow-up work to be done by lawyer.	
	10	State next contact between lawyer and client.	
	11	Ask if "Any Other Business" and deal with it.	
	12	Terminate, help out and goodbye.	

OBJECTIONS

There are many types of objections, but they can be grouped into four main categories: "sincere", "hidden", "insincere" and "unnecessary". Only the face-to-face meeting gives a real opportunity to recognise and understand these and overcome them. The sincere objection is a buying signal if it can be met. The hidden objection is usually caused because the respondent is not the decision maker but will not admit it. The insincere objection is the "brush off" using an excuse to terminate the meeting, and the unnecessary objection is frequently caused by offering benefits that are not in reality benefits at all. Sincere objections should be welcomed and encouraged. They are only raised about issues which concern the decision maker. They thus reveal his or her true interests.

To apply the most effective technique for overcoming objections, there must be an understanding of what type of objection it is. Once this is assessed the procedure is simple and, like most other aspects of interpersonal skills, the first requirement is to listen. It is unwise to interrupt and advisable to hear the whole objection through. Apart from showing a courtesy in appreciating the other's point of view, it also encourages the decision maker to listen to the complete answer. Once an objection is met it is bad practice to return to it later in the meeting. Offering apparent agreement does not limit a negotiating position. Such agreement relaxes the buyer, and from this basis it is possible to use the counter arguments effectively. It is essential that, whatever the objection may be, it must be recognised. The objection has been raised to test the reaction of the person making the offer. If the objection is ignored or glossed over the purchaser will be both wary and disappointed.

THE CLOSE

A successful face-to-face meeting is closed with a favourable decision. Again, methods of closing are well tried and successful:

1 *Trial close.* It is never too early to close: "Can we fix up a briefing meeting for next week?"
2 *Alternative.* "Would you like to have the briefing meeting next week or the week after?"
3 *Summary.* Reassurance by track record: "Our partners have been deeply involved in management buy-outs for many years". Where information is public knowledge or can be revealed, client names are very helpful.
4 *Concession.* Adding to or conceding some additional benefit: "A contract placed now will enable us to amortise out-of-pocket expenses by combining the work with another non-competitive project which is currently being undertaken".

5 *Fear.* This is not recommended, even if genuine, if it can be avoided. "If we are to act for you, we will need a quick decision because there is a strong possibility of being retained by another potential client which would create a conflict of interest".

6 *Possession.* Talk as though the favourable decision has already been made. "When we meet to discuss the approach...".

7 *Ask for the instruction.* Do not be reluctant or hesitant.

No contract can be obtained unless a deal is closed. The practice representative should give as much attention and care to the closing stages of a meeting as to all other aspects of interpersonal contacts.

SMALL TEAMS

There is a distinct trend among professional service firms to create small teams for marketing and for presentations. There are many advantages in doing this. It encourages a high degree of focus in marketing. By the pooling of non-billable time budgeted it creates a practical aggregation of financial resources for marketing. As in many other aspects of professional practice, peer pressure is an excellent motivator for action on time and within budget. Within a team, each member can concentrate to maximum effect on their existing skills. If the team is correctly balanced, any deficiencies will be made good by other members of the team. A marketing team provides the opportunity for encouragement, mentoring and skill transfer while at the same time, properly managed, internal competition provides a strong motivation to succeed. Small teams, by avoiding a feeling of isolation, encourages the broadest participation from all parts of the firm and from all levels of seniority. In creating teams, it has already been inferred that balance is necessary. However, while there should be a mix of skills and interests, there has to be a commonality of interest.

Where individuals coalesce naturally because of common interests, they are most effective. Usually, however, there will have to be a team leader or facilitator in order to bring the individuals together. Teams, while stable, should not be permanent. The advantage of changes, which include the introduction of new ideas, skills, dynamics and critical reviews of past activities, certainly offsets the learning curve loss caused by movement of personnel.

Planning activities to be undertaken is important if the team is to be effective and all the rules of planning as set out in Chapter 27 have to be followed, that is: a resource check; identification of problems and opportunities; clear and preferably quantified objectives; a strategy and tactics for achieving the objectives; monitoring; and control systems. In short a concrete plan, time and money budgeted must be created rather than a "wish" list. The team leader must secure contracts for action. Peer groups to review plans and projects are a useful adjunct. All plans must of course fit into the overall corporate plan and other teams' plans.

PITCHING FOR BUSINESS

One other aspect of the application of interpersonal skills requires comment—the much disliked "beauty parade" or pitching for business. This is where the prospective client invites a number of competitive practices to present their services, usually to a selection committee. Although the request is, in a real sense, an invitation to adopt an extrinsic approach, it must be resisted. No presentation should be attended unless the client has been carefully researched first. Even if it is not possible to uncover confidential information, a great deal can be gleaned which will enable a focused presentation to be made concentrating on the client not the practice.

The guidelines for successful presentation can be described, but obviously different circumstances may require different approaches. Some considerations will, however, be common to all submissions and high among these will be to obtain an understanding of what the meeting is about, that is, the client's objectives and the presenter's objectives. Next is the need for as much information on the client or prospective client's situation as possible. The checklist on pages 282–4 provides a list of the topics which, under most circumstances, should be considered and researched.

A salient decision is: Who will represent the practice? Chemistry and skill in equal proportions are needed. It is also important that there should be agreement about who speaks on what subjects and when and that any possible areas of disagreement between the presenters is resolved before the meeting, not during it. Date and time must be confirmed as well as how long has been allocated for the presentation. Here it is worth remarking that it is not uncommon, when meetings run late, for some practice representatives to be asked to shorten their presentation. This must be resisted politely but firmly. A 45-minute submission reduced to 30 minutes at short notice is most likely to fail. Information should be sought and given concerning room layout, numbers attending on the client side and equipment required such as flip charts, computer, slide or overhead projectors and video. While it is not possible to demand that the client uses badges or place cards, the presenters can do so, so that the clients know who is speaking. It is, however, a valuable contribution in creating the right ambience to note the names of everyone present at the outset and their position in the room and to address them by name where possible.

There is much to be learned from a successful as well as an unsuccessful presentation, just as there is from lost clients (Chapter 23). The following checklists can be used as a framework for a creative inquest on any presentation:

- What new information was obtained on the clients and their business needs?
- Were the right subjects addressed? Was too much or too little material covered?
- Did the right practice representatives attend?
- Did we succeed in addressing the client's concerns about our services?
- Was the setting appropriate? Too formal or casual?
- Were we over- or under-represented?
- How could the presentations be improved?
- Who should do the follow up, and what should be done?
- How do we develop better relations with the client?
- Do you think the firm will receive work from this client? If not, why not?

CONTACT REPORTS

Perhaps because practice representatives who have client contact do not want to see themselves in a sales role there is a reluctance to report on meetings. This is in contradistinction to the enthusiasm with which most professional firms carefully note subject and time spent on fee-paying consultation including telephone calls and letters. For most products and commercial services salespersons, contact reports are mandatory. The time spent in completing them is more than justified in the great value which can be placed on the reports in terms of client knowledge and actions to be taken. All meetings with prospective clients, and that term includes new business from existing clients, ought to be appropriately logged to provide key information.

There is little virtue in suggesting a detailed reporting format since each discipline, each firm and each practitioner's needs will vary. It is, however, useful to suggest the types of information for consideration. A simple contact reporting form can be developed by using relevant items in Appendix 7 combined with relevant items in the checklist on pages 282–4. But in addition to those items included there should also be an entry giving date, duration of the meeting and who was present, the subject of the discussion, who else should see the report, the next action required by whom and when. The system should then ensure that the report is raised before the appropriate date for action and the persons involved warned.

Discipline in completing forms rapidly builds up a dossier on client contacts which ensures appropriate actions are taken and that information on the client is completely up-to-date. This has an especial value in direct mail most particularly if relationship and database marketing are being used or developed (see Chapter 5 and Chapter 26, pages 313–14).

Because practitioners do not like filling in forms of this type, they must be persuaded to do so. The greatest encouragement which can be given is to demonstrate just how the information is used and any benefits that have resulted because of what was provided. Apart from making this obvious to the person who obtained and recorded the information that led to positive beneficial actions, everyone else should be notified *pour encourager les autres*.

Of the many marketing tools available under conditions of de-regulation, the one most likely to yield the greatest rewards from its mastery is the development of interpersonal skills, which goes beyond building on those mythical qualities of empathy and ego drive so beloved by trainers. Interpersonal skills are more than charisma and are not endowed at birth. They must be learned.

ACTION POINTS

- Be certain everyone with client contact understands the roles they must adopt and see that they act accordingly
- Train and encourage all personnel to adopt an intrinsic approach in all personal contacts
- Encourage personnel to develop reasons (and client benefits) for agreeing a meeting
- Be sure the objectives (client and own) of every meeting is known in advance
- Listen creatively
- Train in objection handling
- Communicate and monitor best practice in presentation techniques
- Devise reporting format and encourage and monitor use

NOTES

(1) Although boisterous in style and related to goods rather than services, some practical ideas for "cold calling" will be found in Schiffman, S. *Cold Calling Techniques*, Kogan Page, London (1988).
(2) Sherr, A. *Client Interviewing for Lawyers*, p.21, Sweet and Maxwell, London (1986).

25

A Review of Some Practice Development Tools

Three factors have inhibited the imaginative use of the many marketing and communication techniques which can be adopted for practice development. The first is a widespread feeling among professionals that most forms of promotion are not suitable for the discipline they practise and, as such, they would clash with their self image and the culture of their professions. The second is that they either do not know about the techniques or if they do, do not understand them. Third, universally almost all marketing tools are regarded as too expensive.

It is, perhaps, as well to start this review by demolishing the barriers to the adoption of wholly suitable cost-effective techniques. Certainly if marketing is associated with hard selling and many types of consumer goods advertising, the techniques are not suitable. Cartoon figures with squeaky voices, provocative sexual images and expensive location settings are inappropriate. The message, however, does not rule out the technique and some firms have already discovered that the majority of the tools of marketing can be applied with skill and sophistication and are not brash and intrusive.

That practitioners should not know about particular marketing tools other than the most obvious ones and that they do not really understand those they do know about is, of course, easily explicable in terms of their training and past experience. There is, however, nothing magical in acquiring the appropriate knowledge and certainly it would require infinitely less time and application than was called for to achieve their professional recognition. The view that all marketing tools are too expensive to be appropriate for professional practices is totally incorrect. The vast majority of promotional tools can be adopted and adapted to bring them well within the budgetary constraints most firms have relative to their development. If media advertising is seen as full pages in the national press or 30-second slots in prime time television, then it is too expensive. But, as is shown later in this chapter, media advertising costs can easily be as low as three figures and still be effective.

PROMOTION: CRITICAL QUESTIONS

No matter what level of promotional activity is adopted and given that there are few accurate ways of measuring the effectiveness of any particular technique, it is important to use a system for at the very least assessing what has been accomplished, even if this cannot always or even usually be accomplished in the short run. In considering non-personal promotion, as with most other activities concerned with improving the practices' performance, the first stage is always to set out what it is intended to achieve. (These should be considered in conjunction with the communication guidelines set out in Chapter 10, pages 91–9.) The marketer must ask some critical questions:

- Which are the targets for this particular activity?
- What is the activity proposed?
- What is the purpose of the activity?
- What is the budget in time/money terms?
- Who will be responsible for its timely and satisfactory completion?
- What criteria will we use to assess the effectiveness of the actions?

The format used in Appendix 27B, page 367, can be easily adapted for the purpose of promotional planning. The column headings are obvious enough but, so far as "achievement" is concerned, different techniques will have different measures. If the objective was to prove a greater awareness among potential clients, research will reveal the extent to which this has succeeded.

For example, in a target group for a building surveyor of, say, estate agents as a referral source, research finds that the awareness level has risen from 42% to 58% following a promotional campaign, judgementally at least the campaign can be said to have had some success. If, however, the purpose was to obtain referrals and there was no evidence that the referral rate from estate agents had increased, the campaign, at that moment in time at least, had failed. With an objective that is to raise inquiries from the public for an in-store offer by opticians, a measure would be the number of people entering the premises or inquiring about the offer. If the purpose of the promotional activity was to improve sales of higher-priced spectacles then, over time, the "before and after" comparison can be made by internal analyses of stocks, sales, revenue and profitability. A damage limitation public relations campaign cannot be judged by whether sales were increased, only by whether it reduced or stopped the haemorrhaging of customers or irrevocable damage to the organisation's image.

However, in assessing results, it has to be accepted that the market place is not a laboratory. It is not possible to adjust one variable while all else remains unchanged to see the effect of the changes. Neither is it possible to either anticipate or control competitors' activities which could impact on the marketing effort. A campaign to promote immunisation services provided by a medical practice could alert potential patients to visit their own doctors for this purpose. The campaign "owners" would regard their efforts as a failure if the purpose was to market *their* immunisation services and it marketed those of competitors. But the greater danger is for the fortunate practice that obtained the new business to believe that it was their marketing which induced the demand. Both beliefs threaten the robustness of the assessment of effectiveness and accomplishment.

While a direct mail campaign can be evaluated within weeks, a brochure may not be capable of evaluation for effectiveness while at the same time can have a longevity running into many years. A public relations campaign will show within days, for example, how many column inches were achieved or radio and TV mentions. It will only rarely be possible to identify business actually gained by such a campaign but its contribution to the image of the firm and the creation of an ambience that attracts new clients, while largely beyond measurement, is nevertheless very real.

Why then, if the assessment of promotional efforts is so difficult and so imprecise, bother at all? The answer has to be, that which can be measured should be, that which can be evaluated should be and, for those activities that defy both, judgement must be used to at least avoid the grosser errors. The guidelines are precise: all promotional methods should be clearly defined and agreed throughout the firm; the message must be comprehensible and convincing to the target audience; there should be feedback or checks on the receipt and impact of the message; decision on the coverage—national, regional, local, specific segment or individuals—needed to achieve the objectives; what frequency should be adopted for the techniques to be used; what continuity will optimise the effort and expenditure.

BUDGETING

The question invariably arises as to how much a practice should spend on its marketing and what sort of return could be expected. Asked by the General Council of the Bar to provide an estimate of the benefits of marketing expenditure, a leading accountancy practice estimated as a "rough but defensible" figure some 20% return on their marketing expenditure. That is, for each pound spent on marketing, barristers would receive 20 pence profit.[1] Reality suggests that such a high return, even if it could be calculated, is unlikely and, in any event, there must be a situation of diminishing returns.

There is, of course, no standard figure for expenditure or return if only because there would be big variations between a launch situation and campaigns to simply maintain "visibility", between the year in which a brochure was produced and the years when its stocks were used and because of the values of the beyond-profit element. However, in terms of expenditures a very crude overall figure, which is generally accepted as practical, is between 1.5% and 2% of revenue and this is to include all time involvement that might otherwise be devoted to billable or other work. Unquestionably, personal contact will absorb a considerable amount of the appropriation.

A method for setting marketing budgets with precision has eluded even the most sophisticated of fast-moving consumer goods marketers. All systems of arriving at marketing budgets are inadequate when the effect of individual promotional tools is not traceable. The marketer must select the least inadequate alternative which stems from three requirements—least marketing waste, least risk to firm, best estimate of result. Within this cautionary framework, it is possible to consider a number of methods all with positive and negative attributes, as shown in Table 25.1.

Table 25.1 *Setting marketing budgets: principal methods*

Method	Advantages	Disadvantages
Percentage of previous year's turnover.	Always affordable so long as earnings are consistent.	No provision for growth or exploiting opportunities. No allowance for inflation of marketing costs. No flexibility if competition increases marketing effort. Assumes inertia in market.
Percentage of value expected engagements.	Allows for growth. Encourage stability in marketing.	Engagements appear to cause marketing. Can lead to over or under spending in growth or declining markets. Treats marketing as a constant factor irrespective of service position on life cycle.
Percentage of profits or profit excess.	Extra profits invested in marketing offset against tax, therefore subsidised.	Profits appear to cause marketing. Plan will be unstable and can vary widely from year to year. Risk of marketing appropriation being cut can cause premature allocation.
Matching competition.	Stabilises marketing wars. Creates a sensitivity to competitive situation.	Competition appears to cause marketing. Comparable expenditures difficult to estimate. Expenditure level and quality of marketing not correlated. Time lag to respond.
Objective and task method.	Forces detailed consideration of marketing objective.	Problems in attributing results. Difficulty in establishing weight and form of marketing to reach objective.
Equivalency.*	Historic performance gives reasonable and realistic guide to input levels and cost.	Changes in personnel's performance and in markets may make historic situation unreliable.

*Equivalency budgeting is explained in Chapter 12, pages 119–20.

To illustrate the interconnection of the three components of promotion—objectives, methods and media, and targets—some are exampled in Table 25.2 but, needless to say, the list is anything but complete.

Table 25.2 *Variables in the promotion "mix"*

Objectives	Audience	Method and Media
• increased awareness of the practice	• clients	• press, radio, TV, video, audio tapes, film
• heightened comprehension of the message	• potential clients	• public relations activity
• greater conviction that the service will be delivered	• own professional bodies	• inter-personal network (referrals)
• improve the image of the practice	• other professional bodies	• newsletters
• promotion of the service irrespective of who provides it	• community opinion formers and leaders	• seminars and conferences
• improve extent and quality of work obtained	• special interest groups	• sponsorship
• higher client retention	• institutions	• audio visual presentations
• improved conversion rate of inquiries to contracts received	• central and local government	• direct mail
• changed ratio of private to corporate clients	• financial organisations	• outdoor (poster) advertising
	• stakeholders	• inward visits
	• referral sources	• entertainment
	• educational bodies	• demonstrations
	• intermediaries	• exhibitions
	• suppliers	• brochures
		• signage

However, if the targets and objectives are tightly defined, the alternatives in terms of methods and media can be sufficiently narrowed down to manageable proportions. A promotional campaign to increase knowledge of the firm among local businessmen would obviously be uneconomic if national TV advertising were to be used, whereas direct mail or a seminar is much more likely to be cost effective.

The framework within which marketing should be conducted was given in Table 6.2, page 60, which listed some 30 different methods of marketing and the enabling functions which permit the methods to be used, such as marketing research and fee and range strategies. The two important ones for most types of professional service firms have already been dealt with in some depth in Chapters 20 and 24. The more important and frequently used of the others listed are considered here.

BROCHURES

Brochures do not, for the most part, contribute directly to obtaining or retaining business so much as help to build up knowledge and perceptions which are conducive to a firm being retained. The most practical way to consider brochures is to view them as large and exceptionally glossy business cards. They fulfil the same function plus offering the possibility of providing prospective clients with a wide range of information on the practice.

Before the time and expense of producing a brochure is invested, a decision should be taken as to what role in marketing the brochure is to fulfil. Who are the target audiences? Is it for clients or prospective clients or both? Should it be used for general mailing or only in response to a direct inquiry? Perhaps its use would be confined to distributing after a face-to-face meeting with prospective clients. Each decision has an impact on just what the brochure should contain and what it should look like.

Whatever its function the brochure must clearly emphasise the benefits clients receive, not the features of the service which produce those benefits. The accent the whole time must be heavily on the reasons why that particular client should retain the firm and there is only one reason why they should do so—they can clearly see the advantages of using them rather than appointing any other practice. Chapter 10 places considerable emphasis on this translation of features into benefits and Table 10.2 illustrates the point.

Brochures, as all other practice development messages, must be client centred and the desire to write a history of the practice and to extol its virtues has to be resisted. An opening statement that will immediately attract attention might fall under the heading, *"You and/name of firm"* or something similar. Next a statement of the "who we are" variety (which describes the firm now, not its history). Sequence can usefully follow, "How we work for you and with you" is a possible generic heading or "taking your instructions". Obviously there must be a list of services and explanations of special expertise, resources, facilities and experience to which clients can relate. The client will look for indications of the quality of communications—how, when and why the practitioner communicates with them, progress reporting procedures reminders and other issues. There should be a statement on how fees are charged and billing policies. It is always useful to take a posture on quality control and how complaints are dealt with. Biographies of members of the firm can be added. It is helpful to give precise details of location with a map and indication of or where parking is available. Life does not end at 5.00 p.m. on Friday afternoon. For those services where an urgent demand can arise at any time—health care, law and veterinary services are three obvious examples—an emergency contact number is always appreciated. Design and quality of the brochure is obviously of considerable importance and it is far better to leave these issues to professional designers and to printers unless, and this is unlikely, there is expertise and skills in these areas within the practice.

Both copy and design are always subject to the most intensive consideration, argument and amendment. The typical time for a brochure to go from conception to completion is over 12 months. That this should be so stems from the fact that the copy and design are circulated too frequently and amendments are amended. The most efficient way to produce a brochure is to give the task to one person who commands the trust and respect of the others in the firm. The draft should then be circulated once only and any amendments and changes incorporated. After that it should go to proof stage without further consultation and then be circulated once more but only for typographical corrections and minor amendments. The basic requirement for brochure production is to establish a benevolent autocracy. Frequent and wide consultation is costly and ineffectual.

A useful precaution is to copy test the material at the various stages of production using a member of what is seen as the target audience. Apart from the general reaction, they should be interviewed and questioned to establish just what it is they understand and do not understand, what they feel they require and is missing: what they consider is too lengthy or boring should also be investigated.

In summary, a good brochure must be literate, honest, visually attractive and reflect the image which the firm wants to project. It should also be up-to-date. The average life of a brochure is about 18 months. That is not to say major changes will usually be needed. Most of the copy can be retained with adjustments where necessary—changes in personnel, services offered, new offices and so on.

SEMINARS AND CONFERENCES

Three types of meetings can be considered:

1 Being invited by another organisation to speak on their platform. Such an invitation to which actual or potential clients may attend is a public recognition of the individual's (and through him or her their firm's) expertise in the subject matter.
2 Own sponsored meetings. These can also include non-members of the firm as speakers, their presence adding something to the objectivity of the occasion and perhaps their reputation also contributing to the firm's image.
3 Unacknowledged sponsored meetings. This is where an outside contractor is instructed to organise the event, either on a fee basis or on a profit basis with a guaranteed minimum return. This type of meeting gives the sponsor control as well as the apparent recognition of their expertise.

Across all professions there is a consistent success story relating to the advancement of seminars and conferences, public and in-house, as sources of generating new business. However, these meetings have to be a great deal more than a promotional vehicle for the firm. There has to be a clear benefit to anyone prepared to devote their time to attending. Neither the organisers nor the audience will react kindly to a sales pitch for the practice. Any benefits the practice offers should be deducible from the presentation which is made and not be its purpose. If this is to happen, the speaker *must* know something of the audience. Addressing information or opinions to an audience with little or no interest in the subject can only be counter-productive.

Since a speech is highly perishable it is useful if the organisers agree to hand out copies of it or of visuals used as a reminder of the subject, the speaker and the practice. One practical idea is to provide only limited paper but offer copies of any visual material shown or parts of the speech not reprinted to anyone who wants them. This will immediately identify interested audience members and provide a very suitable and valid reason to contact them with the material and a suitable covering letter offering further information, a brochure or a meeting.

A speaker at a conference is the human evidence referred to in Chapter 15, page 154, they must therefore be a true representative of the practice. The speaker must have a knowledge commensurate both with those whom he or she is addressing and those within the practice. A poor speaker, poor material or poor presence will damage the firm and, through the interpersonal network which operates both for good and evil, make such damage almost irreversible.

Particularly for meetings sponsored by the practice, numbers have an important psychological impact. Too few attending will signal to those present that the subject is of little interest to the firm's main clients or that their client base itself is extremely small. Too many at a meeting and important clients may well feel neglected by the senior members of the sponsoring firm.

A method of widening the audience to include prospective clients is to extend the invitation to the "customer's customer". That is, the clients are invited not only in their own right but are encouraged to bring their own favourite client or customer with them. This gives the direct client a double reason to attend—the intrinsic value of the programme and the opportunity to spend time with their own clients while extending the benefits to them. This technique is particularly productive if the seminar includes an outside speaker of repute.

Calling the event a "seminar" or workshop should mean that there will be audience participation: "conference" or "briefing" are better titles for straight presentations. The subject should clearly indicate the content. *The In-House Legal Department—justifying your existence* leaves little doubt about the subject coverage whereas *Future Directions* is vague.

When a member of the firm is invited to speak at a public event, then clients who might be interested in the subject matter should be informed. It may even be worthwhile purchasing places and giving them as invitations to selected clients and prospective clients. It is important, however, that the places are taken up both for reasons already given and, of course, to ensure money is not wasted. Thus, these types of invitations should be two stage, first asking if the person would like to attend giving them details and, only when they have expressed an interest and made it a commitment, sending the invitation.

None of this, of course, precludes taking seminars and other meetings into client premises. One well known international accountancy practice offers its major corporate clients lunch time seminars for their senior managers on personal tax planning, investments, pensions and other financial matters without charge. It is a technique much approved by the client firm since it provides a valued service to valued members of the firm, it is appreciated by those who attend who receive high quality advice from a major practice and, of course, the practice itself frequently acquires the individuals as high quality private clients.

One particular seminar subject, although of recent origin, has proved to be particularly successful in obtaining valuable private and some types of commercial clients. This is the *Wealth Seminar*. It has been used by accountancy and other financial services, legal, property industry professionals and others. The purpose is to present to a highly select group of individuals a series of ideas related to the generation and protection of wealth.

First, a list is made of firms in other professions with whom the practice would like to work, perhaps a solicitor, an estate agent, investment adviser, insurance broker, building society manager, and others (possibly an expert on collectibles would be a useful addition). All these professionals are interested in cross marketing. One acts as a facilitator to get the group together to discuss a joint programme for, say, either A or B socio-economic groups or for businesses of a defined type or size.

A 10-minute presentation of each profession represented is agreed directed towards the generation and protection of wealth, each of the participants explaining what *their* service has to offer. There are two aspects to the presentation. The first is to explain the money-making or protection idea simply and clearly so that everyone in the audience can understand it, and the second is to ensure that it is not explained completely. If the audience are told exactly what to do and how to do it, then they will not need the professionals' help—and that is not the point of the seminar. They should be disturbed or stimulated by the idea and then shown just as much of the solution as needs to be revealed to demonstrate that there are ways to increase and/or protect their wealth.

This is a cross-marketing exercise and to cross market it is necessary to share clients. Thus, there will probably be three or four of the facilitator's clients and another fifteen to twenty people who are the clients of the other professionals. The participating practices will, of course, invite their most important high quality clients and because of the excitement and interest this type of meeting generates, there is usually little difficulty in getting acceptances. Experience has shown that about half the audience will, within a year, use one of the other professionals making a presentation. Thus, it can be expected there will be two to three approaches from potential new clients of just the type most firms want since each professional will only have invited their worthwhile clients.

There are two additional benefits. First, those who are not currently using the other practices will almost certainly hear favourable comments from each firm's clients and third party endorsements are of enormous value. Second, the facilitator will improve both the links and the quality of relationships with the other professionals who may well be the source for other interprofessional referrals. For a wealth seminar to succeed there are certain steps and certain precautions which must be observed. These are set out in a checklist in Appendix 25.

PUBLIC RELATIONS

This is one of the more commonly used tools in practice development and, since its use did not directly offend many of the restrictions on marketing that existed in the past, it is a tool with a relatively long history within the professions. A survey among solicitors practising in the United Kingdom showed that over half were using public relations while less than 20% were advertising.[2] Familiarity with this method has not, however, led to any noticeable sophistication in its use, largely because it is an area of activity where many organisations feel they have the ability to undertake the necessary activities themselves. It is, however, a high skill area and one which is often misunderstood by the confusion of the initials PR meaning public relations with press relations.

The official definition of public relations is "the determined, planned and sustained effort to establish and maintain mutual understanding between an organisation and its publics". "Publics" are not just clients and potential clients but any individual or group who have an interest or involvement in the activities of the organisation and whose attitude can materially affect its performance. Thus the publics of most professional organisations is much wider than is generally conceded. Table 16.1 (page 161) identifies both the publics of a firm and the publics of their profession as a whole. It can be seen at once that, to be effective, public relations has to have an impact in the form of creating goodwill towards the practice among those groups or individuals who represent both potential business or can influence business.

The value of public relations rests in the goodwill it generates. Where the interests of the firm and the publics are aligned it produces many benefits. Clients are more likely to return to a practice which is well known, well spoken of and whose services are recommended by those whom they in turn respect. New clients are drawn to the firm for the same reasons. Suppliers who regard the organisation as a good firm to do business with will give that much extra support in the form of quality service and products. The impact on employees and on potential employees is also beneficial in creating a satisfactory quality of work place life and attracting suitable recruits into a stable and happy atmosphere.

Treated as a common-sense approach to developing the practice and as a management aid, public relations can create and maintain for any organisation, and consistently, a high degree of visibility and favourable attitudes towards it. It should not be seen either as a series of one-off campaigns or used only for damage limitation exercises.

With perhaps one exception there are no clear boundaries as to precisely what activities fall within public relations. Many which are listed are regarded by some marketers as techniques in their own right. Some commentators, for example, will include exhibitions, conferences, newsletters, sponsorship while others would not classify such activities as true public relations. The definitions are not important so long as appropriate tools are used.

The one area of public relations where the classification is not disputed is press relations (which, of course, includes radio and television) which is essentially concerned with obtaining editorial

publicity as opposed to paid advertising. There is only one requirement for a successful press release and that is that the information is indeed news which would interest the readership of the
publication, viewers or listeners.

The guidelines for achieving exposure are clear cut:

1 Define the audience to which the release is addressed. The
  opening of a new surgery by a dentist or a veterinary surgeon
  is less likely to be of interest to their respective professional
  press than to local newspapers.
2 The release has to be written in terms that will interest the
  readers and in a style which is editorially acceptable. The
  headline should summarise the contents. Most editors prefer
  to create their own headlines and in any event will not risk
  using the same headline as other media. Not too much time
  should be spent creating clever alliterative statements.
3 Shorter releases have a greater chance of being used than long
  ones. It is quite a useful technique to provide the release in three
  lengths, say, 150, 300 or 500 words or, depending on the contents, the same ratio for longer items. This gives the editor
  options related to space available and reduces the editorial
  work required.
4 Pictures should accompany the release or offer of their availability where illustration adds impact to the story.

The intricacies of creating attractive and usable press releases
fall far outside the purpose of this chapter but there are numerous
textbooks to guide the marketer given that they decide not to use
an agency.[3] The advantage of the latter rests in their skills and
expertise both in extracting stories from the firm and presenting
them in a newsworthy way. Just as important is their network of
contacts thus enhancing the possibilities of use. However, it cannot be denied that agencies do not come cheaply. But an agency
fee which produces results is obviously more economic than a
do-it-yourself effort that yields nothing.

One other aspect of public/press relations should be mentioned—articles attributed to the practice or to individuals associated with the practice. The same rules of course apply; the
subject must be appropriate to the media, shorter articles have a
greater chance of publication than longer ones. There is, however,

a further benefit: features can be reprinted in the form they originally appeared so that there is an easily established link between the article and journal and then circulated to clients and other contacts as direct mail. This ensures the feature is seen by all the appropriate individuals and organisations.

SPONSORED BOOKS

Whether sponsorship falls within public relations or not is a matter of opinion. Since its major purpose is to influence important publics favourably rather than to offer a specific service, which is the object of most other marketing tools, it might well be said to fit under that heading. Sponsorship takes many forms and while some have a high impact, they can be short lived. The financing or underwriting of one-off, as opposed to on-going arts or sports events does not contribute a great deal to long term developments. In contra-distinction the sponsored book has an extended shelf life, sometimes running into years and can often be self-liquidating, that is it pays for itself.

A book close to the firm's services and markets is written either by a member of the firm or by a "ghost" but credited to a member of the firm. This need be the only direct reference to sponsoring, but all examples and illustrations are taken from their services and clients.

There are a number of current, excellent, sponsored books and it is often not appreciated by readers that they are indeed sponsored. Many of them are standard works on their subject and are a constant reminder to all readers interested in the subject of the book of the author and the firm's expertise.

The mechanics are that the book must be published by an established and well-known publisher if it is not to be seen either as pure propaganda or as an ego trip for the author or organisation. Most major publishers have sponsored book facilities. The sponsor underwrites the cost of the book but receives over 60%—a figure which can be negotiated—of the revenue generated by its sale. Some books are given away, perhaps to clients or potential clients, some sold at favourable prices possibly to university and other libraries, and some sold at full price through normal publishing channels. Action must be taken to ensure the book is reviewed in the appropriate media to get maximum exposure and value from the book.

Even if the cost of the sponsored book is not recovered (although it certainly can be), it will be low and the exposure is for a considerably longer period than any other marketing tool can achieve.

DIRECT MAIL

Probably along with media advertising, direct mail has attracted more commentators than any other marketing tool. That it can succeed needs no other evidence than its continued use in massive quantities by all types of organisations. It is certain that if it did not work they would not use it. The only question is whether it is a technique suitable for professional service firms. Used with discretion the answer must be "yes".

The major advantage of direct mail is that it is possible to target the message accurately to individuals both in their personal capacities and within companies. Control can be exercised over the rate and timing of mailings. If response reaches a level which places too great a strain on the firm, the mailing quantities can be reduced or stopped, or if the response is low it can be increased. The third advantage of direct mail is that dispatch can often be timed at a favourable or propitious moment to parallel some event, conditions or circumstance. One of the most ubiquitous uses for direct mail is by the accountancy profession where many firms send their clients information on changes in taxation on the day following the budget. A disaster can stimulate direct mail for firms offering insurance against that particular risk or a legal judgement may create the opportunity to alert clients to a favourable or unfavourable change in their market or life style.

The question of reliability of sources of addresses is of prime importance. A firm's own client and prospective client list ought to be the most accurate one available, but the reality is that these are often out of date. An example of this is a solicitor's practice which wrote to every client for whom they held a will but with whom they had had no contact for the last five years, suggesting that the will should be looked at in the light of the client's present situation and current conditions. Among the replies were several from personal representatives which indicated that later wills had been made which the practice did not hold nor had they any knowledge of. The only interpretation that can be placed on such a situation is that the firm could not distinguish between inactive and lost clients and thus their own mailing list was inaccurate.

Another internally generated list which must also be checked for accuracy is that of non-client contacts—individuals or organisations who have made inquiries about the firm or who are perceived as potential clients. Beyond this it may be necessary to revert to directories to obtain mailing lists. It is, unfortunately, more the rule than the exception that many compilations on which direct mail plans are based are taken from directories and other sources which can be as much as 40–50% inaccurate. This is caused by removals, deaths, changes of occupation, status, home ownership in the case of individuals, or discontinuances, relocations, mergers, start-ups and a wide range of other reasons among commercial concerns. However, such a high order of inaccuracy does not have to be accepted if direct mail users take care in ensuring that sources are relevant, of recent date and that the lists have been "cleaned" and monitored regularly. Although the majority of mailing-list firms are willing to pass a credit for returns, this does not completely compensate for time lost and other efforts associated with a mailing campaign.

The advent of information technology has led to a technique which produces a much higher direct mail response rate through more accurate targeting. This is database marketing.[4] Database marketing has an ability to analyse client characteristics and purchasing habits and procedures which permits a detailed profile of prospective clients to be devised. This can then be matched to geodemographic databases and then used to drive the marketing strategy. This is of particular value for the private client sector, but also has applications for corporate clients. As can easily be deduced, database marketing is an important tool if relationship marketing referred to in Chapters 5 and 7 is adopted. Client profiling is explained in Chapter 11 and Appendix 11A gives some of the inputs which could be used for database marketing.

Whether using database marketing or not, once a good list is established it should be monitored routinely. This makes sure changes are recorded, for example the appointment of new personnel, changes of title and address, acquisitions, divestments and other corporate activities while, for private clients, births, deaths, marriages, removals, house ownership changes all contribute to list accuracy.

The contact report referred to in Chapter 24, pages 294–5, makes a considerable contribution to keeping information on clients and non-clients up-to-date and any changes noted should be transferred to both the client data sheets and mailing lists.

For the three dominant reasons given—accurate targeting, control of timing and topicality—but also for other reasons, direct mail can be one of the most economic methods of practice development but can also be one of the most extravagant. With control over the target audience and timing, economy can be ensured, but if the message itself is unremarkable the mailing will be totally wasted. The mailing piece is unlikely to go further than the wastepaper basket. Everyone receives a plethora of direct mail of one sort or another, some on such a regular basis that it is possible to discard many of the pieces without opening them since the label or envelope is recognizable.

At any moment in time there are a finite number of individuals and firms considering the adoption of particular services. If a mailing piece arrives at that moment, it will stimulate a reply. For all others it will be wasted as an immediate practice development effort, but might contribute to longer-term prospects. If this is so, it justifies the expense of wider coverage. However, for most practices a policy of ensuring penetration to the right person at perhaps a higher cost per piece mailed is generally the best one. This means that the contents themselves must be attractive and, in the case of commercial recipients, of apparently sufficient importance to pass through the screening personnel of post room, secretaries, assistants and others. One of the most effective ways of doing this and ensuring attention used to be to address the prospect by name and to personalise the message as far as possible. Today however with the advent of sophisticated computer and word processing systems, being addressed by name is not indicative of a personal approach. Other methods are needed to break the three-second barrier.

The three-second barrier is that moment in time when the recipient decides whether to read the material or throw it away. This means the first contents of the envelope must have an attention arresting impact. Whether this is done by a headline, design, format or even a gimmick is of no consequence so long as there is no compromising of the professionalism and culture of the firm and client. Gimmicks are only expensive if they do not work. A spring-loaded cube showing on each side the services offered by a quantity surveyor created surprise. A wristwatch strap calendar sent month by month through the year by a stockbroker, each time accompanied by news items on the firm's activities, is an example of a continuous mailing programme. The calendar was habit-forming and was missed if not received. A light touch can be adopted for perfectly serious services. A regular mailing of wire puzzles to clients and prospective clients by a firm of ergonomic consultants, emphasising their problem-solving capabilities in relation to physical forms of objects, proved to be highly effective in terms of response and recall.

Direct mail gives the firm a greater opportunity to describe its offer than many other methods of practice development. If the effectiveness of direct mail is to be assessed, it will always be necessary to return to first principles and to know clearly what the direct mail campaign was intended to achieve. The importance of precise goals can never be over-emphasised. Thus, if the objective of the mail piece is to persuade recipients to send for further details, its effectiveness should not be measured in terms of business achieved, but in terms of responses for more information. Similarly, if the mailing is to open the way for a personal meeting, the measure of its success is not requests for more information by mail (however useful this may be), but the number of appointments booked. However, even with such narrow goals, it is still not possible to make a totally accurate assessment of achievements since many elements other than the mailing may contribute to the action being measured. For example, the service firm may be known to have successfully undertaken work similar to that which the prospective client is considering, but this information came from the press not a mailing piece. Under these circumstances, the attribution of a new client to direct mail would only be partly accurate. However, even if total accuracy cannot be achieved, a measure of relative success is still more than worthwhile, as it gives at least some criteria for comparison of effectiveness.

Although the arithmetic may seem depressing in general terms a response rate of about 2% is considered to be successful, but in highly focused direct mail a higher rate is not unusual. If 200 pieces are mailed and four inquiries received, one of which is converted to business of any substance, there is little doubt that even the low figures are acceptable.

CHECKLIST

- Will the mailing "pack" gain attention?
- Is the offer appropriate?
- Is there anything exceptional in the offer?
- If not what can be done to create something exceptional or unique in the offer or its presentation?
- Have the markets been identified with precision?
- Is it known what the target group want (relative to the services offered)?
- Does the offer match the need or want?
- What is the immediate attainable objective?
- How will the ultimate objective be reached?
- Is the mailing piece visually attractive?
- What is a favourable reply worth?
- What is a reasonable expectancy of response?
- Is it easy to respond to?
- What will be the cost per recipient?

In direct mail the formula for success is a mixture of accuracy in targeting, appropriateness of the message, realistic expectations of target reactions, credible promises of real benefits, ease of response, requirement for initial minimum commitment. If the mailing piece is carefully appraised, perhaps by both copy testing and piloting, it reduces the possibility of errors and heightens the likelihood of success.

MEDIA ADVERTISING

With the possible exception of some financial services, there is little evidence to show that media advertising has been very successful for most other types of professional practices. Following a burst of activity after the US Supreme Court decision (Bates and O'Steen v. State Bar of Arizona) in 1977 and first stages of de-regulation in 1985 in the United Kingdom, in many professions there has been a good deal of disillusionment about this particular method. The cost is high, continuity is vital, results tend to be long term and difficult to measure.

The media advertising figures for two of the major and largest professions presented in Table 25.3 tell their own story:

Table 25.3 *Expenditure on advertising by solicitors and accountants*

	£M
Year to December 1988	3,480
Year to December 1989	3,855
Year to December 1990	2,376
Year to December 1991	876
Year to December 1992	1,162
Year to December 1993	2,662

Source: Media Expenditure and Evaluation, London (1993).

Allowing for inflation it can be seen that, in terms of total advertising expenditure, the sums spent are minuscule and declining. They become even less significant if the composition of advertisers in 1988 and 1989 was repeated in the other years, namely about 25% of total expenditure was incurred by only six accountancy firms, and in 1993 over 30% by three firms.

If a distinction is made between surveyors and estate agency advertising of property which, in any event, is usually paid for by the vendor and the advertising of their own services, then once again the sums involved are insignificant even taking into account local radio, door-to-door literature drops and direct mail. For many other professions which have been referred to in this book, media advertising can be said to be non-existent.

It has been suggested that, in deciding to advertise, five decisions are called for and these have been put together as a schematic or flow diagram (Figure 25.1) which clearly shows the sequence.[5] If the sequence is followed, while there can never be any guarantee of success, it will certainly avoid the grosser errors.

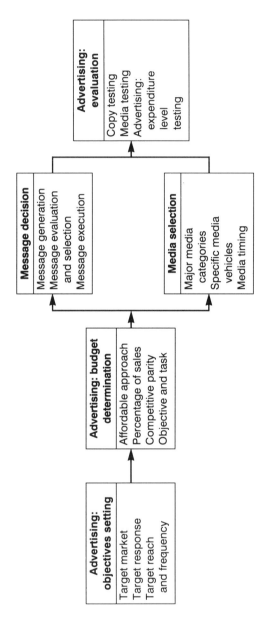

Figure 25.1 *Major decisions in advertising management*

While major display advertising appears to have lost favour, there are two possibilities which smaller firms might well consider and where cost is low. Classified advertisements (and small display advertisements) appear to generate a fairly high number of inquiries but mostly for what is seen as low quality work. While there is no reason why a practice cannot organise itself to undertake such work profitably, it is not usually a prime practice development objective. A survey of classified advertisements by professional firms shows a pattern of this type:

Profession	Work type advertised
Solicitors	Matrimonial
	Wills and trusteeships
	Minor criminal
	Debt recovery
Architects	Conversions
	Renovations
	Planning applications/appeals
Surveyors	Residential property building surveys
Accountants	Disputes with taxation authorities
	Tax return completions
Human resource consultants	Outplacement
	Career counselling
	CV preparation
Dentists	Cosmetic treatments

The other low cost media are special interest and enthusiast journals such as church, school and club magazines. Space costs rarely exceed double figures and while the audience is small the readership is intense. Advertisements in these media show the firm's commitment to the special group and this type of loyalty is often reciprocated by the readership.

On the border between media advertising and directories are *Yellow Pages* or classified business directories. For many smaller firms, this represents a principal source of new business but the fact that a few major practices can also be seen to advertise in these publications indicates that they can yield business of the type larger firms also find attractive.

Again there are guidelines that can assist a firm to obtain maximum benefit from *Yellow Pages* advertisements, and this arises from research into their use. It is claimed there is a direct relationship between size of display and response. Research shows that 60mm x 90mm display advertisements will produce five times as many responses as 30mm x 15mm while it is stated that 120mm x 170mm will produce fifteen times as many. It would seem that the top right hand corner of the right hand page gives a better result than in any other position by a factor of four. Whether the figures are accurate or not, there is little doubt that the relativities are in the correct order of magnitude and that an ordinary entry has far less chance of being chosen than display advertisements or even bold type.

The usage patterns appear to be to review display advertisements first and the choice of the firms closest geographically to the inquirer, and then alphabetical perusal of the normal and bold type entries and, again, choice is being highly influenced by proximity.

Given an entry is made, then the key for success is to clearly indicate:

- *Who*—identify the firm clearly
- *What*—list services offered
- *When*—times available
- *Where*—location (landmarks)
- *Why*—emphasise difference
- *How*—layout, typeface, logic

A checklist for making advertising as effective as possible is shown in Figure 25.2 and is applicable to all media.

OTHER MARKETING TECHNIQUES

The methods covered in this chapter represent those most usually either considered or adopted by professional service firms and

Layout/copy	Yes	In part	No
1. Attracts immediate attention			
2. Provides reader appeal			
3. Has a professional design			
4. Has a pronounced message			
5. Has a non-standard appearance and appears balanced			
6. Identifies the company			
7. Demonstrates the benefits			

Figure 25.2

which have generally been found to yield satisfactory results. There are, however, other techniques many of which are less common but which, if used and applied creatively, have also proved to be successful. It is an old marketing adage that success stems from either doing something different to everyone else or doing what everyone else is doing better.

Posters have been found to be effective, particularly used at locations within the vicinity of a practice and where people tend to be relatively static, that is railway stations, airports and other termini, sports stadia. Many international professional practices will be found to be using posters or signage at major airports.

Entertainment is the promotional method which has always been used and has never been regarded as anything other than acceptable. It might seem few people need any guidance on getting the best value from entertaining and yet, as with so many other marketing methods, there are ways of improving its utilisation.[6]

Telesales are regarded by most professional firms as the epitome of all that is wrong with marketing and totally at variance with professionalism. Certainly the way this has been used gives support to that belief particularly when "ambulance chasing" is involved. Nevertheless, there are opportunities for telesales which are already used extensively in financial services. Perhaps for professional services it is most effective in combination with other techniques such as direct mail, when it can be stated that the writer will telephone in due course to discuss the content of the letter or the offer. Telesales can assist in identifying specific situations for clients who may not be aware of them—such as new regulatory situations.

Telesales are not always outward. The skills can be used for dealing with inquiries made over the telephone. Usually for a professional practice the objective is to get the inquirer to agree to a meeting rather than to obtain an engagement. It is now commonplace for would-be conveyancing clients to ring a number of legal practices to get the lowest fee. This situation can be handled by what is virtually a scripted text which will enable even inexperienced people to succeed in making the contact a successful one.

Exhibitions. This form of promotion has become much more focused in recent years and can form a useful addition to the range of marketing tools adopted. They attract a well defined commercial audience. Consumer exhibitions may be somewhat wider but both are worthy of consideration. The Environmental Technology Exhibition has had, over the years, an increasing number of stands taken by legal practices as well as environmental and engineering consultants, as might be expected. Human resource consultants are to be found at the Institute of Personnel Management conferences and exhibitions. Like so many other marketing tools, exhibitions can be wasteful unless the purpose is clearly understood before evaluating results.[7]

Pro bono publico work. Undertaking public service of this type can both satisfy personal goals and, at the same time, promote the firm in a most favourable way. The recognition that *pro bono publico* work provides unquestionably adds to the reputation of the individual and the firm, both of whom are seen as good citizens. By a consanguinity of interest it provides benefits to the community or individual and, at the same time, the opportunity of widening the network among potential clients. *Pro bono publico* work is not necessarily confined to providing free services of social value; it can also consist of the loan of equipment or facilities, the donation of research and other educational and training grants, and allowing students to "shadow" professionals.

Packaging is not usually associated with services because of the intangibility of the service. However, most professions at some time in their relationship with clients have to present documentation, and the way this is done is in a sense packaging. A quantity surveyor dropping an untidy bundle of calculations on to a client's desk may provide the information but it does little for the image. Professionally printed and bound with well designed covers and layouts con- tributes to the perception of professionalism and efficiency. Design, typography, the use of colour, illustration, paper quality, binding come together to create a most favourable impression.

A good quality wallet, printed or embossed, "Important docu- ments", with the firm's name and address in which a will or other documents are given to the client will create an excellent im- pression and will be retained and probably used for other personal documents. Thus, whenever reference is made to any of its con- tents, it will be a reminder of the firm at a time when the type of services they provide may be under consideration.

Demonstrations. Although it is generally stated that it is not possible to demonstrate the service without giving it, there is never- theless always the possibility of demonstrating some aspect of the service which stands as an excellent surrogate for the service itself. A number of professions do, in fact, offer some aspect of their service on a no fee or trial basis. The use of this marketing method is most common in law and accountancy. Business "health checks" are sometimes undertaken by management consultants based on the analysis of a completed questionnaire and sometimes by on-site consultancy. The legal audit or preventative law is another area where it is possible to demonstrate at least some aspects of the firm's attributes. At least one accountancy practice is offering "value for money scoping reports" based on examining a single department or operating unit of a large company in order to demonstrate the yield of the technique if applied to other parts of the company. In some respects there is evidence of the use of this approach in dentistry, where an examination of the patient is undertaken to enable an assessment to be made of the risk involved in dental insurance policy for that patient. Demonstrations, where they can be given, are a most effective marketing tool for the firm that is confident in the quality of their service and its delivery.

Directories. Most professions have directories and year books. Entry in some is on a paid basis and others free, while yet others have a mix of free and paid entries. A free entry is always value for money, but whether to advertise requires information on a number of aspects of the publication. What will be the circulation in numbers and by types of recipients, will it be distributed free or have a cover price, what is its expected shelf life, for what purpose will recipients use it, what is the competition and, of course, what will it cost? Care is needed not to devote appropriation to directory advertisements just because the competition does so. As with exhibitions this is not a valid reason for the expenditure. Yet again it is necessary to return to first principles in order to reach sensible decisions. What are the firm's marketing objectives and how will the entry into a directory help achieve them as against the use of resources for other promotional methods? (The suggestions concerning *Yellow Pages* insertions, see page 320, are also applicable to other insertions.)

At a time of skill shortage a directory of the top 1000 law firms was found to be a useful way of attracting recruits, but it is not a publication many people seeking to appoint a legal practice would consult. As a generalisation, with few notable exceptions, professional listings are not as useful as multi-disciplinary/trade directories.

Marketing clubs. A clone of database and relationship marketing, which it is claimed will provide some of the most cost-effective routes to marketing success, is club marketing. This has been defined as "customer groupings with shared interests sponsored by a supplier of goods or services to build and sustain loyal buying behaviour that accepts the sponsor's need to manage the relationship for profit".[8] It is most easily illustrated by the various Executive or Frequent Flyer clubs which reward loyalty by providing special privileges to a group of customers. It has not, so far, been used extensively within core professional services but a few pioneer examples can be found in the financial services sector including accountancy and insurance, computer software, some branches of health care and by educational establishments. The club idea can be extended to include the sponsorship of special interest groups of significance to the professional service firm. Examples are a human resource consultancy which created a club of personnel managers which in turn gave access to special forums, newsletters and providing a network forum for the members.

Mobile Services.   This is a trend adopted in a very minor way by some financial services, but which may intensify and spread. This is taking services to demand sources. In the USA, one bank provides a mobile service, visiting hospitals, factories and housing sites, which is an extension of the now common facility of banks offering services at exhibitions and other public gatherings. In health care, a fleet of vehicles have been fitted out both to provide on-site health checks and fitness training facilities and an accountancy service is offering assistance in making tax returns. The possibilities for new mobile services are numerous and while the "drive through" concept has never really taken off in many countries the "drive to" may hold worthwhile possibilities.

"MAKE OR BUY" IN MARKETING SERVICES

Given that few practices will have all the necessary skills to undertake many of the marketing techniques which are available to them, the question will inevitably arise as to whether external experts should be used. There is no one answer to this question since it depends very much on the objectives set, tools chosen, appropriations available and targets identified.

The need to appoint an agency will not just emerge from any lack of skill. It can also originate from such issues as internal work load, the disposition of the management of the firm, the size of the practice, the ability to be completely objective (for market and image research) and the availability within the firm of personnel capable of selecting and monitoring any agencies appointed.

Having decided to use an agency, choosing the best one for the firm is critical. The battlefields of marketing are strewn with corpses of agencies which have failed to understand their professional services clients' needs and culture and are the victims of clients' failure to begin to understand how marketing agencies work, how to work with them, what they can and cannot achieve.

There are, however, certain guidelines which can be followed to assist in the selection of an appropriate agency. The first rule is always to use an agency of which satisfactory experience has been gained in the past. There are mutual advantages: the marketing services agency will benefit from the exposure they have had to the client and their operations; the client will have some knowledge of the agencies' strengths and weaknesses. Shopping around for agencies is commonplace practice which is wise in moderation but can be time-consuming, confusing and wasteful to both sponsor and agency when carried to excess. If, however, the project is a first attempt at using a particular technique, then it is necessary to check all the available services that appear suitable. It will be found that an initial list for the screening of about 10–12 firms will give a good cross-section of most marketing services organisations.

It is always useful to discuss any proposed appointments with business associates who may have had experience of particular agencies and can comment on their competence and can thus make recommendations for inclusion on the list for consideration. Professional associations and journals are usually willing to advise, based on their own experience or on that of their clients or members. A number of organisations, for example, the Chartered Institute of Marketing and the Institute of Management and their equivalent organisations in other countries, can provide a short list of firms or individuals they consider suitable to handle a particular assignment.

Directories of agencies are not a reliable guide to services or companies. As with most directories, many more claims are made than can, in fact, be substantiated by those appearing in them relating to their ability to provide services. Moreover, since the majority of directories require paid entries they are rarely exhaustive. Directories produced by associations are more often than not just lists of firms which employ a member of that association and as such provide little guidance on the suitability of agencies for the project.

Once a list of agencies has been obtained the next step is to narrow it down to those which appear most likely to meet the needs of the firm. At this stage a very brief outline of the assignment can be given and the agencies asked to indicate if they are interested in being considered. They should be asked to submit their literature and any published material, and to explain the scope and extent of their services and resources. A careful study of this literature will provide further clues to their suitability. From this and other information gathered from other sources it should now be possible to narrow the list down to three or four possible companies or practitioners.

Those judged suitable, on paper, should if possible be visited to establish both how far their claims are born out by the physical evidence of their activities and also to get the "feel" of the agency. An organisation claiming to employ 30 researchers might be expected to occupy more than two or three rooms. Commercial status symbols are not necessarily indicative of top quality work, but then neither is the use of very old machinery and furniture likely to invoke the feeling of a successful organisation to any prospective purchaser of the agency's services.

This is the time for asking penetrating questions about the agency's organisation: information on the qualifications of staff; the extent of specialisation or full service facilities should be checked to ensure the needs of the practice can be met; how they operate in distant markets if this is an issue; back-up available if the person(s) assigned to the project cease to be available needs to be explained. The agencies client and job listings provide very relevant clues, albeit often unwitting, to the prospective purchaser of their services. It can, of course, rightly refuse to reveal the names of clients but it is usual for most agencies to be able to mention at least some clients for whom they have worked and who are prepared to give a reference as to the effectiveness of their work. Prospective clients of agencies should not hesitate to ask for references and to take them up. In seeking to check out agencies, professional firms have the advantage in that the type of information clients seek of them is very similar to that which the firm should obtain from the marketing services agency.

When negotiating with the larger agencies, it is a useful precaution for the sponsor to ascertain which executive will be responsible for the project. This serves the multiple purposes of: removing the faceless aspect of the agency where responsibility is difficult to pin down to that of a personal contact; ensuring that if the project is successful and further work is commissioned, the same executive can again be asked to handle the new assignment; and avoiding the charge, again something not unfamiliar to professional practices, that "you see the top man when they are selling you the service and then you never see them again". Agencies may have a continuous corporate life but the individuals in them change and there is no guarantee of a consistently high standard merely because the same firm carries out a project.

The last step in choosing an agency is based on the submission of a proposal and costs. It is unfair to ask more companies or individuals than necessary to prepare these, but it is wise in most circumstances to obtain more than one quotation. Comparison of fees is difficult because no two approaches are strictly comparable. The final decision must depend upon the appropriateness and quality of the offer or project design, or proposal, how far the fee and time conforms with the needs and the *rapport* that has been built up in the initial appraisal stage of the agency.

The practice might want to hold a "beauty parade". That is, those agencies who have submitted offers are invited to make a formal presentation of their proposals to the partners or other decision makers. These presentations are usually of about 30–40 minutes duration but the time very much depends on the complexity of project under consideration and the number of individuals and marketing services agencies involved. A presentation gives the agency a chance to expand on the documentation and, more importantly, gives the practice members the opportunity to interrogate them on the approach and on the details, including fees.

To reiterate, agencies, like their professional service clients, rely heavily on their reputation to attract clients. By the time they have the end product they have paid for, the choice of supplier has long been made. For this reason, there is a good deal of subjectivity in the choice of agencies. Few spend time and money in advertising themselves on a large scale because, again, like professional service organisations the majority of their business stems from personal recommendations and from continuing business from past clients. This, itself, is proof that it is reputation rather than hard selling and publicity which count.

DANGER SIGNS

The positive aspects of selecting an agency have been given. There are a number of danger signs that can be detected by an observant, potential sponsor. These have been summarised and they are well worth restating:

- *Overselling.* Resist high pressure tactics or attempts to sell a package which is more than is needed or can be afforded. Beware of exorbitant claims about their experience and qualifications which cannot be fully substantiated.
- *Disparagement of competition.* Avoid organisations that tend to "run down" their competitors. Not only is this a poor selling tactic but also a highly questionable business practice. If a client's interests can be better served by using the facilities of a competing organisation, most responsible agencies will tell you so. They may even recommend a rival organisation.
- *Price cutting.* View with scepticism organisations which say they are quoting a price "at below cost" and whose competitive bid for an engagement appears abnormally lower than others. The chances are that the statement is not entirely true; costs can be padded. An unusually low bid may be genuine but may also indicate a weakness in methods or quality.
- *Extravagant promises or guarantees.* As will have become obvious, guarantees cannot be given for many aspects of marketing activity. The same duty of care that most professionals recognise as the guiding principle in their work applies or should to marketing services agencies.
- *Vague ideas of approach, results or final costs.* Exercise caution, in employing an agency that is overtly vague concerning the approach and probable results of the project and does not give a firm fee or estimate. Such an attitude may reflect an uncertainty about how to deal with the problem.
- *Reluctance to be specific.* Organisations that refuse to put on paper the specifics about an assignment should be regarded with suspicion. Most commitments are entered into in good faith by mutual agreement of both parties.

Even though a number of marketing tools have been described, the list is by no means complete. While it is unlikely that any really innovative new marketing tools will have immediate application for professional services, the creative use of existing and tried methods will distinguish one practice from another and create the conditions of market leadership or obtaining and sustaining a profitable niche in the market.

ACTION POINTS

- Decide the purpose for every promotional effort made or technique used
- Define the criteria which will be used to judge success or otherwise
- Establish a clearly defined overall budget—time and money—and allocate it to the various methods to be used
- Devise a system for regularly monitoring and control of each method adopted
- Decide which activities will be dealt with internally and which by agencies
- Consider all appropriate tools methods and media against time and money constraints
- Decide the appropriate message for each target group
- Copy and media test all promotional messages

NOTES

(1) General Council of the Bar *Strategies for the Future*, p.39, London (1990).

(2) ICL *The Future of the Legal Profession*, London (1991).

(3) Jefkins, F. *Planned Press and Public Relations*, International Text Book Co., London (1986) covers most aspects of the mechanics of public relations.

(4) A useful introduction to the subject and bibliography will be found in Fletcher, K., Wheeler, C. and Wright, J. "Success in Database Marketing", *Marketing Intelligence and Planning*, No. 6, p.10, Bradford (1992).

(5) Kotler, P. and Bloom, P.N. *Marketing Professional Services*, p.246, Prentice Hall, Englewood Cliffs (1984).

(6) Green, M. *Improving Results from Business Entertaining*, Kogan Page, London (1984).

(7) For an excellent exposition on the use of exhibitions as part of the marketing activity see Alles, A. *Exhibitions—a Key to Effective Marketing*, 2nd edition, Cassell, London (1988).

(8) The best detailed exposition on the use of clubs for marketing will be found in Wills, G. and Wills, J. "Journey to Marketing Clubland", *Marketing Intelligence and Planning*, Vol. 10, No. 2, Bradford (1992).

APPENDIX 25

CHECKLIST FOR MOUNTING A WEALTH SEMINAR[1]

- Keep the arrangements simple.
- Have the meeting on neutral territory so the other presenters do not feel themselves disadvantaged.
- The subjects chosen must be those which will interest the audience. This is *not* a presentation of the firm but a presentation of a wealth generation and/or protection idea.
- Know what other presenters are going to cover and co-ordinate.
- Get a confirmation those accepting will attend. The ambience will be spoilt if the session is under attended.
- Have refreshments available both before and after the meeting.
- Be sure to have a supply of business cards, brochures and data sheets or explanations of the subject covered. Give the audience plenty of paper. If it is possible a full pack containing all the presentation material in a folder of good quality will add to the professionalism of the occasion.
- Put out a few less chairs than there are people and bring in extra chairs as others arrive. No empty chairs indicates to the audience the success of the seminar.
- Try and arrange parking. Lack of packing space is one of the main reasons people do not attend meetings, most particularly in town centres.
- Timing is important. Agree with other presenters but late afternoon other than a Friday has been found to be one of the most productive time slots.
- The role of the chairman is critical, he or she must be independent otherwise it will set up tensions and jealousies among the presenting firms:
  - keep remarks short
  - welcomes guests who are going to *share* ideas with a panel of experts to help them generate and/or preserve wealth
  - explains the procedure, e.g. 10 minutes per presentation and then questions, usually at the end of all the presentations
  - explain presenters will answer questions and provide consultation on an individual basis—usually while refreshments

are served at the end of the session—since many matters will be regarded as confidential
- each speaker should be introduced as the best in the profession or in the particular city where the seminar is held. It is both easier and better for the chairman to deliver the encomium than the individual who will sound as if he or she is boasting
- thank attenders and the speakers
- the following day write to all those attending, again thanking them and listing the presenters' names, their firms and addresses and the subjects on which they spoke. (This letter is of course produced by the convener for the chairman to sign.)
- if a personality can be obtained as chairman, for example a local radio station interviewer, this adds to the attraction as well as the efficiency of the meeting

NOTE

(1) Marsh, W. "Sharing Your Clients Around", *The Australian Accountant*, Sydney, June (1992).

26
What's New about the Future?

The idea that the professions have reached a plateau, having undergone major changes in so far as activities have been re-structured to meet current needs and attitudes and that now is a time for contemplation and consolidation, is comforting but incorrect. The turmoil of the last decade is not about to calm and the clamour for further and even more adjustment to meet client/patient needs is very likely to increase.

Practice development, while it certainly has an immediacy and urgency is also something which has to be planned over time spans. The most practical are: "*at once* meaning this week; *short term* perhaps 3–6 months; *medium term* approximating to a year; and *long term* 2–3 years, maximum 5 years. These may seem to the conventional forecaster ridiculously short-term thinking. This is an argument that might be accepted had their own long-term forecasts not been universally and often wildly inaccurate.

Even short-term forecasts have most frequently been unable to accommodate violent and uncontrollable forces which impact on every practice and every individual. The sudden and considerable rise in oil prices after the Six Day War almost overnight changed whole economies. The collapse of financial markets also overnight in October 1987 precipitated the slide from the expansive 1980s to the constrained 1990s.

Forecasting, or prediction, is as old as mankind itself. Prophesy, witchcraft, necromancy, superstition, were the trading skills of the Sibyls, Old Testament prophets, Merlin, Lilith and Nostradamus;

philtres, fire and the entrails of the freshly killed pigeon their materials. The desire to peer into the future, like the desire to achieve a state of invisibility and to fly unassisted by machines, is as fundamental to human nature as is the need for personal acceptance and recognition.

Forecasting techniques are not yet such as to lead to the belief that a wholly accurate method is yet within the grasp of the seers even in such well-established and scientifically advanced fields as meteorology. At the present time, the tools available have narrowed down the areas of error but not to the extent that a forecast can be developed and safely used without the application of the human qualities of judgement and understanding.

Forecasting is the probabilistic assessment, on a relatively high confidence level, of future developments in the area or activity under review. Current studies are already historical analyses by the time they are ready. Although the lessons of the past are of vital consequence, it is the course of future events which is of primary concern in planning for and operating practices.

THE BUSINESS ENVIRONMENT

The nature of business demands that the future be constantly scanned and, equally, that plans for the future also be under unremitting surveillance. Markets are perhaps one of the most hazardous of all areas to forecast, the variables being as great as in any other discipline and the movements perhaps more volatile and unpredictable than most. Nevertheless, the difficulty of the task is not a reason for not undertaking it in a methodical manner and applying best judgement to situations that defy stricter analysis.

Given the unreliability of forecasting techniques, it could well be asked why busy practitioners would bother with this arcane activity (not to be dignified with the name "discipline"). The answer has to be that if it is not possible to forecast with accuracy the expected condition of the business environment, then it is necessary to at least have contingency arrangements to deal with those circumstances which could occur.

Most professionals know a great deal about their firm, have a lively knowledge of the immediate environment and market in which they work and can respond sensibly and effectively to

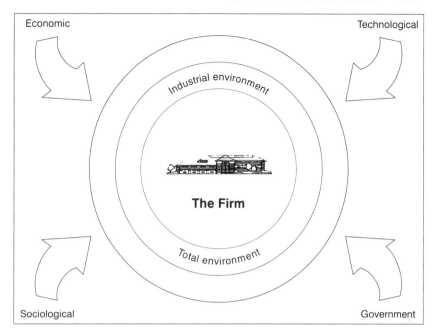

Figure 26.1 The business environment

change: what is frequently lacking is an understanding of what might be termed the "outer environment", where four major forces of change are at work. As shown in Figure 26.1, these are government activities, technological change, sociological change and economic change—all irresistible forces in their own right and all intertwined with each other. The impact of these forces on the outer environment must cause shock waves impacting on the business environment and, in turn, within the firm itself. No organisation can ever be insulated from its environment.

The effect of *government intervention* has already been documented in previous chapters. But among those issues which could impact heavily on the professions would be change in law to permit limited liability, direct professional access, mixed discipline practices, the need for small company audit. *Technological change* has certainly not passed by the professions; all of them without exception have been affected by the availability of new tools and new techniques. Moreover, for the professions which charge on a time basis, technology represents a particular dilemma. Heavy investment in the latest equipment to reduce the time it takes to complete clients' work leads to lower returns. It may well be that pressure from technological developments may force these disciplines on to a different billing method. *Sociological adjustments* have produced a more knowledgeable, more questioning and indeed more litigious private client situation. The impact on fees of professional negligence insurance premiums is considerable and this, in turn, can produce another sociological effect in reducing the viability of professional services to a large part of the population. The information explosion is widening choice—choice not just between different professionals and different professions but also where products can substitute service and where services have become so de-skilled they can be carried out by non-qualified practitioners or the clients or patients themselves. The structure of society is itself changing; more women in the workplace, the ageing population, the increase in ethnic minorities and the shrinkage of the middle classes. *Economic changes* have led to fee pressures on established disciplines, the need for new services and the emergence of new activities clamouring for professional recognition. Superimposed on this are the violent swings of economic and business activity.

None of this is to suggest that every practice must produce its own macro-economic forecast, input–output tables and all the esoteria of forecasting, only that they must be sensitive to the likelihood of changes and their impact on their own businesses and activities and have an in-built flexibility.

The plethora of books on professional service marketing which have emerged in the last decade all emphasise the need for forward planning but very few of them give advice on how to forecast the situation for which the forward plan is devised. This is barely surprising since there is no body of knowledge which can be said to be vaguely practical on forecasting techniques for professional service firms. At best it is heavily dependent on product, usually business-to-business, forecasting.

It should be said at the outset that precision forecasting, even if it were possible, is a luxury few practices can afford or need. While, in forecasting, the demand for a sea water distillation plant does not leave much room for error if it is to be viable, the demand for professional services requires only that best judgement suggests the probability of an event or trend occurring or not occurring has to be within a wide band of acceptable values.

THREAT AND RISK ASSESSMENT

A simple technique, but with high implementive value although originally developed many years ago by SRI (previously Stanford Research Institute), has not been widely adopted despite having been found to yield excellent results at a very low cost and thus justifies its place among the techniques which are suitable for professional service firms to adopt.[1] This is called *vulnerability analysis* which substitutes a precise and disciplined methodology for emotional or even hysterical reactions to emerging threats or, at the opposite extreme, a "don't let's look, it might go away" philosophy.

Vulnerability analysis is a simple, inexpensive diagnostic process that is usually undertaken on a group basis within a firm. It does not use complex concepts, elaborate models or massive data inputs. Rather, it uses the expertise and the judgement of the group's participants who are drawn from throughout the organization. Since the approach can be cross-disciplinary, the technique makes participants aware of conflicts in their planning assumptions—both implicit and explicit. This awareness, in turn, improves interdepartmental communication.

The method is simple. It commences with the identification of those factors, circumstances and resources which must exist, or not exist, for a firm to operate successfully. These are called *underpinnings*. At its simplest, and using a "people resource" as an example, if there were no new entrants into a profession, a practice must eventually cease. Thus a supply of suitably qualified personnel is (or could be) an underpinning of that practice as in (2) below. To take another example, the prosperity of a solicitor's practice could be heavily prejudiced by changes in legislation introducing no fault liability, registrable divorces or direct access to barristers, as in point 10 below.

Some 12 critical factors have been identified but there may be others specific to professional services which have yet to be identified:

1 *Needs and wants*—traditionally applied almost exclusively to clients but necessarily must be extended to stakeholders and employee groups in firms.
2 *Resources*—refers to all people, physical assets, materials, systems and services employed in running a practice.

3 *Relative costs*—the relationship of a firm's key cost elements with those of competitors.
4 *Client base*—this relates to the number and composition of the client base.
5 *Technology*—this concerns technologies which impact on the services in the way they are performed and by whom performed.
6 *Special abilities*—the ability of one firm significantly to outperform its competition in certain ways (see Chapter 8).
7 *Identifying symbols*—logos and other means whereby the client's services are identified.
8 *Artificial barriers to competition*—various laws and regulations which eliminate markets or exclude competitors.
9 *Social values*—those clusters of social values which create demand for specific services.
10 *Sanctions and supports*—the enabling permission or public endorsement given to professions by governments and other groups.
11 *Integrity*—the basic trust a client places in a service.
12 *Complementary products/services*—products and services which are essential to the performance of the services.

The group must identify which of the underpinnings relate to the firm's activities. It certainly will not be all or indeed many of those listed. The test of an underpinning is whether, if it were removed, the practice would cease to be able to operate or could only be operated under the most adverse and unsatisfactory conditions.

The next stage is for each individual engaged in the vulnerability analysis exercise to identify the threats which could attack the underpinnings. Here the imagination need not be bounded by what is likely so much as by what is possible. Individuals are invited to consider each threat and to locate them on a grid in terms of likelihood of their occurring (horizontal axis) and the severity of their impact (vertical axis)—see Figure 26.2.

A consensus is then taken of each threat by grouping on to one matrix the judgements of the individuals involved of each threat in the exercise. If there are wide disparities of views, each person is asked to give the basis for the position he or she has allotted the threat and, through re-cycling, a Delphi forecast is produced. The same grid is used both for individual personal assessments and consensus results, as is shown in Figure 26.3.

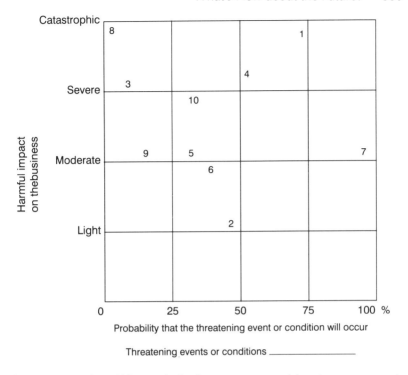

Figure 26.2 *Vulnerability analysis: threat assessment (showing one person's assessment of 10 different threats)*

The grids containing the consensus for each threat can then be segmented to isolate them so that the appropriate actions can follow. In Figure 26.3 the grid is divided into three sections. Threats in crescent A require immediate, urgent avoiding strategies. Crescent B threats must be subject to contingency planning so that if they move either upward making them more dangerous, or to the right whereby the risk of their occurring becomes greater, no delay will occur in dealing with them. Crescent C calls for monitoring of any threats within it to be ready to reconsider their significance and any actions necessary should their position change.

Vulnerability analysis is a simple exercise and combined with the SOFT or SWOT analysis will give a reliable profile for strategy formation and market planning.[2] SOFT (Strength, Opportunity, Fault, Threat) and SWOT (Strength, Weakness, Opportunity, Threat) are alternative acronyms for the same self-analysis technique.

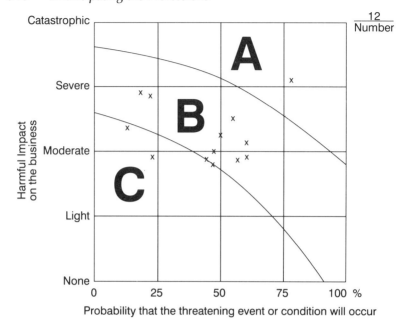

Figure 26.3 *Vulnerability analysis (showing composite of evaluations for sample threat)*

OPPORTUNITY ANALYSIS

Although SRI have not extended the technique to forecasting opportunities there is no reason why the same methodology cannot be adopted; that is, using an audit of the basic skills and resources of the firm instead of the underpinnings and then identifying what circumstances and events could lead to the opportunity for their greater profitable exploitation.

In the financial services sector firms are at risk through non-compliance with the plethora of new rules and conditions self-regulation generates. The opportunities this opens out for the practice of preventative law or "company health checks" is considerable. Accountants have the skills to offer forensic support services and quantity surveyors' expenditure programming and resources allocation. The opportunities emerge from environmental factors created by the influences of the four major forces of change.

An intelligent appreciation of these forces with an on-going monitoring of the practices market environment will yield valuable and usable information and data to enable sensible and practical planning to occur. At the very worst it will avoid many unpleasant and unexpected surprises although it is useless to attempt to make contingency plans for every possible violent change.

The Appendix to this chapter provides very useful guidelines for obtaining the maximum yield of highly implementive ideas from vulnerability or opportunity analysis process and they are based on observations made during sessions conducted for a wide variety of organisations.

Forecasting the course of de-regulation is fortunately not too difficult a task since it will almost certainly go forward worldwide, only the pace of change varying. While it cannot be envisaged that the professions will ever be a complete free-for-all—no one would benefit from such a situation—regulations will continue to exist in terms of entry, professional conduct and continuing professional development. It can be said with considerable safety that control of marketing will be confined to the basic needs to be decent, truthful and legal irrespective of the tools or communication methods used or whatever messages are carried by them.

ACTION POINTS

- Identify lead indicators in the economic and business environment which can impact on the practice, monitor them and prepare contingency plans to deal with eventualities (some examples of lead indicators will be found in the next chapter, page 359
- Create a vulnerability analysis interdisciplinary or inter-departmental group
- Appoint a strong invigilator
- Identify the underpinnings of the firm and agree them
- Identify threats to the underpinnings
- Both individually and consensually assess likelihood and impact of threats and plan to exploit or avoid situations arising

---

NOTES

(1) The explanation is based on the work of Hurd, D.A. and Riggs Montfort, E. and is summarised in *The Evolution of Vulnerability Analysis*, SRI, Menlo Park, CA (1989).

(2) Descriptions of SOFT or SWOT analyses can be found in many books on planning although not necessarily related to marketing. A concise explanation is in Wilson, A. *Practice Development for Professional Firms*, pp.48–9, McGraw-Hill, Maidenhead (1984).

APPENDIX 26

SOME GUIDELINES FOR CONDUCTING A VULNERABILITY ANALYSIS

- Draw participants from several functions and/or departments within the organisation.
- Conduct the session with 8 to 10 participants if possible—6 minimum; 12 maximum.
- Only one person should speak at a time. (If two conversations start, some valuable information may be lost.)
- Every participant should be encouraged to suggest both underpinnings and threats (and opportunities).
- Idea-killers, of which there are many varieties, are not admissible.
- Participants should not waste the group's time by trying to educate each other or the leaders about their activities or their problems.
- Start the search for underpinnings with the *wants and needs* and the *resources* groups because they are the most easily identified.
- Title a separate sheet of easel paper with the name of each *class* of underpinnings. Tape the sheets to the walls of the meeting room. Record the underpinnings in their appropriate groupings as they are suggested.
- Do not be concerned about the category into which a particular underpinning is put. The main point of the first step is to identify as many as possible.
- Some overlapping between categories of underpinnings will exist. Sometimes underpinnings may be identified from the perspective of one group that were overlooked in another category.

- When the group cannot think of any more specific underpinnings in one category or class, go on to the next. Other underpinnings can always be added later.
- No evaluation of a threat should be made at the time it is suggested. Evaluations should always be made independently on worksheets by each member of the group.
- Initial evaluation must take place before open discussion.
- The leader should present the group pattern before inviting open discussion.
- Concentrate first on achieving consensus; if a new perception of the event emerges, evaluate it immediately.
- Evaluate events in groups of 10, taking each group through to final evaluation and discussion.
- Treat maverick votes as you would uncut diamonds.
- To lock in the group's memory and commitment, ask each member to summarise the results of the workshop and obtain written action commitments from the appropriate authorities.

27
Bringing it Altogether: the Master Action Plan

"Would you tell me please, which way I ought to go from here?"
"That depends a good deal on where you want to get to," said the Cat.
"I don't much care where…" said Alice.
"Then it doesn't matter which way you go," said the Cat
Alice in Wonderland—Lewis Carroll

What was true for Alice is equally true for the practice developer. But apart from having a clear idea of where it is the firm wishes to go they must also have an equally clear idea of the route to that destination.

Just as market planning was beginning to find acceptance in the professions, the worldwide depression led to the ceremonious tearing up of elegant and sophisticated five-year plans in favour of very short term survival. Crisis management, which has few virtues, was substituted for strategic thinking and action. While it is true that it is not possible to foresee every change which occurs, it is certainly possible to prepare contingency plans for given circumstances. Alternative scenarios are infinitely better than crisis management which is tactical, short term and with the limited if important objective of survival at almost any price. This should not be the option facing a firm which plans both its corporate future and, within it, the marketing activities needed to achieve it.

Planning is essentially a forecasting exercise with highly practical and checkable results but the hazards of forecasting were set out in the previous chapter. As with other aspects of marketing, the difficulty of the task is not a reason for failing to undertake it. It is a challenge that must be met.

Many of the marketing suggestions and ideas which have been presented in this book will certainly work as free-standing activities but their value is considerably enhanced if they form part of a coherent and comprehensive plan. A marketing plan, as valuable as it is, must be seen as part of the wider corporate or partnership plan. Market planning in isolation is better than no planning at all, but not much better. Unless the marketing objectives and the overall objectives—long, medium and short term—are aligned then problems are certain to arise in terms of co-ordination, disputation over the allocation of resources, disagreements about the range of services to be offered and, perhaps stemming from this, the manpower planning.

This chapter is concerned with market planning but it begins with the caution that only in the last resort should it be prepared in isolation from the overall practice plan. A stand-alone marketing plan can, however, be used as a lever to persuade others in the firm to create both departmental and total corporate plans by providing the starting torque for a bottom-up planning system. That is, each activity or department creates its own plan which is then recycled and co-ordinated to create the master plan. Because it is so easy when concentrating on marketing to assume that this represents the most significant part of the organisation's activities, it is necessary to clarify its role. It is not the dominant activity, as is often claimed, because the firm cannot operate without its market; but then neither can it operate without finance (the financial plan), people (the human resource plan), premises (the facilities plan), service development (service R&D plan), and other areas of activity to embrace administration, quality control, information technology and other aspects of the firm's operations which must be monitored and controlled.

Plans are not just what top management and senior departments do every few years; they are everyone's concern and should be on-going. They provide a direction for action—a benchmark against which to measure progress. They enable a firm to adjust without trauma or disruption to changing situations and to demonstrate to staff and clients alike that they are in control of their activities and destinies. Everyone, without exception, should own a plan and be committed to it. To achieve this *desideratum* everyone should have a role, however slight, in its preparation and its implementation.

All organisations from one man firms to major international practices have to plan if they are to maximise their resources and opportunities. For the smallest practices the danger rests between not planning at all and turning planning into a time consuming in-house industry. Neither polarities are necessary. Planning can be a simple systemisation of what is being done or should be done.

Business strategy has been defined as the pattern of objectives, purposes or goals and major policies and plans for achieving these goals stated in such a way as to define what business the firm is in or is to be in and the kind or practice it is to be. There are several fundamental steps which precede the formulation and adoption of a practice development strategy. At their simplest they would involve:

- *Formulating the task*
  - defining its scope
  - identifying the reasons it is being undertaken
  - defining the characteristics of the answers sought
  - considering alternative methods of procuring answers
  - selecting method of solution based on cost–value analyses and resource availability
  - listing the information required for solution
  - specifying the action required to develop the information needed
- *Developing the inputs*
  - assembling the facts
  - forecasting or postulating the uncertainties
  - developing the alternatives to be considered
- *Evaluating the alternative courses of action*
  - converting alternatives to terms that can be compared
  - establishing criteria for making a selection
  - comparing alternatives
- *Deciding*
  - objectives
  - strategy

- tactics
- control methods
- *Translating the decisions into statements*
  - why the action is required
  - actions and resources involved
  - consequences expected and when
  - to accommodate what and when
  - controls for interim measurement of progress by identifying critical forecasts and conditions to be monitored and prescribing necessary performance standards, schedule met and budget requirements.

This framework now requires converting into a document which acts as a blueprint for the whole planning process. By breaking down the process into a series of steps, the planner can ensure both that the correct sequence is adopted and nothing is omitted. Moreover, by planning on this basis it provides the opportunity for everyone to contribute to the plan and thus the much greater possibility of its acceptance through ownership. The following planning steps have to be carried out if the realistic and realisable objectives for the practice are to be achieved:

- *Situation analysis*—relevant significant facts about the services, the firm, the clients, the competition, the business environment, relevant technology
- *Identification of problems and opportunities*—these will emerge from the situation analysis
- *Objectives*—the intended outcome of the plan in terms of revenue, profit, volume, growth, positioning quality of assignments acquired, new services and skills as well as the image of the firm
- *Strategy*—segmentation: clients must be segmented by their volume, growth prospects, quality/service expectations, profitability, needs and other significant criteria
  —service "mix": this is influenced and controlled by what is reasonably sure is required and can be delivered at a sustained level of quality
  —marketing "mix": the tools of marketing must be selected both for their short term impact and the contribution they will make in the long term towards achieving the objectives

- *Tactics*—selection and timing of methods, media, and messages
- *Monitoring and control*—methods for assessing the effectiveness of the strategy and control mechanisms for adjustments

The processes described will reveal any quantitative and qualitative resource gaps which must be filled to achieve the targets. Their existence and other factors will lead to a recycling of the planning steps including revision of objectives until the hoped for optimum matching of opportunities and resources and the timespan required for their achievement is practical. It is from this point that the practice expansion strategies can be developed.

SITUATION ANALYSIS

The first step in creating a marketing plan is to ensure that the use of existing resources are maximised and missing resources are identified. This requires undertaking an examination of precisely what the practice possesses and what gaps need to be filled. The review can range from a simple summation to a full scale internal inquiry which is known as the marketing audit or by the use of SWOT or SOFT analyses (see page 339). The former is a technique which identifies, classifies, evaluates and interprets in practical terms the range, extent and quality of existing resources that can be utilised for marketing. From this analysis it is possible to focus on ways of achieving improved results by their application. The internal marketing audit is a rapid, low cost method of obtaining the maximum value from un-utilised, under-utilised or wrongly-utilised resources which every firm possesses in some measure. The technique is based on extracting and interpreting information already within the firm.[1] It does not necessarily seek original external facts and, therefore, no market or other research, which can be expensive and time consuming, is involved. Any lack of data identified can lead to appropriate action for obtaining recent, detailed and better information from within the firm's resources.

In conducting SWOT or SOFT analyses only those resources or capabilities which would be recognised and valued by the target clients should be included. Forcing executives to confront the differences between what they think is important and what the client thinks is important is a substantial contribution to the success of the technique.

The areas within a typical professional practice where tangible and intangible assets are to be found will usually group under the following generic headings:

- Personnel with their skills, experience, interests, contacts and qualifications
- Clients with a requirement for but not utilising the full range of the firm's services and who could also be valuable for networking, non-clients and referrers
- Infra-structure comprising offices, equipment, vehicles and other physical assets
- Information held by the firm in terms of know-how, client and market data, continuing professional developments, controls, and administration systems
- Finance—its application and manipulation
- Service range and skill available
- Intangibles, most particularly image, quality controls, client care systems

All of these resources have been dealt with in some depth in the appropriate chapters.

While the *marketing* audit will reveal available resources, it should also include some element of *market* audit. The difference is not just semantic. *Marketing* audits are concerned with the identification of resources which can be utilised for marketing and checking on how well they are performing. A *market* audit is concerned with the configurations of the market: its size; rate of growth or decline; market shares; extent of business passing through intermediaries; ratio of private to corporate business; international trading data; and the performance of competitors: in fact, all quantitative aspects of a market that will assist in planning.

For most practices the cost involved in establishing a market size is rarely justified. Unlike the motor industry or fast moving consumer goods, most professional practices are not volume sensitive in terms of cost and there are few if any disciplines where one or two firms meet the bulk of market requirements. Although it is relatively safe to ignore such aspects as market share and size, it is unwise to do the same to overall growth or decline trends and to competitors' activities. A vital part of the position analysis is a detailed and timely knowledge of direct and indirect competitors.

PROBLEMS AND OPPORTUNITIES

Since the purpose of the plan is to resolve or avoid problems and to exploit opportunities, which will lead to profitable growth, it is obviously of importance to identify both phenomena. The techniques suggested in the previous chapter will contribute to this identification but it can be safely assumed that, within practices of any size, there will always be differences of opinions as to what are the actual threats and opportunities and resources the firm commands. It is obvious that a plan must be predicated on the basis of specified and agreed weaknesses and strengths of the practice, its markets and its competitors. Such an agreement is not necessarily going to be achieved without discussion and advocacy. It is, however, no use proceeding with the plan unless there is indeed a consensus. Without this, enthusiasm and co-operation will be missing. Moreover, given the propensity of most professionally trained personnel not to be amenable to direction towards goals they do not share, there is every chance that consciously or unconsciously the plan will be ignored.

A profile of the typical professional suggests, and observation tends to confirm this, that they are unable and unwilling to manage other people and substantially they are only interested in the freedom to develop their professional skills. They are difficult to integrate into a management structure. The good ones will have developed styles and concepts of their own and are often unwilling to accept the ideas of others or new rules.[2] In problem and opportunity identification, these are not the characteristics most likely to achieve a consensual view so that the task at even this early stage of planning is a difficult one but must nevertheless be accomplished.

Just as was stated earlier that solving a problem a client does not recognise exists wins no accolades, solving problems that are not significant for the firm will achieve neither better performance nor praise. Equally, identifying opportunities that are unreal or failing to see those that offer substantial prospects of more and better quality business will not improve the well being of the business or the professional.

Thus, in the planning process no strong base can be laid without the agreement throughout the practice as to precisely the problems and opportunities that exist or are emerging and thus the actions to be taken to solve, avoid or exploit them.

OBJECTIVES

Objectives, the core of managerial action, provide direction to the practice development by defining objectives and goals (objectives are general aims, goals specific aims). They can be stated in many ways, but basically they group into time or scope dimensions, or relate to a designated activity within the firm. Objectives can be expressed for any functional area such as marketing or organisational level considered important as well as for the firm itself. A pre-requisite for developing suitable strategies, as is obvious from the foregoing, is the acceptance by all concerned of the mission statement and the objectives of the practice as a whole. From this, the *marketing* objectives can be decided as well as the route to be followed to achieve them over a given time scale. Without this prior agreement, the likelihood of any strategy being successful, or of objectives being achieved in a structured rather than a reactive manner, are diminished. This again emphasises the earlier reference to everyone "owning" the plan. If the processes described in Chapter 6 have been followed, then the practice will already have a mission statement such as those used in the examples given on page 53. The firm then knows its purpose for being, what it is and what it wants to be and thus what marketing is to achieve.

The broad objectives of the firm must be related to key-result areas, that is those which are vital to the firm and which can be measured or evaluated preferably against quantified objectives. Key objectives are obviously such performance indicators as revenue, profitability, rate of growth, increase in billable time. But beyond these there is a hierarchy of sub-objectives which are also important for direction and performance monitoring and in providing both functional and individual objectives. All these have to be considered in setting marketing objectives and goals.

Objectives and sub-objectives need to be recycled to make them practical and so that everyone involved including the lower levels of management have their personal and departmental goals, all of which are compatible with the overall objectives. It is necessary to compare them horizontally and vertically so that there are no omissions, duplications or inconsistencies.

As will be obvious, the span of objectives can be extremely wide from the macro (increase practice profitability to £...) to micro (increase profitability of work undertaken for XYZ Company). Most guidance on objective setting tends to be confined to providing crude guidelines rather than stating the objectives themselves. The following are, however, suggested as a starting point for consideration and can be used as a basis for extending them to key result areas. It is, of course, always arguable which are corporate as opposed to marketing objectives since some, such as increasing profitability, is not wholly within the control or influence of marketing:

- Increase fee income to £... by 199?
- Increase profitability by ?% by 199?
- Improve conversion rate of enquiries to quotations (or presentations) to engagements
- Increase billable time by ?%
- Identify and concentrate on key clients
- Introduce new services to account for ?% of fee income by 199?
- Widen knowledge of the practice to targeted publics
- Increase the number of clients for each (or specified) service(s).
- Engagements from non-domestic markets to represent ?% of turnover by 199?
- Upgrade technology
- Extend and increase activity of referral sources
- Develop services with anti-cyclical demand characteristics
- Achieve improved image profile
- Reduce identified vulnerabilities
- Improve ratio of new to repeat instructions
- Identify and remove blockages to progress
- Increase cross referral business to ?% of revenue
- Improve ratio of commercial to private clients
- Open ? new offices by 199?
- Extend continuing professional education and introduce management and marketing training by 199?

The implication that all objectives have the same time span is clearly impractical, and while they can be divided between the overriding purpose of the organisation and the sub-goals which make up the hierarchy of objectives, they will require to be classified into short-, medium- and long-term goals. Just what these time spans mean in weeks, months or years depends upon the scope of the overall plan but those suggested in the previous chapter, page 333, have been found in use to be practical. The level of speculation beyond five years, given the inaccuracy of forecasting in the present turbulent times, makes detailed planning past this point unrealistic. However, all plans should be "rolling" so that the five-year "end of plan" period is constantly moved forward and the programme adjusted in accordance with changed internal and ambient conditions and resources.

All objectives should be ambitious enough to stretch the capacity, capabilities and energy of those within a practice charged with expanding it and who will be held responsible for the successful achievement of the plans. Equally, objectives must not be so unrealistic as to be demotivating in the sense that they are unachievable and therefore not worth striving for.

An effective if somewhat crude way or arriving at a first rough profit or revenue target is provided by gap analysis. That is the projection of three-to-five years' past performance on a surprise free basis to establish where the firm would be if the present course is maintained. It can be modified to some extent by known variances in the past history as compared to the present, for example the impact of new legislation, unusual economic conditions, the removal or arrival of substantial competition or one-off opportunities. The position can be compared with the desired target and decisions taken whether any gap between the surprise free projection and the target can be filled. If not the target has to be reduced.

STRATEGY

In looking at the strategy for the practice, an initial division is required: that is, how much resource and effort is to be directed to obtaining new clients and how much to retaining clients which the firm already serves. The headlong rush for new clients which followed the major steps of de-regulation, allied with the fact that clients began to use their countervailing power to play off one practice against another, led many firms into a marketing trap. Given the significantly higher cost of obtaining a new client than in keeping one it should have been, but was not, obvious that the marketing strategy ought to have been directed to holding and

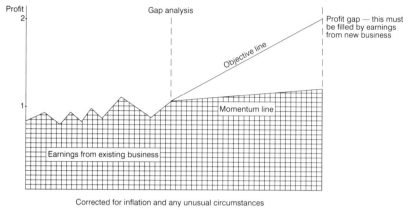

Figure 27.1 *Gap analysis*

expanding the business of existing clients. That is not to say new clients should not to be sought (indeed they are the life blood of any organisation), only that the nurturing and retention of existing clients should not be sacrificed in pursuit of the new. In most organisations recognition of practice development effort and success tends to concentrate on new clients being obtained. There should be equal reward and recognition for client retention and systems should not discriminate between success with either groups of clients.

Although outside the field of marketing the rider that the key to client retention is employee retention has to be considered. Many companies unnecessarily reduce their opportunities through their human resource policies which lead to high employee turnover. Those practitioners who deal with clients on a regular basis have a pervasive favourable effect on client loyalty. Any strategy should reflect the balance of effort required to achieve an optimum new:old ratio. Chapter 13 discussed this issue at some length.

The first element in the strategy is segmentation—already dealt with in Chapter 6. Particular reference to Table 6.1, page 56, gives some practical segmentation targets. Chapter 8 reverses the position by examining any aspect of the firm which has a particular advantage to any specified client group, thus making identification of the target more precise in terms of the likelihood of the offer being taken up.

The second element in the strategy concerns the "mix" of services which are to be offered to achieve the objectives. There are two dimensions involved here. First the "width" of services offered: that is, the service range. This might be from high specialisation or boutique to full range or one-stop shopping. The other dimension is the depth of each service: that is, the extent and sophistication of the service. A human resource consultancy might confine itself to a single service of outplacement counselling or its offerings could also include career reviews, research, assistance in writing *curriculum vitae,* self-marketing, job search, presentation training. Superimposed on this could be skill level of the counsellors, trainers, writers, providing everything from a luxury top quality service to a bare-bones assistance. Many practices could usefully consider offering full life cycle services: that is, having available appropriate services for clients at different stages of their career and personal life cycles. For a financial institution this could range from simple savings accounts ultimately to pensions. For a medical practice paediatrics to geriatrics. Full life cycle services use, to the fullest extent, client loyalty to the service provider, and highlight the benefits of obtaining "life time" clients.

The third dimension of strategy relates to the various communication methods which are to be adopted the marketing mix. As Chapters 20, 24 and 25, most particularly Table 25.2, show the choice is wide, the permutations massive and the decisions difficult. Nevertheless every plan must indicate without equivocation which tools are to be used and when.

TACTICS

Tactics are concerned with short-term goals and while these may be related to the three basic strategic issues, segmentation, service range and communication content, they tend, so far as professional practices are concerned, to be concentrated on timing, the selection and use of communication methods, media and messages.

The tactical, as opposed to the strategic, decisions concern such issues as the form and content of the message in the sense of offering specific benefits to different segments of the market, and the adoption of those media and methods to which they are most likely to be exposed to and influenced by. If it is intended to develop the image of the whole practice rather than a specific aspect of the practice's services then the message will emphasise the totality of the firm while the media might be press, radio and perhaps (but somewhat unlikely given its very high cost) television. If the purpose is to obtain market acceptance of a new therapy to be adopted directly by clients rather than through medical practitioners, press and public relations might be the best carrier of the message and, although it may also promote other providers of the therapy, it widens the market as a whole with the firm obtaining what it is hoped would be a reasonable share of that market. If one of the broad objectives is to obtain more high net worth private clients, then a tactical approach would be the *Wealth Seminar* explained in the Appendix to Chapter 25, pages 331–2. This would be a highly appropriate tactic.

It is at the tactical level where the majority of professional and support staff become involved. If the whole range of activities is displayed to them and an element of choice is permitted as to which they personally will involve themselves with, then support for the plan moves from theoretical to practical. Those with the appropriate skills and interest will choose those tactical issues they feel best able to accomplish, and those with enthusiasm but no knowledge and experience can be exposed to both the appropriate training to exploit their enthusiasm and can also be mentored by others.

While strategies would normally only be changed at wide intervals, and then perhaps only incrementally unless a major circumstance warranted diverging or abandoning the original plan, tactics can and should be adjusted in the short term both in response to their impact and to changes in the firm's environment—competition, regulation, social changes and technology (see Figure 26.1, page 335). The decision of the British Government to contract out £1.5 billion of services previously undertaken by internal departments caused many firms to widen marketing targets and marketing efforts to what was a new segment for many of them.

One aspect of tactics which is often overlooked is the need for monitoring new methods and approaches to promotion. The marketer should be constantly alert to new ideas which appear in any sector of the economy because many of them can be adapted for professional services. An excellent example of a new technique which can be introduced into many services is one devised by a pension company:

> "The company negotiated with a number of businesses to put aside in a retirement account 6% of a consumer's purchase price on all products sold. The arrangement creates a win–win situation for consumer and seller. The business gains customer loyalty, and the consumers pay what they have usually paid (and what other consumers pay regularly), but 6% of what they pay goes into savings. Some grandparents in Florida are directing the savings to accounts to pay for grandchildren's education."[3]

In the not-for profit sector, one arts organisation in Australia has promoted the idea of their supporters taking out life insurance policies in favour of the organisation rather than paying a regular charitable subscription. Although the benefits are long term they are very real and one additional plus is that it avoids quarrels which can stem from straight bequests when legatees do not share the same loyalty as the donor to the organisation. The opportunities for insurance companies of selling this fund raising concept to not-for-profit organisations are obvious.

MONITORING AND CONTROL

Some measurement of total performance, as well as of the performance of components of the practice development activity is necessary. The final part of the practice development plan is the incorporation of methods for evaluating its unfolding progress and for controlling or introducing variances.

There is little point in setting up complex monitoring and detailed measuring systems if there is no intention of attempting to control the phenomenon reported. Performance must be seen as comparative, that is: comparison with the stated objectives and how far they have been achieved; comparison of the methods devised to achieve the objectives and how these methods have been applied; comparison with the performance of the market as a whole and with competition. It is not without significance that measurement (or monitoring) and control are almost invariably taught together and combined in books on marketing. They are insolubly linked because control cannot be effective without standards of performance.

While, in large concerns, the marketing department can often be treated as accountable for profit or loss in its own right, it would be rare to find such an arrangement applying to practice development in the professional service firm. Nevertheless, the contribution activities to develop the practice make to total profitability requires assessment, if only because of the essentially variable nature of practice development costs. The ability of a firm to measure profitability in its various operations, as distinct from the total profitability of the firm, will differ with the firm's size, the complexity and sophistication of its operations, and the range of services offered. For small practices, there is some evidence to show that the administrative and accounting methods installed to measure and control performance are often out of proportion to the results achieved. For professional services firms (and not ignoring the need for at least an outline idea of profit contribution), measurement and control may be achieved through cost control.

Marketing is a front end but continuing investment and if it is simply regarded as an overhead which is being taken from partners' and senior managers' income, it is likely to be among the first economies to be made. This would be a very short term and dangerous view. Marketing must be seen as an investment in exactly the same way as expenditures are made on buildings, equipment and personnel. If a marketing budget is to be acceptable then it must be subject to cost control. This is a necessary operating objective of any firm. One way in which organisations try to achieve their profit objectives is to administer their expenditure to get the maximum results from the cost incurred. Practice development activities, which stem from the strategy, must be subject to cost accounting procedure to enable management to make periodic comparisons of costs in terms of the specific origins of these costs. The statement can be used both as a standard of performance and as an instrument of cost control. A comparison of costs over a period of time, and also with averages for the profession as a whole (where these are available), is one of the more conventional ways to approach the measurement and control of performance and is a critical input for effective planning.

Obviously, the reporting system must be capable of revealing the situation, otherwise there can be no adjustment of activity or of the plan itself. Both the requirement for a touch on the tiller or a desperate grab at the wheel demands detailed recent and accurate information on just how the practice development is progressing and how individuals and techniques are performing. Each firm will need to develop its own signals. For example, in the short term, using the average time between an enquiry and a commission or instruction and the percentage of conversion to actual business as a comparison will indicate an imminent downturn or upturn in business from which information the appropriate actions can be initiated. Where available, interfirm comparisons, benchmarking (explained in Chapter 8) and professional norms may be a practical guide. For some practices there will be reliable "lead-lag" indicators. New housing starts, which provide business for solicitors, financial institutions, possibly surveyors, estate agents as well as many trades, may be a macro indicator of demand.

A checklist of control information with suggested frequency of collection and dissemination, standards and methods of indicating variance as well as internal circulation can be adapted for the purpose of professional practices and will be found in Appendix 27A of this chapter. Control programmes which result from the implementation of the strategy, like control of any other management activity, should be a dynamic process responding to changes as they occur. In short, it is the continuous process by which management makes certain that the strategies are adopted, implemented, guided or restrained to achieve the goals which they have been devised to attain. It cannot be effective if practised in a one-off or reactive way.

However, watching the results of a practice development plan unfold will not assist the situation unless a contingency plan exists against anticipated variances. Such a plan should identify actions which must be introduced in the short, medium or long term to exploit or avoid the consequences of any deviations from the plans or the assumptions on which they are based.

MAKING THE PLAN WORK

The whole planning process from position analysis to monitoring and control can be summarised in a schematic (Figure 27.2). If the

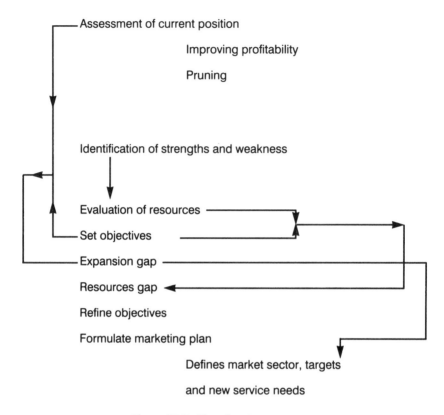

Figure 27.2 *The planning sequence*

objectives as revealed by the gap analysis (Figure 27.1) show the need for more resources to achieve them then there is also a resource gap. Objective and resource gaps must be recycled to arrive at the optimum position.

In the final analysis when everyone who is or should be involved has been consulted when the plans have been recycled and when general approval and "ownership" has been obtained, all that the practice developer has is a document. Nothing will happen unless there is now a determination to make it happen.

The first stage is decomposition. Every action that is implied in the plan from the most fundamental to the most trivial must be identified and each one allocated by name, scheduled for satisfactory completion and monitored. Some amplification to that statement is needed. "By name" is important. There must be no misunderstanding where the responsibilities rest. Volunteers are better than conscripts, most particularly when they are allowed to take on tasks which they have ability to perform or in which they have an interest. Moreover "by name" enables the most powerful motivator of all to come into play—peer pressure. If everyone knows what everyone else is supposed to be doing internal pressures build up to ensure that it is done. There are few individuals who do not want the approbation of their superiors, peers and subordinates and thus the motivation to carry out the activity even in the face of other pressures, mostly professional, is high.

Scheduling, where it is possible, should be left to the individuals concerned. If they set their own time they cannot subsequently claim it was unreasonable to expect them to complete the work by the agreed date. While they may not always achieve their set dates, again peer pressure will create an atmosphere where the greatest endeavour will be made to meet the original or revised dates. Mostly people do not want to ask for additional time too frequently.

Finally, monitoring helps concentrate the mind. If no one is responsible for seeing the plan into its activity state then the likelihood of it happening is remote. Appendix 6, page 63 can be a format for a personal action plan which each individual can use set out their own programmes and their contract for action. It avoids the risk of "wish" lists and is a clear commitment to action. Appendix 27B, page 367, brings together for the practice developer the personal plans and provides an overview of what is happening and what is to happen. A summary in the form of that given in Appendix 27B is circulated to all those with agreed tasks, then it is possible for everyone to observe who is and who is not complying with their commitment.

Before the plan is finalised, it is as well to subject it to some intensive questioning both as to the underlying principles and also what it is hoped to achieve and its practicality. A valuable checklist in Appendix 27C will give the planner guidance and will help identify any weaknesses that are unintentionally built into the plan.

ACTION POINTS

- Formulate the planning task and appoint a senior person to write the plan
- Undertake a position analysis
- Involve as many people as possible with the purpose of developing a sense of ownership in the plan and being committed to it
- Set realistic but high targets
- Decide the strategy in terms of segmentation, service and communication mix
- Devise, initiate, operate and monitor an evaluation and control system

---

NOTES

(1) For a full description of the marketing audit technique with appropriate checklists to aid extraction of the information see Wilson, A. *Marketing Audit Checklists*, McGraw-Hill, Maidenhead (1992).
(2) Sveiby, K.E. and Lloyd, T. *Managing Know How*, p.59, Bloomsbury, London (1987).
(3) SRI International Business Intelligence Program, *Scan*, p.59, Menlo Park, CA (1992).

APPENDIX 27A

MODEL FOR REQUIRED CONTROL INFORMATION

Performance information	Report frequency: W = weekly M = monthly YTD = year to date	Standard	Variance shown by	Executives receiving reports: C = control purposes I = information purposes		
				Marketing partner	Departmental head	Senior partner
1 Value of engagements:						
total sterling	W or M/YTD	Forecast	Value	I	C	—
by service	W or M/YTD	Forecast	Value	C	C	—
by region	W or M/YTD	Forecast	Value	C	C	—
by nominated accounts	W or M/YTD	Forecast	Value	C	C	—
2 New accounts:						
total new accounts opened	W or M/YTD	Forecast	Value	I	C	—
by service	W or M/YTD	Forecast	Value	C	C	—
by region	W or M/YTD	Forecast	Value	C	C	—
by nominated accounts	W or M/YTD	Forecast	Value	C	C	—
3 Profits:						
net for firm	M/YTD	Forecast	Value	I	—	C
gross margin	M	Forecast	Value	I	—	—
by service	M	Forecast	Value	C	C	—
by region	M	Forecast	Value	C	C	—
by department	M	Forecast	Value	C	C	—
by individual	M	Forecast	Value	C	C	—
4 Expenses:						
total marketing	M/YTD	Budget	Value	I	C	C
by service	M/YTD	Budget	Value	C	C	—
by department	M/YTD	Budget	Value	C	C	—
by region	M/YTD	Budget	Value	C	C	—

Performance information	Report frequency: W = weekly M = monthly YTD = year to date	Standard	Variance shown by	Marketing partner	Departmental head	Senior partner

Performance information	Report frequency (W = weekly, M = monthly, YTD = year to date)	Standard	Variance shown by	Marketing partner	Departmental head	Senior partner (Executives receiving reports: C = control purposes, I = information purposes)
5 Fee/discounts: amounts of variance from planned fees						
by service	W or M	Plan	Value	C	C	–
by region	W or M	Plan	Value	C	C	–
by department	W or M	Plan	Value	C	C	–
6 Marketing activity:						
total quotations to engagements ratio	W or M	Plan	Number	C	C	–
by service	W or M	Plan	Number	C	C	C
by existing/new clients	W or M	Plan	Number	C	C	–
by region	W or M	Plan	Number	C	C	–
by department	W or M	Plan	Number	C	C	C
by key clients	W or M	Plan	Number	C	I	–
non-billable time expenditure	M	Budget	Value	C	C	C
7 Clients:						
number gained by region	W or M/YTD	Plan	Number	C	C	–
number lost by region	W or M/YTD	Plan	Number	C	C	–
net change by region	W or M/YTD	Plan	Number	C	C	–
number gained by service	W or M/YTD	Plan	Number	C	C	–
number lost by service	W or M/YTD	Plan	Number	C	C	–
net change by service	W or M/YTD	Plan	Number	C	C	–
ratio of corporate to private clients	YTD	Plan	Number	C	C	C

Performance information	Report frequency: W = weekly M = monthly YTD = year to date	Standard	Variance shown by	Executives receiving reports: C = control purposes I = information purposes		
				Marketing partner	Departmental head	Senior partner
8 Client service:						
complaints by type	W or M/YTD	Acceptable standard	Number	C	C	—
complaints by service	W or M/YTD	Acceptable standard	Number	C	C	—
complaints by region	W or M/YTD	Acceptable standard	Number	C	C	—
by practitioner	W or M/YTD	Acceptable standard	Number	C	C	—
refunds and allowances	W or M/YTD	Acceptable standard	Value	C	C	—
9 Credit:						
number and value of accounts outstanding over 10/30/60 days	M	Objective	Value–Number	C	C	—
by service	M	Objective	Value	C	C	—
names of accounts over 60 days		—	—	C	C	—
10 Billing:						
invoices issued			Value–Number	C	C	—
work completed not billed			Value			
advance payments			Value			
11 Marketing activity by function:						
media advertising	M/YTD	Budget	Value	—	C	C
meetings and seminars	M/YTD	Budget	Value	—	C	C
public relations	M/YTD	Budget	Value	—	C	C
by service	M/YTD	Budget	Value	—	C	
status report on marketing functions, literature, exhibitions, direct mail etc.	Quarterly	—	—	C	C	C

Performance information	Report frequency: W = weekly M = monthly YTD = year to date	Standard	Variance shown by	Executives receiving reports: C = control purposes I = information purposes		
				Marketing partner	Departmental head	Senior partner
12 New service development:						
status of each project pending	M	Plan	Number of weeks	C	—	—
new projects started	M	Plan	Number of weeks	C	—	—
projects completed	M	Plan	Number of weeks	C	—	—
projects in market test	M	Plan	Number of weeks	C	—	—

APPENDIX 27B

Marketing Plan

Period   Date of issue

Target group	Actions	Objective	Budget		Person responsible	Plan completion deadline	Time schedule												Achievement
			3	Time			J	F	M	A	M	J	J	A	S	O	N	D	
		Total																	

APPENDIX 27C

SOME "FRIENDLY SCEPTICAL" QUESTIONS TO APPRAISE A STRATEGIC PLAN[1]

- What special capabilities do you plan to have that your best competitors cannot match?
- Why can't they match them?
- What actions will you take to put these capabilities in place?
- In what way are your investment priorities likely to be different from those of your competitors?
- How do you know the clients will like what you're planning? What field testing have you done? What client testing have you done?
- Who will be in charge of executing each component of the plan?
- Who was involved in the development of this plan? Is everyone in agreement? (Who was not consulted? Do they have a role in executing the plan?)
- On whom will you be dependent for the execution of this plan? Do they have sufficient incentive to do their part? Is it in their interests to do what you want?
- Do you have to modify your reward systems to make this happen?
- Specifically, which 5 or 10 clients, by name, represent your most *likely* source of expanded business for the next few years? What actions do you plan to take to get closer to these clients?
- Which new clients are at the top of your priority list? Why? What makes you think you can get their business?
- What is the one most significant thing that each of the main competitors are doing that will affect you? What do you plan to do as a response?
- In what way do you plan to take advantage of the firm wide network? How do you plan to get the co-operation of others?
- How do you plan to contribute to the firm wide network? How will what you are doing benefit them?
- What are the staffing implications of your plans? Where will you get the staff from?
- What are the main assumptions on which your plan is based? Which is the most "risky"? (i.e. if it can go wrong, where will it go wrong?)

- How will we know if the plan is working? What indicators can we agree on, and when shall we review them?
- What early warning signals will there be if the plan is not working? What contingencies have you put in place?

NOTE

(1) Maister, D.H. "How to Create a Marketing Strategy", *The American Lawyer*, New York, June (1990).

Conclusion

The purpose of this book has been to present ideas and techniques which can be adopted by any profession within the practice rules which may be imposed on them by their professional associations. Nothing which has been suggested is beyond the resources or skills possessed or acquirable by a typical practice. Indeed, when compared with the training undergone to qualify in professions such as quantity surveying, medicine or accountancy, they shrink into insignificance. The difference between developing abilities in marketing and obtaining professional recognition is substantially that of motivation not the capability of absorbing the training.

No book can, on its own, provide motivation which is not based on sound reasons or, to use a word which had appeared in most chapters, benefits. These benefits to the professional are very real when the threats to their futures are intense and imminent. Prime among them is the intensification of direct and indirect competition from the qualified, semi-qualified, unqualified, new technology and from products. To suggest a profession or a practice cannot succeed against competition without formal marketing would be a hyperbole but if survival is not the issue then the quality of life most certainly is. With lower revenue, lower margins and lower profit, work satisfaction is threatened as are living standards.

For the unconvinced this book has attempted to set out what can be achieved and how. It is then left for the individual practices to decide if they want or need marketing. Then, at least if there is rejection it will be based on facts and not a distorted view of what marketing is supposed to comprise and that it is the antithesis of professionalism.

The next decade will see more and faster adjustment than the professions have ever experienced. It is better to prepare for the challenge rather than wait until the threats are translated into reality. The changes which will be embraced or forced on the professions will require management and financial skills not just marketing ability but, above all, for those who have yet to be convinced a transformation in attitude and culture.

Winston Churchill, asked on his birthday what it felt like to be 80, replied that it was better than the alternative. None of the adjustments which will be necessary will be comfortable but they will be better than the alternative.

Index

Note: Page references in *italics* refer to figures; those in bold refer to tables.

Index compiled by Annette Musker